Youth, Education and Risk

Youth, Education and Risk: Facing the Future is a provocative and valuable insight into how the dramatic social and economic changes of the last twenty years have affected the lives of Western youth. Covering young people's attitudes towards and experiences of work, education, relationships and health, Peter Dwyer and Johanna Wyn provide a comprehensive perspective on young people in Western society in the 1990s.

The book is divided into two parts. Part One is a comprehensive review of ten years of research, policy and practice, as related to the 15–30 age group, comparing data from the UK, Australia, the USA and Canada. Part Two goes on to argue for the need to develop new research and policy frameworks that are more in tune with the changed conditions of life for Western youth. It questions approaches that measure youth life patterns with reference to the norms of the past, when such norms are largely redundant in the light of changes in Western societies in the post-1970 period. At once comprehensive in its coverage of research and challenging in its conclusions and recommendations, *Youth, Education and Risk* sets out the conceptual basis for a new approach to youth and the practical implications for research, education and youth policy in the new millennium.

Peter Dwyer and **Johanna Wyn** both teach at the University of Melbourne's highly regarded Youth Research Centre. Peter Dwyer's previous books include *Opting Out: Early School Leavers and the Degeneration of Youth Policy* (1996) and *Confronting School and Work* (1984). Johanna Wyn's previous books include *Rethinking Youth* (1997).

Youth, Education and Risk

Facing the future

Peter Dwyer
and
Johanna Wyn

London and New York

First published 2001
by RoutledgeFalmer
11 New Fetter Lane, London EC4P 4EE

Simultaneously published in the USA and Canada
by RoutledgeFalmer
29 West 35th Street, New York, NY 10001

RoutledgeFalmer is an imprint of the Taylor & Francis Group

© 2001 Peter Dwyer and Johanna Wyn

Typeset in Sabon by
Florence Production Ltd, Stoodleigh, Devon
Printed and bound in Great Britain by
TJ International, Padstow, Cornwall

British Library Cataloguing in Publication Data
A catalogue record for this book is available from the
British Library.

Library of Congress Cataloging in Publication Data
A catalogue record for this book has been requested.

ISBN 0–415–25778–6 (pbk)
ISBN 0–415–25777–8 (hbk)

Contents

List of tables and figures   vii
Introduction   1

PART I
The context of change   7

1   Balancing options   9

The ambition paradox 13
Patterns of change 18
Priorities 25
The idea of transition to adulthood 32

2   Outside the mainstream   35

What alternatives? 39
Being an outsider 46
Policy disjunctures 51
Concluding remarks 55

3   The policy gap   57

Mainstream: the image of success 59
Masking outsiders 63
Training beyond the mainstream 66
Continuing inequalities 70
The policy gap 74

4   Coping with change   76

Elements of convergence 80
A perplexing optimism 83

Choice biographies 86
Participant research 89
Concluding comment 95

PART II
Problems of transition   97

5   **Student hopes and outcomes**   99

Future prospects 100
The impact of change 110
The life-patterns project: 1991–6 113
Uncertain outcomes 119

6   **The gender factor**   123

Gender and work 124
Gender and education 131
Gender and identity 136
Conclusion 143

7   **'At risk'**   145

Whose problem? 146
Whose solution? 159
One-dimensional lives 166

8   **Life-patterns and careers**   169

Complex lives 175
Career choices 179
Rethinking careers 184
Choice or constraint? 187

    Epilogue   195

Foreclosed options 195
Multi-dimensional lives 199
Active voice 201

References   206
Index   219

Tables and figures

Tables

1.1	Changes among total student participants	19
1.2	Respondents combining work and study	19
1.3	Attitudes towards work/study combinations	20
1.4	Sample items of preference diversity	21
1.5	Current work	22
1.6	Characteristics of adult life	26
1.7	Personal priorities	27
1.8	Main practical commitments in life	32
3.1	Industry distribution of employment: 1986 and 1996	75
4.1	Changing social indicators	77
4.2	Multiple transitions	82
5.1	Positive indicators	103
5.2	Optimist/pessimist break-down of total sample	107
5.3	Contrasts: 16-year-old optimists and pessimists	107
5.4	Personal troubles	108
5.5	Views of 16-year-olds about continuing with education	110
5.6	Percentage responses on negative indicators	111
5.7	Study intentions and outcomes	115
5.8	Sample compatibility: 1996–2000	116
5.9	Enrolment	117
5.10	Career expectation contrasts	117
5.11	Permanent full-time career outcomes: 1999	118
8.1	Priorities 1996–9 (VOCAM)	178
8.2	1998 qualifications and job outcomes	182
8.3	Per cent vocational integration (1999)	183
8.4	Career outcomes (1999)	184
8.5	Favoured aspects of a career job – 2000	186
8.6	Important goals in adult life	190

Figures

2.1	Income source on leaving school	48
3.1	US 1992–3 college graduates	61
3.2	Educational outcomes for 19-year-olds	64
5.1	Priority contrasts	104
5.2	Lifetime priorities	105
5.3	Main youth issues	109
5.4	Outcomes in first year after school	115
8.1	Vocational integration of 3-year Canadian graduates	181

Introduction

Most of the established studies on young people in Western societies have been devoted to an understanding of their transition within their families and schools towards adulthood and their working lives. Attention has also been given in some of the writing to the specific problems that young people confront (or create) as they go through different stages in their transition. More recent research in Europe, North America, the UK and Australia indicates a growing mismatch between the established models of transition and the actual attitudes, choices and experience of young people themselves. The significant social and economic changes that have taken place since the early 1970s in all of these countries have introduced elements of uncertainty, unpredictability and risk into the lives of this new generation, which their parents and others from previous generations often find difficult to explain or understand. The purpose of this book is to draw together the threads of this more recent research with particular emphasis on its implications for educational policy and practice.

Our experience with teachers, students and their parents in a variety of countries indicates that the increasing importance being placed on extended education participation has raised many problems for them. In particular, the strong emphasis being placed on post-compulsory education as an essential precondition for adult lives and careers has increased the pressures and expectations of 'growing up'. An understanding of how students themselves are responding to and reading those pressures is therefore an important concern for teacher training and practice. At the same time, young people are much more than students – for many of them the other aspects of their lives are even more important – and so our ability to bridge the gap between policy and practice in education depends on our readiness to take those other priorities and interests seriously. In this book, therefore, we do this by looking back over a variety of international studies as well as those we ourselves have undertaken during the 1990s. Our aim is threefold: to move beyond more localised national perspectives and develop an international perspective on young people's lives and educational expectations; to take seriously the impact of globalisation on the life experiences of the post-1970 generation; and to reflect on what the main findings tell us about how the young people who have grown up in the post-1970 years have been responding to changes in their education and how they have been shaping their lives.

There is growing evidence from both small-scale and large-scale research projects at both local and national levels which at times causes the researchers to puzzle over the lack of 'fit' between the accepted models of 'growing up' and what their research reveals. A large part of that puzzlement is due to the fact that the evidence which would assist our understanding is fragmented into separate domains. For example, evidence about new family formations, new levels of educational participation, new lifestyles, and the growing contingency of work tends to be kept separate from the growing evidence that young people are now taking these factors into account in their educational choices and the shaping of their own futures. What is not recognised is that not only have significant social and economic changes occurred during their lifetime but that members of this new generation have learnt through personal experience that they can no longer rely on the traditional 'markers' of transition to adulthood and the previously assumed stability of established social institutions which enabled previous generations to find their own place in the world. In this sense, the transformations occurring on a global scale can no longer be seen as mere 'life-cycle transitions' that can be neatly incorporated into the traditional interpretations of the experience of youth and the outcomes of schooling. Yet the assumption persists that, while the social realities and reference points of transition may have become much less certain, 'youth' is still the same sort of experience that we, the teachers, the parents and the policy-makers, went through ourselves. We read our own pasts into an experience that we, in another voice, say has been transformed.

The central aim of this book is to examine this paradox of a new generation growing to a new adulthood in a changed world. Throughout the 1990s we have had the opportunity to work with researchers in the US, the UK, Europe, Canada and Australasia, and have become increasingly aware of common strands of evidence about the lives of young people in the different nations. We have also become aware that the common threads have not been joined together – they remain disconnected because of the priority that is given to particular national research traditions or the respect that is held for the established and 'authoritative' local literature. A random perusal of the bibliographies in recent books or journal articles on similar topics but emanating from different nations reveals how limited and parochial the acknowledged sources can be. Even a failure to cite the appropriate local 'expert' – or what is read as an over-reliance on a non-local one – in submitting an article to a particular national journal can draw a sharp rebuke during the review process. This practice can create the impression that young people growing up in Western nations today are cut off from each other, or at the very least that research on young people in one part of the Western world has nothing to learn from – or contribute to – research on an identical issue and an identical age group in some other nation. Yet the common themes are there in the research, even if their significance gets lost and is seen at best as a 'subtext' in the general findings which still pay court to the accepted local research perspectives and established national literature.

If, however, the imagery of globalisation and its acknowledged impact on the life-chances, lifestyles and education of the young are to be analysed seriously, some attempt must be made to break through these localised research preserves and make connections between the developing strands in each. More simply, if there is considerable evidence available from a variety of quite independent national studies that points to similarities between the new life-patterns in their younger generations and their attitudes towards their own education and future careers, it is important to draw that evidence together for our own understanding of their lives *even within* their own national settings. If young lives are different now, our own understanding of what they will make of their education and how they will shape life in the future for themselves and those who come after them are also at stake.

The advantage of drawing together the international and local research findings is that it enables us to learn how the participants in those projects have been shaping their lives in a period of unsettling change. The material in the book is divided into two parts: the first is largely devoted to the elements of change affecting the lives of young people during the 1990s, and in particular to the educational issues and concerns that during those years tended to dominate policy debate; the second looks more closely at young people's transitions beyond school, and is particularly concerned with a widening disjuncture between education policy and actual outcomes which became increasingly evident towards the end of the decade.

The book draws on some major research projects undertaken by the authors as part of the work of the Youth Research Centre in Australia. The Centre places an emphasis on consultation with and participation by young people themselves in the belief that, although young people are often the specific 'objects' of major policy decisions, or narrowly defined 'target groups' for study and research, they are often denied an active voice in the shaping of those policies or in the evaluation of the study or research findings. Many of our projects therefore have been deliberately designed to fill the gap in existing knowledge about the sense young people themselves make of the pathways they take: whether the stated goals of policy square with their aspirations and outcomes; whether the delivery of programmes takes sufficient account of changes of interest and vocational focus on the part of particular individuals; and whether sufficient allowance is made for the ways in which students balance their studies alongside a range of other equally important commitments in their personal lives. Assumptions adopted at a policy level need to be tested against the actual choices of the participants.

Those choices have been central to the research that we have been engaged in over the past ten years. That work could not have been begun or successfully completed without the assistance of many colleagues. Particular mention should be made of Roger Holdsworth who has worked on a variety of our projects in a variety of roles, of Elizabeth Holden whose work on our early school leaver project was outstanding, and of Debra Tyler and Aramiha Harwood who have worked consistently on our large-scale longitudinal study titled the Life-Patterns Project. Dianne Looker of Acadia University in Canada has provided professional input in a number of ways. Above all we owe a great debt to all those who have participated in our different research programmes. For purposes of anonymity we have used pseudonyms in all references by name to actual participants in our various projects.

In all the chapters we have drawn on a variety of international studies. We are aware that this kind of cross-cultural story will present a challenge to some of our adult readers. For them, learning about their own nation, how their own young are coping with change, and what problems they are presenting for the nation as a whole, is often more important to them than what might be happening to other young people in some far-off place. We are, however, also aware, from our own experience in research involving young people from a variety of national settings, that young people themselves are in fact eager to learn about what is happening in the lives of their own generation elsewhere; to find out how what they themselves are doing in their lives – and the puzzlement or concern it arouses 'at home' – is something that they share with others and not just something that is 'strange'. Within the limits of copyright we have therefore made as much use as we can of research from different Western nations, but because of those limits we have also unashamedly used our own research as a unifying thread in the weave of what is a significant cross-cultural story. For this reason the book has drawn upon some of the reports of our research that have previously appeared in academic journals: for chapter 2, material from *Australian Journal of Education*, 1995, (39)3; for chapter 3 *Discourse*, 1997 (18)1; for chapter 4, *Journal of Youth Studies*, 1999 2(1); for chapter 5, *Unicorn*, 1994 (20)2; for chapter 6, *Australian Journal of Public Health*, 1994 18(1); for chapter 8, *Journal of Education Policy*, 1998 13(3); and for the epilogue *International Social Science Journal*, 2000, 164.

Part I
The context of change

1 Balancing options

Vince grew up in an outer suburban area of a large metropolitan city. He was undecided about a range of options on completing school in 1991, and was interested in physical education, forestry and photography. He decided on the third of these as his first choice but was unsuccessful and so began a course in computers and applied physics 'to keep occupied'. He soon gave it up ('wasn't really interested in it') – but was also doing some volunteer work for a National Park environmental group and so moved to a horticulture course ('a lot of outdoor work – which is what I wanted') and then a certificate in resource management. He started a correspondence course at a regional campus in Parks/Recreation/Heritage in 1994 – used local resources and went up to the campus for two weeks a semester to do the required labs etc. – 'self-motivation and interest in what you're doing is the main thing'.

Vince has continued his volunteer work in National Parks and through that got a job as a park ranger – as he put it in 1997: 'I'm now glad I didn't get into photography because I am now doing exactly what I want'. By 1998 his contract had run out so he found work as a landscape gardener, but is actively looking for work as a park ranger, is listed with four agencies, and intends caravanning around the country to see if he can pick up work as a park ranger. He would prefer to work in his home State but is so focused on his chosen vocation and intent on it that he 'would take a job anywhere' as a ranger.

Vince's career focus is not necessarily shared by his peers. Oscar, for example, is ready to turn his hand to anything – having a job with a steady income is what matters to him. Oscar's father has a university degree and worked in a rural community. Oscar was not happy at school and 'wanted to get out'. His parents said 'get a job or stay in school – either–or'. One of the teachers at school showed him brochures on a pre-apprentice course, so instead of doing his final year, he moved to another country town, and did the sixteen weeks pre-apprentices course at a vocational college. 'I liked it but would've rather been doing work – it was a good idea if it got me out of school – I would've been willing to do anything'. He moved back home when finished and applied for an apprenticeship as a fitter and turner in another local town, which he got and has been doing that ever since – commuting ninety minutes a day and attending college through a day-release programme. Oscar will try to get a job locally, but 'if not, might go up and see my cousin up north or head out west and try my luck out in mining settlements'.

Like Oscar, Clare grew up in a country town and went to a government school. She wanted to do something which wouldn't require her moving to the city 'at least in [the] first year' after her final school year. Initially she wanted to do 'something in the law area', to help change the law. She did legal studies in her final year and wanted to follow on from this, because she liked it and was interested. Clare was unsuccessful in getting into a criminology course, so took a college enrolment as a second option. She decided to do something 'practical', and because 'shifting from the country to the city was a big deal', she tried to delay it until feeling 'able to cope'. Wanting to do something worthwhile which would lead to a job, she enrolled in an office administration course at a country campus.

The following year she transferred to a city college and 'found the transition very hard'. She was not able to get much help, found accommodation through an ad on the college noticeboard but 'didn't get on at all with the new flatmate' and felt isolated from her classmates. Commenting on shifting to the city she said 'I look back now and don't know how I survived'. Because of exemptions she started in the second year of the course, so she didn't know any of the other students. 'Found it very lonely.' Half way through the year things improved as she began to make her own friends. But she still did not really like city life, and so on finishing her course she has since moved back to live and work in a country town.

Annette also attended a government school and, as an only child, she 'had to be the boy for dad'. She had an uncle who was an engineer, and she herself wanted to do engineering, 'always interested in bridges and dams'. She was very ill in 1992 but enrolled in a local regional institute to study engineering. As the only girl in the class, she had a 'problem' teacher who forgot about her in the class, 'only addressed the boys'.

Illness and subsequent absences from study affected where and in what to enrol, and because the college started being 'difficult' about running classes for only a few she started looking around for other options. She was offered an opportunity to go to Scotland to train for Scottish dancing teaching qualifications, and so she did this. 'Situation (i.e. health problems) was beyond my control, but I learnt a lot about engineering and dancing'. On returning from Scotland, the restaurant where she had been working part time asked her to be manager. She was 'rapt' and put her studies on the backburner. 'I have a fantastic job as manager of the restaurant, have a good car, now dancing is my first interest'. She has since married, plans on having children, and after that 'develop my interest in Highland dancing and be a teacher – nothing to do with engineering!'.

This pattern of change is also evident in the case of Moira. She had grown up in a large city where she had attended a private school for girls. She went on to a university and undertook a double degree in music/arts: 'had always been a musician so I suppose it was generally accepted that I would follow on in this path'. Life to her seemed very straightforward at this point – living at home, financed by her family and with a scholarship for her studies. Finding suitable employment related to her studies was a different matter. 'I won't get work easily with the double degree I have'. Moira insists that 'there is no one priority in my life – my study, my family, my part-time work are all important'. She also thinks that if you put all your eggs in the one basket or become too optimistic 'you only get disappointed'. She is quite happy to have a mix of commitments in her life – her studies in a double degree, and two part-time jobs, one as a music teacher and one in an office.

Thus, in 1997 Moira was working four hours part time as a music teacher, and in office administration for twenty hours. By 1998 the office wanted someone full time and she was still studying, so now she is looking elsewhere. She says, though, that if possible she 'doesn't want to teach and doesn't want to work in the music area'. She is a bit vague about the sort of job she wants but does not seem that concerned 'as it will not be a job that I will have to do for ever'.

These mini-biographies illustrate the importance of paying attention to the diversity of experience that characterises the lives of these young people. They belong to the same generation, were all born in the early 1970s, have grown up in the same country and have gone through the same schooling process, but they have emerged with different aspirations for the future and have made different choices about their personal interests and priorities. They are all part of one of our major research studies known as the Life-Patterns Project. This is a ten-year longitudinal study based on an initial group of

30,000 students completing high school in 1991. The study was originally designed to examine the sense young people themselves make of the pathways they take, and whether the goals proposed to them by their elders square with their own aspirations and outcomes as they move into adulthood.

By 1996 it became evident that there was a growing mismatch between the changing priorities and choices of the young people involved in our study and the linear assumptions often made about their transitions into adulthood, and that this had parallels in studies from other countries as well. An example would be a study of young people in the United States (Schneider and Stevenson, 1999) which has used an informative blend of quantitative and qualitative data to examine their lives and ambitions. In this chapter therefore we want to examine in greater detail some of this evidence on young people's transitions through post-compulsory education.

For a start, one of the strongest messages that comes across in our interviews with the young people in our Life-Patterns Project who have now arrived at their late twenties is a sense of persistence and determination in the face of frustrated expectations. Many of them had believed that their future was assured – 'finishing my degree will provide me with employment, regular income, independence and enable me to be up to date with my friends who are already working'. Then, after graduating, they discovered that the outcome did not go according to plan. Unemployment and the increased competitiveness for employment is often mentioned in this context:

> I am concerned that my friends cannot find jobs and what it is doing to them emotionally and how degrading it is to them. No wonder they turn to alcohol and drugs and go on the dole;

> Since leaving education, it makes you aware how hard it can be out there when you become an adult, it can also make you harder.

Being 'harder' means making pragmatic decisions about what to do; not only 'making do' but also learning how to keep your options open and how to balance a number of different commitments (study, work, relationships, leisure pursuits, membership of community, religious or sports organisations) – becoming adult in different ways but holding on to a determination to achieve particular personal goals. Some researchers read this in a positive way as a sense of 'agency' (du Bois-Reymond, 1998), others see it as a sense of individual choice that seems puzzling in the way it underestimates the risks (Rudd and

Evans, 1998), while our data suggest 'pragmatic choice' as a better way of summing it up.

One thing is clear: after graduation the participants in our study are finding it harder than they had expected to establish themselves in adult life. For some there is a great sense of frustration that all the work they did at school or since at a college or university does nothing for them in the real world, 'establishing a healthy social life has been easy, a happy work lifestyle has been a lot harder'; while others express feelings of disillusionment that many have not been able to achieve employment in the area they trained in, 'many of us who did the same uni course are having trouble finding work, even though we were promised jobs as graduates'. Are these reactions typical? How do others respond to the uncertainties they face? What kind of decisions have they made? How have they set about the task of balancing their options for the future? These are the kinds of questions that concern us in this chapter.

The ambition paradox

The upheavals affecting the lives of the post-1970 generation introduce us to a paradox displayed by the widening gap between the way young people are assessing their future options and the way other people interpret their choices (Wyn and White, 2000). On the one hand, the research data display some common themes in the personal comments of members of the post-1970 generation from Britain, Europe, Canada, Australia and the United States, which point clearly to their need to make choices within a context of risk and uncertainty. On the other hand, there is a persistence in the social science and education literature that continues to explain and reinterpret young people's choices with reference to predetermined or established perspectives about what it means to 'grow up'.

A recent study from the United States (Schneider and Stevenson, 1999) is a good example of an attempt to address this paradox. It is one of the best contemporary accounts of the lives of the post-1970 generation, which makes good use of both large-scale quantitative data and detailed personal accounts from interviews with a wide range of young Americans seeking to find some kind of future for themselves. The authors note how the combined pressures of a growing insistence on post-school credentials and increasing uncertainties in the labour market have heightened the levels of 'ambition' for this generation by comparison with those which shaped their parents' lives.

The magnitude of the change we were describing was dramatic, and it appeared to be occurring among both males and females, as well as adolescents from different racial and ethnic groups. The rising ambitions were not limited to students from high- and middle-income families.

(Schneider and Stevenson, 1999, p. ix)

This change in outlook leads the authors to define the young people as 'the ambitious generation' and to acknowledge the disparity between their heightened aspirations and their likely or eventual achievements. But the authors can also see an 'ambition paradox' at work here, and it forms part of a subtext in the book – the teenagers are not only ambitious but, unfortunately as the book's subtitle would have it, 'motivated but directionless'. Why directionless? Because many of them lack 'aligned ambitions'; they are 'drifting dreamers' who 'are unaware of steps they can take that may help them achieve their ambitions' (1999, p. 4).

The book provides a very up-to-date account of the lives of this generation and in doing so not only brings out the obvious diversity of their ambitions and the choices they are making, but also demolishes many of the myths about youth lifestyles, pastimes and peer relationships that are so much part of the persistent media 'teen' images inherited from the past.

Popular media images often portray adolescents as 'slackers', drug users, and perpetrators of violent crimes. The overwhelming majority of teenagers, however, graduate from high school, do not use hard drugs, are not criminals, and do not father or have babies while still in their teens . . . Most young people are worried about their futures and believe attaining a college degree is critical for finding a first real job.

(1999, pp. 3–4)

Television shows and recent small-scale studies that are not longitudinal present a traditional 1950s view of adolescent peer groups: enduring circles of close friends with strong social ties. These groups are seen as having strong norms that influence the behaviour of members and make them readily recognisable to outsiders. Evidence from the Sloan study suggests a strikingly different view. Adolescent friendship groups are highly fluid, changing from year to year during high school.

(1999, pp. 197–8)

This theme of change and the need to make choices for yourself runs through much of the interview material – not surprisingly given that 80 per cent of them are already working and gaining a degree of economic independence during their high school years (p. 170) and that they actually spend 'more time alone than with family or friends' (p. 192). The theme of change is also evident in the uncertainties of the labour market which are helping to shape this generation's choices of college courses and desired future careers.

> Today's teenagers see their future work lives as filled with promise and uncertainty. They believe in the value of technology, in the importance of being flexible, and in the need for specialisation; they also believe that they will change jobs frequently and change careers occasionally. Teenagers accept the volatility of the labor market and believe that the way to create a personal safety net is to obtain additional education.
>
> (1999, p. 11)

This contrast between promise and uncertainty is central to the ambition paradox the authors are investigating. The paradox emerges because much of the analysis in the book is organised around the link between the concepts of 'aligned ambitions' and 'social mobility' – measuring their ambitions against their likely prospects of 'moving up the economic and social ladder'. What are these aligned ambitions? They are characterised by the fit or correspondence between established educational and occupational goals – 'students with aligned ambitions know the type of job they want and how much education is needed' to get it (p. 6). The authors advocate this type of approach because it strengthens prospects of social mobility and also gives direction and 'a sense of order' to teenagers' lives.

> We have found that life plans that are coherent with detail and realism are especially useful for choosing a path that increases the probability of success in adulthood. They provide adolescents with a sense of order, encourage them to engage in strategic effort and to sustain high levels of motivation, and help them to use familial and organizational resources.
>
> (1999, p. 7)

At the same time there are problems associated with this assumed link between aligned ambitions and social mobility. As the statistical data presented by the authors on pages 72 to 78 show, educational ambitions and occupational outcomes are not as directly related or as easy to match as young Americans have been led to believe. As a result, some teenagers overestimate the amount or type of education they will need for the future while others underestimate the kind of qualification that will be required of them. More than half of the members of this study belonged to these categories of 'misaligned ambitions', and only 43.7 per cent could be said to have 'aligned ambitions' or an accurate assessment of the 'fit' between education and occupation. The authors strongly advocate this fit and empha-sise its importance, but their evidence also casts doubt on whether it would in fact lead to more successful outcomes for everybody. They acknowledge that students with aligned ambitions are 'more likely to be able to chart a path towards their career goals' (p. 263), but their data on the extensive restructuring and fluidity of the current American labour market tend to call into question the extent to which the imagery of 'a path' leading to a 'goal' is appropriate in a contin-ually changing employment market.

> Since 1955 there has been a steady increase in the percentage of seniors aspiring to jobs in the professional category. The greatest increase occurred from 1980 to 1992, when the percentage of students desiring professional jobs increased from 54 percent to more than 70 percent.
>
> (1999, pp. 75–6)

> The number of adolescents aspiring to become lawyers and judges is five times the projected number needed; the number who want to become writers, artists, entertainers, and athletes is fourteen times the anticipated openings. High school students are much less likely to aspire to work in service and administrative occu-pations, and the number of jobs projected in these categories by 2005 exceeds the number of adolescents who want to fill them. There will be five times as many administrative and clerical jobs as there are adolescents interested in such work. The picture is also skewed for service jobs, with seven times as many jobs as there are teenagers interested in them.
>
> (1999, pp. 77–8)

What is of concern here is that these aspirations of young Americans, however 'misaligned' they might appear on analysis, were scarcely of their own making. As with their counterparts in other Western countries, they became 'ambitious' because their parents, teachers, public officials, social commentators and policy-makers told them that they needed to be or else they would be putting their own futures at risk. The knowledge society, the 'highly skilled workforce of the future' and the needs of industry for the new millennium were so much part of the imagery influencing their own growth towards adulthood that it is not surprising that they took it so seriously. What they were not told and what they did not therefore take into account in ambitioning professional careers was that the realities of the labour market did not fit the imagery surrounding them.

Misaligned ambitions are a direct product of the misleading claims promulgated so enthusiastically by the proponents of the knowledge society. In their unqualified pride about all that their generation has achieved, they boast that now the largest group in the workforce is composed of those who apply their knowledge and skill in problem-solving, creative enterprise and the management of information. If only it were so! The recent Report on the American Workforce by the Bureau of Labor Statistics (1999) introduces a much-needed element of sanity by means of a considered analysis of the impact of 'skills' on the American labour market. Its authors acknowledge the increase in skills levels of the labour force, employer demand for higher skill levels for vacant positions, and the spectacular rises in financial remuneration for the most highly qualified in the most highly skilled positions and professions. At the same time, they caution that over the past decade bachelor degree occupational positions have increased by less than 2 per cent (from 20.3 per cent to 22.1 per cent) and that '2 of every 3 jobs created over this period were in occupations that do not require a degree' (Bureau of Labor Statistics, 1999, p. 55). In terms of skill requirement, the largest numerical growth (41 per cent) has been in 'short-term on-the-job training' (p. 49), which is related to the fact that the 'most rapid growth in employment over the 1986–1996 period was in the services sector (40 per cent)' (p. 51). The report also indicates that these patterns are likely to persist, so that while jobs which require an associate degree or higher 'are expected to grow faster than average over the 1996–2006 period, the majority of occupations with the largest expected job growth will require less than an associate degree' (1999, p. 61).

Schneider and Stevenson have accurately identified the mismatch that exists between the persistent promotion of the knowledge society and the actual distribution of skilled and unskilled jobs in the service society. The analysis by the Bureau of Labor Statistics demonstrates that the mismatch owes more to the realities of the market-place than it does to misguided or 'directionless' ambition on the part of 'drifting dreamers'. The authors have also accurately identified the potential that life-plans and aligned ambitions have with regard to successful career outcomes, but some caution needs to be recorded about measuring young people's ambitions in terms of alignment without some detailed discussion of how contingent the US labour market has now become. What do 'aligned ambitions' mean when the proportion of 'contingent' workers (i.e. those without regular full-time jobs) had increased to 30 per cent of the American workforce by 1997 (Mishel, Bernstein and Schmitt, 1999; Rifkin, 1995)?

Patterns of change

There are many similarities between much of the information in the American study and the findings of our Life-Patterns Project. The themes of change and the mismatch between aspirations and outcomes are ever present. The Project is a ten-year study of 30,000 students leaving school in 1991 at about age 17, and who completed a 1992 follow-up survey on what they had done since leaving school. In 1996, a representative sample of 11,000 was resurveyed and then narrowed down to form a subsequent annual interview sample of 100 and questionnaire sample of 2,000. The sample was both urban and rural, covering a representative range of school (60 per cent from government schools) and ethnic (with one-third of parents born outside Australia) backgrounds, and a variety of parental educational attainment (close to half not having completed high school).

Our ongoing sample is drawn from two separate groupings: a 'Studying' sub-set who went on to further study at the end of school; and a 'Non-Study' subset who chose some other alternative. However, it is significant that of these 'Non-Study' respondents, by 1996 as many as 80 per cent had returned to study in the intervening years. It is also significant that over 50 per cent of our sample had made a change of some kind (institution, course, deferral etc.) during their years of post-school study rather than staying on a linear track (table 1.1).

A further change affecting their lives that is often overlooked within prevailing policy settings is the fact that the majority of students have had extensive work participation – even going back as far as their final years in secondary school. On this particular issue the participant responses definitely call into question established understandings of career paths that are based on a definition of labour market participation as a consequence of participation in various post-compulsory education pathways. Unfortunately, this masks a significant overlap

Table 1.1 Changes among total student participants (n = 1717)

Changes 1992–6	Number	%
Changed institutions	351	20
Changed courses	425	25
Interrupted studies	250	15
Discontinued	264	15
Total excluding multiple changes	887	52

between study and work that for many of the participants is in the forefront of their experience. They do not view study and work in the sequential way implied in the customary models of transition. When we look at how the respondents describe their actual situation during the course of their studies, we find a complex pattern based on combinations of study and work commitments. This was true for respondents from both city and rural areas. In fact, the majority of both had combined work and study most or all of the time since leaving high school, and at most only 20 per cent had rarely or never had a job during their studies (table 1.2).

Over 60 per cent of them had full-time jobs at some stage since leaving school, some have continued in those jobs after graduation, and a third have drawn unemployment benefits at some stage as 'labour-force participants'. There may have been an element of constraint in this blending of study and work commitments, which is perhaps reflected in another aspect of the findings which indicates a reversal of the trend prior to the 1990s for growing numbers of young Australians to move into independent living situations for themselves. Not even completion of post-school studies or the gaining of full-time employment has prevented them from continuing to rely on their parents for support – with 63 per cent of them still at the parental home in 1996 (including 58 per cent of those who had completed their studies). This appears in line with trends elsewhere.

Table 1.2 Respondents combining work and study

Combinations	Rural (%)	Urban (%)
Continually	31	32
Mostly	22	22
Sometimes	27	26
Rarely	11	9
Never	9	10

The Swedes have even invented a new term (mambo) for those who remain in or return to the parental home after age 18, Canadians for example refer to 'boomerang kids', and Belgians refer to 'hotel families'. In Britain, Jones (2000) notes that young people now 'may leave home more than once' and that the link between leaving home and getting married is now less obvious. While the situation in the United States is more complex and thus more difficult to analyse, recent research (Goldscheider and Goldscheider, 1999) indicates that a reversal of the 1960s trend is taking place there as well.

In our research we had included a range of questions about how the participants assessed the transitions they were making and how they were balancing their personal commitments. The findings provide a significant insight into the ways in which they are endeavouring to shape their futures. For example, we had asked whether they had any difficulties with combining their commitments to both work and study (table 1.3). At least at a pragmatic individual level, the participants are building up their own picture of how to manage a range of personal commitments. The combinations of work and study and the varying attitudes towards those combinations indicate that there is a degree of over-lapping in their lives between the two worlds of study and work, and more importantly that the combinations assume different meanings for different students and that there are different ways in which the combinations are negotiated and balanced.

It is significant that most take some kind of combination for granted, and that even in terms of preferences 'work without study' or (despite its implied priority at a policy level) 'study without work' do not attract majority support. These results were confirmed in various other items scattered throughout the survey which called for responses about personal preferences to do with particular life

Table 1.3 Attitudes towards work/study combinations

Difficulties	%
Work tends to take priority	23
Need to work, but would prefer full-time study	19
Prefer to do both	28
Need both, but difficult to combine	25
Like both, but trouble finding job	8
Would prefer work without study	16
Would prefer study without work	29
(Percentages exceed 100% due to multiple responses)	

Table 1.4 Sample items of preference diversity

	%
Priority for staying in local rural community	20
Interrupted or discontinued studies	20
Preference for parenting/home duties	6
Happy with only irregular work	12
Give lesser importance to qualifications	26

contexts, individual priorities and reactions to possible future scenarios. Some examples of these items are displayed in table 1.4.

Is this pattern of mixed commitments unique to the particular sample that constitutes our Life-Patterns Project or is it a pattern that has now become the norm for students in contemporary society? During 1998, we have examined this issue with an entirely different group in three different colleges in three States. The research involved surveys of about 1,400 entry-level students, as well as interviews with about 50 students in each of the participating institutions. The majority (68 per cent) were 19 years old or younger, and males made up 54 per cent of the sample (Dwyer et al, 1999).

Up to two-thirds of the students surveyed were in some form of either paid or unpaid employment. The majority were working on average two or more days per week. Only 14 per cent had no intention of working while studying (table 1.5).

They were aware that future employment now depends on both qualifications and experience, and so they saw their involvement in both paid and unpaid work as a necessary means to establishing a work record for themselves to complement their eventual training qualifications. There was also a noticeable gender difference in attitudes to work and study – males were twice as likely to 'prefer work without study', while 17 per cent of females and only 10 per cent of males would 'prefer study without work'.

The 144 interviews brought out in much clearer detail the complexity of the study/work combinations in the three localities. It was generally agreed that being in the workforce did, of itself, enhance one's chances of finding work in one's chosen field. Paid work was a stated need by all concerned, while unpaid work was a chosen strategy aimed at gaining a foothold in a desired career, a chance to gain experience and to 'prove oneself'. As one student said, 'It all looks good on your resumé!' Combining study and work was also

Table 1.5 Current work

	%
Intend to get a job	32
Have a full time job	10
Have a regular-part time job	29
Have a number of jobs	5
Have occasional employment	9
Not intending to find job while studying	14

viewed as essential for those looking to 'upskill' or move into new career paths. More of the females saw that their job may provide skills or experience leading to their desired careers. On the other hand, unpaid employment – work undertaken by students on their own initiative – was frequently looked upon as important and it was this work that was seen by some as providing the most promising route to the desired career.

In general, the students regard working part time as a valuable experience irrespective of the type of job. They feel that employers wish to see young people being productive and responsible, so their resumés must show this. Working part time has a short-term benefit – an income – but in the long term its purpose is also beneficial, in that the employer can see their qualifications plus their industriousness, independence and initiative. From this, applicants stand a better chance of securing full-time employment in the future.

Overall, there was considerable variation in the type and extent of study/work combinations, which was influenced by the availability of jobs in particular locations. For example, there were some important gender differences in the rural sample. Young males from farming communities were more likely to be engaged in paid or unpaid work on the family farm, whereas young females looked elsewhere for jobs, in such areas as childcare or retail outlets. Young males from small towns were largely unable to find employment and tended to join their peers in larger towns where both males and females found occasional or part-time employment in the service sector. In one of the cities employment opportunities for both males and females were restricted, and only 43 per cent of the sample had work of some kind, mainly in retail outlets, with some casual work such as lawnmowing, babysitting, or as attendants in car parks or a sports arena. Hours worked ranged from eight to twenty-four hours per week. This range was similar for the participants from the other major city, but they were the most successful in obtaining work, with 68 per cent employed, many in jobs they had held for three or four years. Some were working two jobs but the most common configuration was weekend work including a Thursday or Friday night-shift. The following case studies provided by our regional researcher illustrate the patterns of choice adopted by the participants.

Gordon, 18 years of age, lives on his parents' farm outside a large country town. He is doing a course in plumbing, and plays a lot of football for which he is paid a small income. The football takes up about six to seven hours a weak, and Gordon made the comment that it perhaps helped with his attitude to team-work and also gave him many contacts in the various trades for possible future employment. On his parents' farm he is heavily involved in general farm duties, amounting to some twenty-hours a week or more. The work is mainly with sheep but also fencing and farm maintenance and is done because of family need. He enjoys this work but prefers his other unpaid job, with a local plumber, where he gains valuable experience which he hopes in the future to turn into an apprenticeship. He states that it also helps to make sense of the plumbing course he is doing.

Previously Gordon had had only farming work or his football for income, and concluded that this was mostly due to his locality and family life-style rather than particular choices he had been faced with. Choosing to take up plumbing was in response to suggestions from the school careers adviser who noted his handiwork while in his final years of high school. Gordon feels 'pretty good, I know what I'm doing now'. He has decided to put more of his effort into the plumbing course, being convinced that this is to be his future direction. Study and plumbing take priority for now and 'footy has backed off a bit'. Between the work and study, work is the main priority as he hopes to gain an apprenticeship out of it but study is still very important. He finds that it all 'mingles in pretty good . . . always got time for footy' and that work aids his study and vice versa. In five years time Gordon hopes to see himself as a qualified plumber, still living at home but doing less farmwork and still playing football. Main priority, however, is to 'get that apprenticeship'.

Then there is Amanda, 17 years of age, doing a course in hospitality operations. She share-rents a house in one small town but returns to her parents' home in another on weekends.

Amanda works a number of jobs in her efforts to self-finance her education and gain experience in her chosen field. On weekends

Amanda puts in eight to fifteen hours at a supermarket in her home town and when not there she works at her parents' cafe doing another six hours. This pays for her week's accommodation in the town where the college is located, some three-quarters of an hour away. In addition Amanda works casually through the week at a caterers there, averaging another three to four hours. Amanda doesn't mind the supermarket delicatessen work in her home town as she feels the experience is still relevant to her career aim of being a chef. The caterers work she loves and would do more. The cafe work Amanda also likes and would do it to help out her parents, paid or unpaid. In addition, she sees it as relevant experience.

Whenever she can, Amanda likes to work at the local childcare centre in her parents' town for anything up to six hours. She does this to keep in touch with her fall-back career aim (her primary aim before working part time at a caterers) which is childcare.

Amanda finds that 'sometimes it's demanding . . . studying in one town and having to be at work an hour later at another'. In addition she must sometimes make a decision between working at the caterers in one town, which she enjoys the most, and working at the other in the supermarket, her main source of income. She cannot afford to lose her job at the supermarket nor refuse catering too often. She finds the caterers work particularly valuable to her studies, and the supermarket will one day be her main work reference in gaining an apprenticeship. It is this juggling between her jobs and her travel which makes life most difficult at present.

Amanda is representative of her peers, though perhaps slightly larger than life in that representation. Not all do quite as much as she does, but many do similar if less. She has given everything a go, yet still is not in full-time employment, and it grates. Like her peers, she has studied, worked hard at casual jobs, worked unpaid for experience, changed direction and tried again, still to no avail. Despite this, also like many of her peers, Amanda is still optimistic and planning – unlike the males of her group who are much less positive. The driving that Amanda must do is also reasonably typical of rural groups in that the course she desires to study is in one town and she lives in another.

There are some obvious similarities between Amanda's busy life and some of the North Carolina teenagers in a recent American study. She has her counterpart in Vickie, an 18-year-old with a full-time job at a fitness gym, a part-time job as a drugstore clerk and a weekend job at a video store. Vickie works a sixty-hour week and, as the author notes, while she and others 'have long-range goals' many seem unable to save any money 'even though I'm working all the time' (Willis, 1998, p. 354).

Priorities

When we look at the life-patterns of students like Gordon and Amanda or that of Vickie in North Carolina we become aware of the complexities of life that are now taken for granted by many in the younger generation. Many young people are now, so to speak, creating their own portfolios in preparation for later life. This type of approach has important implications for teachers at the secondary level. Thus the design of education systems in most parts of the industrialised world still reflects the thinking about the relationship between education and society that was current in the immediate post-war era. School is still seen as the prior educational setting where 'learning' occurs and work is the subsequent setting, where learning is 'applied'. One of the implications of the contemporary pattern for young people to mix school and work is that, rather than school being a preparation for work, the workplace is providing young people with a pragmatic perspective on education. They see that life elsewhere is different. In most workplaces, the lessons that young people learn are that there are few 'careers', most work is short-term, and much of it unskilled. To be successful in employment, people must be flexible and proactive, and this more pragmatic approach on the part of young people can begin to affect their attitudes towards school.

This is evident in a recent study of young people in the UK (Raffo and Reeves, 2000) and the ways in which they were making their own decisions about how they relate to their schooling. Not only were they making decisions about their levels of participation in the classroom, they were deciding which lessons they would attend. Even during their school years these young people are making very active choices about when they intend to leave school, whether they would take time out from education and which qualifications to study for. The evidence suggests that young people are developing a perspective on schooling in which education is only one of a number of options which they are managing. Furthermore, in making decisions about how they will manage these options, they are making very pragmatic choices about which school subjects are relevant to them. This suggests that perhaps the American authors of *The Ambitious Generation* were missing something when they described many in their sample as 'directionless' and were closer to the truth in noting how aware their sample was concerning the paradoxes of 'promise and uncertainty' (Schneider and Stevenson, 1999, p. 3).

This process of individual assessment of possible choices in life is also reflected in the way young people weigh up their future priorities. In our 1996 survey of the participants in our Life-Patterns Project, we asked about priorities in life and at that stage items related to personal autonomy were given greatest weight (table 1.6).

In 1998, we followed up this line of inquiry and provided a list of fifteen priority items to be rated in terms of their level of importance currently in the respondents' personal lives. The two dominant items were 'having a steady job' and 'family relationships' – but there appeared to be some differences in interpretation by contrast with responses to other items. Table 1.7 shows the contrasts.

Thus it is interesting to contrast the variations in ranking for somewhat related items in this list. A re-examination of the overall ranking of the different issues displays some subtle distinctions between items that might be expected to be similarly ranked. Thus, while 'having a steady job' is given top ranking, it appears that a distinction is being made between the element of security this provides and actual levels of attainment such as career involvement (ranked 7), doing well in studies (ranked 8) or earning a lot of money (ranked 10). Similarly, a distinction appears to emerge at the level of personal relationships. While 'family relationships' (ranked 2) scores at virtually the same level as 'having a steady job', and is closely followed by 'developing friendships' (ranked 3), these notions of family and friendship do not seem to necessarily equate with either 'marriage or

Table 1.6 Characteristics of adult life

n = 1908	High support
Financial independence	1450
Making own choices/decisions	1310
Emotional maturity	1283
A secure job	1219
Taking responsibility for things	1155
Getting on well with people	1124
Sticking to one's principles	885
Owning one's own home	791
Academic/training qualifications	602
Becoming a parent	533
Having authority over others	97

Table 1.7 Personal priorities

n = 1430	Rank
Having a steady job	1
involvement in work as a career	7
doing well in studies	8
earning a lot of money	10
Family relationships	2
Developing friendships	3
marriage or living with a partner	9
having children	12
Involvement in leisure-time activities	4
Owning your own home	5
Travelling to different places	6
Being physically attractive	11
Working to correct social problems	13
Involvement in community activities	14
Staying in my local area	15

living with a partner' (ranked 9) and 'having children' (ranked 12). It is also interesting to note that while 'owning your own home' (ranked 5) continues to be an important priority for Australians, 'involvement in leisure-time activities' (ranked 4) and 'travelling to different places' (ranked 6) were considered just as important.

Obviously, these contrasting results could prove to be extremely significant, not only for our understanding of young people's priorities but also with regard to likely future outcomes if those priorities are held on to over the coming years. What we can say immediately, particularly in light of the interview data, is that the distinction between 'having a steady job' and 'involvement in work as a career' carries considerable weight with many of the participants. There is evidence in our interviews that echoes some of the attitudes towards work revealed in an American study of 'teens at work' in North Carolina. The researcher indicated that 'the most strongly held notion about work is that horizontal mobility through a variety of meaningless jobs constitutes autonomy' (Willis, 1998, p. 351). As one of the teenagers put it, 'independence is having a pointless job that I can quit any day', or in the words of a young male from a professional family 'freedom is not having to take your work home with you'. There are also within our interview sample signs of some of the reactions that surprised du Bois-Reymond in her study of young people in the Netherlands. She commented that some of her respondents 'do not like adulthood', particularly if it means 'nothing but work' until they are 65 by which time they will be 'old and knackered' (du Bois-Reymond, 1998, p. 74). While our respondents have been less forthright they do make comments which suggest that they have wider priorities in their lives.

One unsuccessful student who had wanted to become a welder (and dreamed of being a musician) had taken a few years off 'to see the world' and now works as an administrative assistant. He is now planning to quit the job 'before the end of the year' because it is 'human nature to move on – you get stale when the routine sets in'. Another male who had a successful career as a golf professional and then became a sports writer says, however, that he 'doesn't like the idea of goals – you just want to keep going and finding new things to attain'. A young woman with an arts diploma and a steady job gives her busy social life top priority and is critical of her parents who 'told me to do an accounting or secretarial course – like a good little migrant girl. Now they are moaning about a marriage with a good boy'. A qualified accountant who was recently promoted wants to give up his job and go overseas 'backpacking in Europe' – after all 'you could get retrenched tomorrow' anyway. Others, both with and without jobs, want to travel – 'get out of Moe, get out of Victoria, get out of Australia, have a look at the world'.

The interview material in particular demonstrates how complex the planning of life's priorities has become for the participants. In working back over our data, our key researchers demonstrated that it is not an easy task. The participants are very much aware of pressures on them from family, teachers and their peers which affect their personal goals and to some extent at least predetermine their expectations.

Comments from the 1996 survey explicitly focused attention on pressure from parents and family to accomplish particular goals – 'It is a social and family expectation that I marry one day'; 'There is the expectation that one should get married and have children and that one should start saving for their future to buy a house and a car and save for a rainy day'. Others made reference to a general pressure to do certain things in life; whether this pressure comes from specific friends and family or from society in general was not made clear – 'Feel pressured to gain financial independence'; 'Too much pressure to strive for success'; 'Pushed into university system straight after school'. Although not always sure of where these pressures come from – whether from the family, friends, teachers or the general community – respondents at times have an awareness that there are external expectations which operate on their own life-choices.

Another factor that could be involved is the desire, on the individual's part, to 'keep-up' with their friends and contemporaries. Many respondents seemed to be concerned that their friends had jobs, or better-paid jobs than they had. One person felt so ashamed at going nowhere with his job that he had changed his name and denied his identity to past friends he had met on the street. Others were aware of the social pressures on them, but tended to shrug them off. Thus there seems to be particular emphasis on individual choice and self-determined life biographies reflected in the commentary of some survey respondents – 'I have learned not to take too much notice of what people have to say'; 'If society is so mixed up, why not reject it?'; 'I see myself as the trunk of a tree of opportunities, with thousands of branches beginning to grow'. Despite the hopes and worries which many of these people share, they still maintain an attitude of agency in terms of their own life experiences and their future.

At the same time, they had a sense of the degree to which economic constraint affected individual decisions and expectations. Where people have come from, who they are and how they see themselves in relation to the constraints that they may perceive in contemporary society was a recurring theme in the commentaries of the 1996 survey. Some respondents could see that society is stratified by socioeconomic factors, which may limit the potential outcomes of younger people – 'Environment plays a role. Poor people keep getting poorer'. There was the argument that study could help one escape the limits of one's social class –

> I come from a working class background but studied hard and made the most of every opportunity and now I'm going to become a lawyer and I'm nearly a qualified lawyer.

There was also the perception that studies could be limited by one's economic/financial situation – 'Formal training should be made more available at an economic rate for the people who have to start off economically disadvantaged'; 'Even though I might not be doing the right course I can't afford to change my mind even though I'm barely out of my teenage years'; 'Financially I needed more help at school'; 'How is anyone supposed to learn when you can't even get a foot in the door, that's what I want to know'.

Despite the pressures, broader concerns remain uppermost. 'Cruising and comfortable' was the comment of a female hairdresser when asked about her ambitions in life, while another accountant insisted that he 'works to live, not the other way around – quality outside hours'. A male apprentice was excited about becoming a father – 'I'm more interested in my home life; setting up a great place to live and working on a family'. There are those with an added commitment to helping other people. One young woman is a qualified fashion designer and 'keenly committed to the Maltese community' in which she does voluntary work and finds it 'much more rewarding than the paid work', and there is the young man, now married but in and out of jobs, who had paid his own airfares to work on Christian missions in Africa and India and currently does volunteer work in Australia. A qualified nurse, who likes to 'party hard' on the weekends, loves her work with alcoholic and psychiatric patients but her 'parents keep hassling me to find a better job – Dad thinks I'll end up as crazy as the patients'.

For most, the financial security that employment provides is obviously important. Some are much more ambitious and determined 'to rise to the top', but others, when given the chance to comment about their ambitions, indicate that wider priorities are the matters that really count. A woman from outside the metropolitan area of Melbourne had got up at six every morning to travel into the city for a hospitality course and then worked an evening shift on returning home. She now works at a local hotel and 'couldn't imagine living anywhere else – this is where my friends and family are (these are the most important things for me)'. A social work graduate could not get work in his area of specialisation and has moved from job to job in restaurants and hotels. He is currently working as a waiter, but also works part time in a community centre on a voluntary basis – his view of work is 'where he would feel satisfied about making a contribution to people's lives and making the world a better place'. Another young woman at a childcare centre has recently taken a drop in pay, but 'the quality of where I work is more important than anything else – not just financial gains'.

This shift of perspective on the part of the participants raises an important challenge for the ways in which we conduct research about their experience of life. Particularly in a longitudinal study, there are questions that, on reflection, needed to be asked in the initial stages but were not, and for which answers which rely on recollection of past events may lack validity. This limitation not only applies to the specific items that are included in an ongoing survey instrument designed some time in the past, but also to the assumptions that are then made that the questions asked some twenty years ago have the same meaning now as they did then (Andres *et al.*, 1999). This is particularly true of questions concerning occupational categories and outcomes, and in other cases where significant changes are affecting the lives of the participants. The complexities associated with their decisions and the influences on those decisions are often not adequately dealt with by such survey techniques.

We became particularly aware of this when we began to uncover anomalies between our interview material and the statistical data we were dealing with in our annual surveys. The surveys had begun as an investigation of student 'pathways' and almost inevitably had locked us into a linear sequence of analysis that had begun to 'bracket out' what we thought were inconsistencies in the responses. On revisiting our material we discovered that they were not in fact inconsistencies but evidence of complexity in the assessments the participants were making and the 'non-linear' factors that they were taking into account.

In our year 2000 annual survey we explored these apparent inconsistencies in greater detail. When asked to rate from low to high how much practical importance in their lives they placed on selected items, both males (75 per cent) and females (87 per cent) placed a high priority on 'developing personal relationships'. Males (80 per cent) were more likely than females (76 per cent) to emphasise career, while females stressed family/home life (93 per cent) more than the males (67 per cent). Two-thirds of the males placed great importance on 'leisure/recreational activities' and three-quarters of both males and females emphasised 'health and fitness' issues. Their responses confirmed the priorities indicated earlier in table 1.7, with a strong emphasis on the importance of more personal issues (such as relationships with family and friends) alongside their work or career concerns (table 1.8).

Evidence such as this demonstrates how a narrow preoccupation with just the two dimensions of study and work in the lives of young people leaves out so much of what really counts in their lives and gives a false picture of the choices they are making and the reasons underlying them. What is most striking in the interview material is that these wider priorities in life transcend the actual circumstances of the participants – whether they are highly qualified or unqualified, highly paid or unemployed, successful in their area of specialisation or working somewhere else, significant numbers of both the males and the females see life as multi-dimensional and have a range of personal commitments that they regard as central to their lives.

In commenting on the contingency and uncertainty of the new job

Table 1.8 Main practical commitments in life

n = 1109	High support
Developing personal relationships	918
Family/home life	891
Pursuing my work or career	852
Maintaining my health and fitness	824
Leisure/recreational activities	683
Being environmentally aware	528

market that young Americans of her generation face, Naomi Klein makes a similar point.

> Because young people tend not to see the place where they work as an extension of their souls, they have, in some cases, found freedom in knowing they will never suffer the kind of heart-wrenching betrayals their parents did. For almost everyone who has entered the job market in the past decade, unemployment is a known quantity, as is self-generated and erratic work. In addition, losing one's job is much less frightening when getting it seemed an accident in the first place. Such familiarity with unemployment creates its own kind of worker divestment – divestment of the very notion of total dependency on stable work. We may begin to wonder whether we should even want the same job for our whole lives, and, more important, why we should depend on the twists and turns of large institutions for our sense of self.
>
> (Klein, 2000, p. 271)

The idea of transition to adulthood

The 'ambition paradox' identified by Schneider and Stevenson has a deeper meaning. It points to a conflict between established understandings of young people's transitions into adult life and what the authors identify as attempts by the current generation to come to terms with 'promise and uncertainty' (Schneider and Stevenson, 1999, p. 11). The conflict suggests that young people's individual identities which are shaped in the current circumstances are very likely to form the basis of more generalised adult patterns and approaches to life. In other words, the choices they must make in response to the widespread changes that have affected their lives foreshadow life-patterns and personal and social predispositions that will endure beyond the transition period identified as 'youth' and not be limited to the merely individual narratives of particular agents. Otherwise we trivialise their experience. If those narratives are now different from those of the past, we need also to ask how different will 'adult' lives and identities be as a result. The ever-lengthening time designated as youth and the increasing importance of elements of choice stretch the credibility of the idea that this is simply a 'transition'. The experiences of change and the aggregation of these in people's personal histories have continuing implications for the construction and meaning of adult identities. Structural conditions (for example, those which affect labour markets), and perhaps the longer-term implications of globalisation, will significantly shape people's lives in the future, because they have changed the circumstances of adult lives as well as youth.

Hence, the emerging understanding of what growing up means in young people's lives today also requires a more critical examination of whether the meaning of adulthood has also changed. The recent research on young people's patterns of study, work and other life experiences suggests that to the extent that there is a reshaping of the way in which youth is experienced it is a reflection of a reshaping of the meaning and experience of adult life that is already affecting older generations. Many of the prevailing assumptions about what 'growing up' means actually owe their legitimacy to parallel assumptions about the predictability and permanence of the established institutional structures of family, education, industry and the state. Because the same degree of permanence and predictability can no longer be guaranteed, the present generation is living out, and perhaps struggling to come to terms with, the consequences. This makes it imperative to distinguish between those features that are part of a broader, fundamental change in people's lives (shared by older people as well as youth), and those features that could still reasonably be attributed to a transition stage between childhood and adulthood.

The examination of the different effects of new social forces and established processes of growth into adulthood also has implications for our understanding of the changing role of education in the processes of transition. While some writers have been willing to suggest that the discourses around current educational goals may be progressive, in that they recognise individual difference and perhaps offer young people the opportunity to develop self-realisation, it is also important to acknowledge the extent to which other agendas of power are at work within these discourses. Instead of education being framed as a social investment for 'the common good', current educational policies are framed to emphasise education as an investment in the self. Under the versions of human capital theory that currently inform the governments of many Western countries, education and training are conveniently seen as an individual responsibility, a question of individuals and their families making 'rational' choices to secure their future positions. Here, the notion of 'free' choices taken by individuals in effect glosses over questions of power and disadvantage.

The tendency towards individual choice which has been identified amongst many of the young people in our studies indicates that they are 'fitting in' with this approach – perhaps shaped by the discourses, in which the idea of the free market dominates and where polarisation between poor and wealthy continues to grow (Côté, 2000). All of these elements are part of a dominant discourse of power which has redefined the context of young people's lives and the purposes, practices and outcomes of their education. It has also become part of their own 'stories', although to what extent there are other sides to their stories needs also to be considered. If we want to find some clearer answers, we need to begin by asking new questions about young people's identities. In addition to employment and education, other priorities regarding locality, living arrangements, lifestyle, experimentation, leisure and multiple personal commitments are also seen by them as part of their 'human capital' and are already being taken into account in decisions about study and career outcomes.

2 Outside the mainstream

Mark grew up in a small rural township in a supportive family. When he was aged 11 his family moved to a new suburban development on the outskirts of a large city and he had to change schools.

> All my troubles started when I left this little country school. The teachers there weren't for learning. Then in grade 6 we moved. It was a real big shock, I was so embarrassed. They were having a times-table race and I didn't know what it was about. I didn't know a lot of the work. I'd never seen it before. When I told the teachers they said 'You should know, you went to primary school'. It was just different. The language around the town was different. It was a big culture shock I'd never come across a lot of the stuff before. I'm glad I left because I was the king clown in the class and everyone was missing out because of me. But, I'm also not glad because if I could've stayed, who knows what I'd be doing now.

So instead of going on to Year 12 and completing his schooling, at age 16 Mark left and began looking for jobs. As he said then:

> I'll take whatever comes along. I'm at the stage that I'm not fussy, I'd take anything. It really helps if you've got a good education. There's heaps and heaps of Year 12s around now. Employers say 'He's got a higher education, I'll take him'. There's not a great deal I can do about it. If a bloke's just looking for a dumb shit kicker, that'll be me.

Before long he ran into trouble with the police and this has coloured his attitude ever since.

The police are arseholes. From day one that I got into trouble, that was it. We'd always get pulled over, blamed for things we didn't do. I've been beaten up by the police – there's nothing you can do about it. The young ones are the worst, they're trying to get respect out of you. The older cops are nicer, they'll speak to you – they get somewhere.

He had similar experiences with the government job service:

They aren't much help. There's not a lot of jobs for my age group. It's for experienced people, or ones with their own car. Welfare is a bit of a pain. When I wasn't working, I was always getting cut off the roll. They reckoned it was my fault, that I wasn't making any attempt.

Frustrated with the way things had turned out, he tried going back to school.

I went back to school because I failed Year 10 the first time, and the second time I wasn't interested. Then when I quit school I was going to places for interviews and I would say I had Year 9. And that was it. They wanted a Year 10 minimum for lots of jobs and apprenticeships. It wouldn't be so bad if you were going back to school and in with your own age group. Last year I was 18 and shoved in a class where the average age was 14 to 15. They were smart arses, trying to be heroes in front of you. Trouble starts again and it's your fault. Now my brother wants to leave school early too. I won't let him. He wants to be like me. I don't want him growing up being a troublemaker and with nothing to do with his life.

By this stage Mark had moved out of home and begun looking for his own accommodation. He was evicted from one place so he:

went to the Housing Commission but they said, 'come back in a couple of weeks!'. So I went elsewhere, sold some furniture and my motorbike and came up with the bond and the first month's rent. I didn't bother with the Housing Commission after that.

He later moved on:

to the Bacchus Marsh Caravan Park two weeks ago. It's a big cabin, better than the other joint I was in. It's like a little unit.

I pay a low sum for rent, phone and electricity. I have heaps of stuff (furniture etc) in mum's garage and dad's old place.

Then followed another re-entry attempt, which got him nowhere.

I don't want to go back to school. I've tried a couple of schools, I just can't handle it. I don't know, I can't get into it. My body's there, but it's not exciting, it doesn't occupy me. I'd have liked to have stayed at school and worked more, though I haven't come across anything I've used from school. You never use what you learnt. Maths and algebra and all that crap. They should be teaching what's out in the real world. I've learnt more out of school. My reading's heaps better now and my spelling's improved. I never had the time for that before, when I was at school. They're just no help at school. I was wasting my time being there. I wanted to try, but the teachers wouldn't give me a fair go.

Discouragement began to take over.

I'm not sure about the future. I'll work until some good job comes along. I take each day as it comes. I'm trying for an apprenticeship. I haven't got my hopes up, because I'm getting a bit too old. I just hope something pops up.

Mark is a good example of a young man who would have had little trouble finding a job for himself on quitting school early – if only he had been born ten or so years earlier. Then, if anything, he would have in effect been part of the 'mainstream' – one of the many young people in Western societies who in the past had been able to establish themselves without completing their schooling or going on further to post-school studies. Unfortunately for him, now that educational credentials are in high demand, as one of the post-1970 generation he has ended up 'outside the mainstream' – a school 'drop-out' entering a collapsed youth labour market without the necessary qualifications or experience to demonstrate that he is 'employable'.

Thus, one of the main effects of current policy in Western societies has been to define young people in terms of their status as students. Whereas in the industrial era the linear model of development placed a strong emphasis on the 'school-to-work' transition, it now incorporates an intervening stage – post-compulsory education – as an essential element of young people's transition to adulthood. The alternatives to the completion of schooling which were taken for granted in the industrial era as part of the school-to-work transition have been called into question as a result of changes to the youth labour market in the restructured economy.

Prior to those changes, 'dropping out' seemed to provide an acceptable alternative route into an adult life for those who were either not academically inclined or were looking to make an early break from school and establish an independent way of life for themselves. In fact, even in the past the transition was not as simple as it appeared, and while leaving high school early was a move which enabled many to take up a positive option that suited the priority they placed on entering the workforce and gaining a livelihood for themselves, for others leaving was an action which seriously limited their possibilities of gaining employment and living independently as adults. The overall effect of the recent changes affecting the youth labour market throughout Western societies has been to increase significantly the likelihood that dropping out will have negative consequences and will fail to open up real opportunities for those who do not complete their schooling.

The fact remains that substantial numbers of young people still do not complete. Mark is not an isolated case – he has counterparts elsewhere. Even in a country such as the US which has had higher school completion rates than most other countries, close to a quarter still leave school early, even though over 40 per cent of these subsequently return or complete the GED (General Educational Development) certificate. Completion rates in other nations are not as high and, depending on the region, between a quarter and one-third of students still do not complete their secondary education. Up to half of these might take up other forms of education such as apprenticeships or traineeships of various kinds. In 1991, for example, outcomes for Australian high school students in one State displayed a virtually even three-way split between those who had entered university or higher education, those in vocational education or training, and those not involved in formal study of any kind. For the nation as a whole those aged 19, without their high school certificate, or other studies or qualifications constituted 23 per cent of the age sample (Department of Employment, Education and Training [DEET], 1993, p. 1).

Comparatively similar data are available from Britain, despite the persistence of high levels of youth unemployment. One detailed study in South Glamorgan in Wales conducted an analysis of monthly figures from February 1991 to April 1993 to identify the proportion of the 16- to 17-year-old age group that were not continuing with their schooling but who were also not included in the employment or training statistics for the area. The proportion made up a substantial minority ranging from 16 per cent to 23 per cent depending on the month in question (Istance *et al.*, 1994, p. 43, Williamson; 1997).

There is a consistency to this evidence from a number of different countries which suggests that, even in the United States where mainstreaming provisions have dominated and participation rates have been much higher than elsewhere, there has always been a substantial number for whom mainstream educational provisions have not been attractive or even suitable. Any realistic planning needs to take this significant proportion of the age group into account, or else runs the risk of delegitimising those who are not yet ready to continue their education or who choose to do something else with their lives. It is the purpose of this chapter to look more closely at what happens to them as a result.

What alternatives?

As we saw in the case of Mark, his experience of schooling had been bad. This had led him to quit but, as we also saw, he was ambivalent about his decision, he made a number of personal efforts to return to a series of different schools, and was also determined that his brother should not end up 'like me'. The consistent evidence about dropouts like Mark from many different countries demonstrates that provision will always need to be made for a significant minority for whom the choice to delay the completion of their schooling remains a legitimate one. One official report noted that:

> staying on in school for some in this group can be counterproductive if it changes neutral feelings about learning into negative ones, and leaves the young person with the wish never to re-enter the training system at a future time.
>
> (Senate Standing Committee on Employment,
> Education and Training, 1992, pp. 37–8)

What this recognises is that for some young people post-compulsory education is only a real option after a break away from school, during which they seek out some alternative for themselves. Unfortunately, to discontinue schooling on completion of the compulsory years is no longer regarded in current official and community attitudes as a legitimate option, which has the effect of increasing the vulnerability of those who are looking for some alternative transition into adulthood that does not necessarily involve continued involvement with school or training. As the South Glamorgan study in the UK indicated:

> This was, indeed, the finding of a recent study of 'status zerO'
> 16- and 17-year-olds: young people who were not in education,
> training or employment (and for whom 'status zerO' is a suitable metaphor for young people who count for nothing and
> appear to be going nowhere). Not only did it confirm suspicions
> that this phenomenon was not restricted to a residual hard-core
> but was a common experience for a significant minority of
> minimum age school leavers, but it also indicated how such young
> people – who were often already disadvantaged by a 'tangle of
> pathologies' – slipped further and inexorably into experiences
> of homelessness, drug misuse and both opportunistic and calculated crime.
>
> (Williamson, 1996, pp. 222–3)

Approximately 16 per cent to 23 per cent of South Glamorgan's 16-
and 17-year-old population 'were not in education, training or work
– at any one time' (Istance *et al.*, 1994, p. 43). As might be expected,
there was considerable movement in and out of work, training or
registering with the Careers Service. Young people became members
of 'status zerO' then moved out, while others moved out and then
later on returned. Viewed positively, the data indicate that opportunities exist to find work or training and there is a regular flow of
'new entrants' who take up these opportunities. Viewed negatively,
the data suggest that the experience of being in 'status zero' is a
much more common experience for the age group as a whole than
is often acknowledged, and that:

> far too many of South Glamorgan's 'out-of-work-and-learning'
> 16– and 17–year-olds are not settling into a constructive long-term experience. They are moving in and out of different experiences; most lack any financial support for the times that they are
> out of training, and they are not acquiring any experience with
> the lasting value that comes from a qualification.
>
> (Istance *et al.*, 1994, pp. 46–7)

What was particularly disturbing in the data is that, of those in 'status
zerO', 'long-term' members far outnumbered the 'short-termers' who
had spent less than six months out of work and learning – only 6
out of the 402 sample (Istance *et al.*, 1994, p. 53).

The outcomes for these 16- and 17-year-olds raise the issue of whether their options with regard to the future are becoming increasingly foreclosed. Despite the lack of opportunity for those without qualifications, leaving school early continues to be a matter of conscious choice for substantial numbers of young people. While progressive educators and policy-makers might contest this, early leavers themselves see their break from school as both desirable and legitimate. Despite very obvious constraints, they still appear to define their lives in terms of choice. As we found in our own three-year study of non-completers, 'most in reflecting back on their decision remained convinced that "at the time it was the right thing to do" or that they were "glad" or "lucky" they left when they did' (Dwyer, 1996a, p. 8). This positive view is supported by another study which found that 91 per cent of all the early leavers surveyed indicated that they were happy to have left, and that this even included over half (58 per cent) of those who had been unable to find any work or training since (Ainley and Sheret, 1992, p. 157). Unfortunately, current post-compulsory education policy ignores this evidence in an explicit attempt to plan and construct an experience of 'youth' that in effect makes post-compulsory education compulsory, not by force of law but by exclusion or disaffiliation of those who continue to exercise choice and thus fail to conform to the policy. A matter of choice becomes a foreclosed option.

The findings from these studies and the more general statistics from the US, Australia and the UK tell us that those 'outside the mainstream' constitute a significant minority close to one-quarter of the relevant age group. What they do not tell us is what happens to that minority at an individual level as a result of the choices they have made and how they have responded to the limited opportunities and obstacles that have confronted them. One of the problems in studies of young people is that an over-reliance on the statistical evidence provides only a limited understanding of what life is like for them. If, however, as many as one out of every four or five young people in these countries do not fit the supposed norm, we need much greater personal detail about them if we are to form a comprehensive picture of what is happening to this generation and what they are making of their lives. A good source of information of this kind is the recent book by Finnegan (1998) which reports on the lives of young Americans in four different communities in different States.

While Finnegan's account lacks the breadth of evidence offered in the other American study outlined in the previous chapter, it more than makes up for this by providing a very comprehensive picture of the lives of particular individuals, their peers, families and local communities. Finnegan in *Cold New World* has chosen to direct his focus 'outside the mainstream'. He provides some vivid insights into the desperation of African Americans in Connecticut and also in Texas, the son of Mexican migrants in Washington State, and some jobless white skinheads in a down-at-heel Los Angeles suburb. He brings out well the ways in which they are operating within limited choices – but because they are disaffected and alienated, the 'choices' (drug-dealing, religious and racial fundamentalism, machismo) have a counter-productive effect. Underlying each of the stories, however, there is the common ground of the prevailing American ideology of 'liberal consumerism'.

> There is certainly no distinct 'culture of poverty'. There are, rather, innumerable adaptations to slight and shrinking opportunities. Some of these adaptations are antisocial or self-destructive. Many are simply survival strategies whose rationales are not always obvious to middle-class outsiders . . . The central ideology of 'mainstream culture', the belief system that most of us share, is liberal consumerism.
>
> (Finnegan, 1998, p. xxi)

While Finnegan is critical of the kinds of choices his confidants are making, he makes the effort to understand how they have been driven towards those choices. Terry in New Haven is a good instance of this. Terry went from being a pizza-box folder earning a meagre $50 a week to dealing in drugs and making $1000 a week, and Finnegan treats his situation sympathetically.

> I am sympathetic to Terry, and to the many other kids in his situation. The fact is that the illegal drug trade offers more economic opportunity to more young men than anything else going in the inner city. Depicting this reality may indeed play into the powerful (and politically destructive) association, in the public mind, of poor blacks and crime. I make a sharp distinction, however (one the law does not always make), between violent criminals and people merely involved in the drug trade. Terry's story is both common and, I think, commonly misunderstood.
>
> (1998, p. xviii)

This raises an issue that is not unique to the United States, nor to African Americans, nor to the inner-urban neighbourhoods of large

cities. The loss of employment opportunities for young people in both
metropolitan and rural areas in the UK, Europe and Australia has
led many of them to make their own way in life by means of the
underground or informal economy largely reliant on the drug trade
and stolen goods. Williamson (1996) and MacDonald (1998) refer
explicitly to this mode of 'livelihood' in non-metropolitan areas in
the UK as do Hutson and Liddiard (1994) in their study of homeless youth. Along with other Australian studies (White, 1995), our
own longitudinal research with early school leavers uncovered
instances of illegal sources of income among our rural and urban
participants. They had come to regard this as their only viable
alternative because of the collapse of the youth labour market in
their locality and the simultaneous tightening of restrictions regarding welfare provisions for the young unemployed. It is hardly
surprising that the combination of hard-line employment and welfare
policies common to all these countries leads to similar outcomes
which are then read as a justification (Murray, 1990, 1994) for even
harder 'zero tolerance' approaches which quite predictably serve to
make matters worse.

Finnegan spends many months in the different communities and,
despite his ready sympathy, conveys a grim picture of waywardness
and false choices as Mindy, the white Nazi skinhead from Los
Angeles, for example, or Juan the macho Mexican American from
Yakima Valley, try to survive and come to terms with feelings of
disillusionment and rejection. For them it is a 'cold new world –
growing up in a harder country'.

> While young people may have no other era with which to
> compare their times, they nonetheless sense the rot in the struc-
> ture of opportunity more acutely than the rest of us simply
> because they are its main victims. For students whose families
> are not rich, it might be the spiralling rise in college costs. For
> those slightly older, it might be the steep decline in home-owner-
> ship among younger families since 1973. Or it might be the even
> steeper (and directly related) decline in entry-level wages. For
> those in trouble, it might be the blood-chilling enthusiasm of offi-
> cials, starting with politicians, for prosecuting, sentencing, and
> imprisoning juveniles as adults.
>
> (1998, p. 346)

For those 'outside the mainstream' the United States has become a
harsher place with widening social and economic extremes and little

understanding or sympathy for the impact that the economic trends and political decisions since the 1970s have had on the disaffiliated.

A different, less personalised but more systematic, analysis of the situation in the United States is that provided by Ianni and Orr in their study of 'dropping out' in a recent book on adolescent transitions (Graber *et al.*, 1996). The authors acknowledge the tendency in many studies to associate dropping out with a range of problems and anti-social behaviours commonly attributed to the younger generation: 'chronic unemployment, drug and alcohol abuse, sexual laxity leading to early parenthood and HIV infection, and aggressive and sometimes violent' behavior to others and to themselves' (Ianni and Orr, 1996, p. 285). They also identify the range of explanations offered in the research literature, including: 'character deficit'; a lack of congruence between the consumer market, the world of work and 'an education system that is not meeting their future interests'; and shortcomings in institutional and social frameworks (including schools, the labour market, economic disadvantage, lack of 'parental and other social controls', and 'delinquent and nonschool peers').

The authors present a thoughtful and measured analysis of these supposed explanations and point to the danger of looking for some simplistic or universal cause or solution that would treat early school leavers as a single category or stigmatise them as 'problem kids' – even though there appears to be an underlying assumption in their analysis that non-completion of schooling is in itself a 'problem'.

> Our own view ... is that the decision to drop out is neither a wilful individual act nor is it the result of irresistible pressure from social forces. Rather, it takes place somewhere in the inter-action between the inner and outer worlds of each student. We are aware, for example, that this problem varies among communities in its size, density, and distribution. As a result, we have concluded, therefore, that the greater the breadth and severity of the problem within a community, the more likely are the broader external forces contributing to the causes of dropping out, thereby creating a need for institutional responses. However, the consequences are experienced individually and regardless of the density of the dropout problem among various communities, some targeted interventions are necessary.
>
> (1996, p. 288)

When they examine the demographic data regarding dropping out they show that it is more widespread than is often realised, and that while particular subgroups of the young are more likely than others to be affected (Hispanics and African Americans, and those from low-income families), the fact remains that the majority of dropouts come from 'middle-income families'.

> Hispanic and African American youth are much more likely than White youth to be dropouts (29% and 14% in contrast to 8%). Yet, 49% of all dropouts are White. Youth from low-income families are more than twice as likely as youth from middle-income and substantially more likely than those from high-income families to be dropouts (25% in contrast to 10% and 2%, respectively). Despite these differences, 52% of the dropouts are from middle-income families.
>
> (1996, p. 290)

This is significant data because it demonstrates how misleading much of the public discussion and imagery about dropouts can be. Statistical distinctions between a functioning 'mainstream' and a small 'at risk' problem-ridden minority are made and are then accepted without question by the general public without realising that it is a distorted picture of social reality that masks aspects of experience that cut across those distinctions. To learn that half the dropouts in America are from white middle-income families would come as a surprise to many.

Clearly, on the available evidence, school performance is a major contributing factor in dropping out, and this helps to explain why neither ethnicity nor family income can be resorted to as the sole explanation. It is important to note that while dropping out definitely places many young people at a comparative disadvantage, and while dropouts are almost twice as likely as high school graduates to be unemployed (22 per cent and 13 per cent respectively), at least a majority of them (51 per cent) eventually settle into stable employment (1996, p. 292). It is also important to note that the predominant reasons indicated in all major surveys regarding dropping out were school-related.

> In the surveys, the youth dropouts revealed why they left. They gave several reasons, most commonly that they left for school-related reasons (43% did not like school, 39% were failing school, 30% could not keep up with the schoolwork, 24% reported that they did not feel that they belonged, and 21% could not get along with the teachers). A substantial percentage of the young women left for parenting reasons (27% were

pregnant and 21% were parents). Many, particularly young men, left for employment reasons (29% had a job and 11% had to support their family).

(1996, p. 293)

One of the most valuable aspects of this study lies in its discussion of the range of theoretical approaches that have been adopted to explain the process of dropping out. After assessing the diverse, complex, and at times conflicting, explanations on offer, the authors conclude that there are

> four major factors that contribute: an adolescent's own devel-opment of self, particularly as a learner; occurrence of role conflict within the school and between the school and other environ-ments; the existence of cultural dissonance for students and staff; and structural deficits and limitations within the school (in partic-ular), families, and communities. None of these factors independ-ently explain why students drop out. Instead they overlap, combining in a variety of somewhat predictable ways to influ-ence whether students drop out.
>
> (1996, p. 305)

Being an outsider

It would be false to suggest that the extremes of desperation identi-fied in America by Finnegan exist to the same extent or to the same degree elsewhere. There are certainly groups within rural communi-ties in other countries, within Aboriginal communities, and amongst the unemployed and homeless, for whom parallels could be drawn. But while the extremes might be narrower or less prevalent, similar economic trends and political decisions have nevertheless had their impact on those 'outside the mainstream'. What is of particular interest by way of international comparisons and commonalities of experience that cross national borders is the similarity between the research of Ianni and Orr and our own work on dropping out (Dwyer, 1996a). This is particularly evident from our longitudinal study undertaken in the early 1990s. As a result of intensive interviews conducted at three-monthly intervals over a three-year period, we are able to 'put flesh' on the statistical data, and form a more detailed and personalised picture of what 'leaving school' means for the young people concerned and what the consequences of their decision are likely to be.

The participants were taken from three different localities: an inner metropolitan area; an outer metropolitan area; and a country region. In total, 508 early school leavers from both government and private schools were identified. The final interview sample was made up of 132 young people including twenty-nine from non English-speaking backgrounds and eleven Aboriginal participants. In the 132 there were seventy-five males and fifty-seven females.

The simple answer to why these students left school before they had completed Year 12 is that it was a negative choice. It is not so much that they left because they saw better options beyond school or were leaving to get a job, but rather because they felt that 'anything is better than school'. Most of their reasons had to do with simply wanting to get away from school, and the two reasons most frequently mentioned were that they did not like the teachers or that they found the work boring. Although the majority did not consider that their own performance in their subjects was a primary reason for leaving, there is a sense in which many of them just 'drifted' into the decision to leave. Not many gave any clear indication that it was a well-thought-out choice or even a positive option for an alternative situation in life. Unfortunately it is also true that only a minority of them (49) indicated that they had received any counselling or advice about leaving, and even in these cases the advice was reported as 'minimal' (see Holden and Dwyer, 1992). The immediate 'fate' of the early school leavers was unpromising (Figure 2.1).

Their comments are illuminating.

- School more or less gave up on me and I gave up on myself.
- I didn't like school at all. I wanted to go out and earn money, earn my own way.
- I left for financial reasons – Mum and Dad wanted me to help the family with money. I was not happy to leave.
- I was not passing. I wasn't there. I got sick of wagging and feeling guilty. I told them 'I'm not coming back'.
- [The school] did nothing at all. They didn't care, weren't interested. They just didn't care about any one at that school.

Only fifty (including seventeen with apprenticeships) had found a job on leaving school. For fifteen of these their weekly income in 1991 was well below the poverty line, 70 per cent lacked any reliable source of income, many of them being dependent on occasional handouts or 'pocket money' from family or friends, and perhaps an

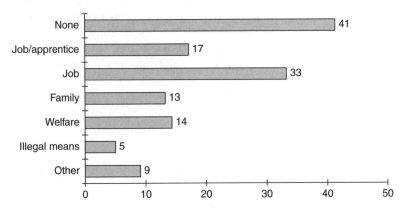

Figure 2.1 Income source on leaving school (n = 132)

occasional loan or even 'illegal' means of some kind. These were some of their comments (Holden, 1992).

−   I regret not doing my final year. I would have only been unemployed for six months now and not eighteen months.
−   Nothing's really happened since I left school. I'm home helping out.
−   We travelled around . . . I didn't stay at schools long enough to get into whatever they were doing and so I didn't really learn much . . . I left my parents [six months before I left school] . . . I didn't have much choice about leaving home. I got kicked out.
−   It's not that easy to get and keep a job. I thought it would be.
−   They wanted an older, more qualified person to do the printing.
−   Someone who doesn't go to school, they go through hell with the money they get. Especially if they're 15. The younger you are, the worse it is. Most parents think: you leave school, you pay rent – you leave school, you turn into an adult. But the government doesn't think that. It's hard going [from] one to the other.
−   Everything's a waste of time. Nothing gets you anywhere. The money you get from one illegal area goes into another. You can't use it for anything constructive.

A few had found difficulties in returning to school when schools proved unhelpful or when past prejudices against the young person resurfaced. Others indicated they would like to return to schooling, but would not return to a conventional secondary school. Most young people had left school early because they experienced problems which are not addressed by the schools and wider community. Leaving not only did not fix these problems, but it created new problems as they attempted to enter a world for which they had not been well prepared. The study found that for this group of young people there are few structured pathways, and few options. For many exit students, the post-school scene was a wild and chaotic one, with a confusing pattern of choices (or lack of choice) and little discernible institutional support. A more appropriate metaphor at this stage would be 'uncharted territory'.

For those in the study the initial post-compulsory pathway was usually intended to be direct entry into the workforce. However, their lives after leaving school could at best be characterised as attempts to make the best of limited options. Most of the young people did not find a successful post-school pathway. Holden has indicated this by reference to the following yardsticks of success:

obtaining employment: young people are accepting positions that do not necessarily coincide with their aspirations;

maintaining employment: young people are staying in exploitative positions because of the restrictive current economic climate;

re-entering the secondary education system: the high incidence of dropping out highlights the unsuitability of the current offerings within the post-compulsory education system;

undertaking further education: again, there is a high incidence of dropping out which underlines issues about the content and lowest-common-denominator factor of many of the courses; and

the establishment of accommodation that is independent of the family: many of the young people in the study are living in substandard accommodation, relying on friends, selling possessions or living in temporary or transients' accommodation.

(Holden, 1992, p. 42)

In terms of these criteria, few of the 132 young people in the study had been successful, and most tended to move in and out of different pathways. Starting with one pathway did not mean that a young person would stay within that pathway, nor did it predict their final point. Experience (or lack of it) in the workforce was a definite indication of this.

Thus, although the motivation for leaving school is frequently associated with a determination to engage with the adult world, few early school leavers in the study were able to establish independent living arrangements for any length of time, even three years after leaving school. In the course of a few years some of the sample had changed course fourteen or fifteen times – a zigzag chopping and changing as they looked in vain for the supposed pathways. There was no systematic movement through education, training, and into employment; the pattern, instead, was one of short-term, lowly paid jobs (when they were available), mixed with living on unemployment benefits and with the support of friends and family (Holden, 1992).

– I've thought about going on the dole, but I don't really want to. The government's in enough trouble as it is ... although it is the taxpayers who pay for the dole. I probably do deserve to get it, but I feel better if I earn my own money.
– I couldn't stand being unemployed again. It was horrible. You get so depressed. There's job interview after job interview and fifty other people are going for the same job.
– Some of the stuff I'm into now – like stolen goods – it's pretty hard to get out of. You think: If things aren't going to get any better, why change?
– It's still hard, with the family breaking up. My relationship with my old man was rocky when I was depending on him for money. Now we're starting to talk. It could be because I'm being more independent.
– Personally, I want to move, but I have family duties here. If I had my own choice I would move out.
– I think I really needed that break from school. I was so immature at the time. I've been out of school so long now it's made me open up my eyes. Being in the workforce has taught me a lot about the real world. My friends who went straight through school and are finished now are so immature. They've been wrapped in cotton wool in their schooling. To be out where you have to pay bills and earn a living, it opens your eyes.

The main options open to them were: education (either re-entry into school or some training course); welfare benefit (reliance on the social security system, mainly after failure of other options); family (living with or financially dependent on parents or other kin); employment (often of a temporary or part-time nature). The main discernible pattern was the decreasing dependence on family or kin and the increasing dependence on welfare benefits. With each 'step' that they took after leaving school, of course, different people moved in and out of the different 'options'. There was, for example, over the first few interviews a core of twenty within the employment option who had continuing employment (even though they had changed jobs a number of times) while various others moved in and out of this option at different stages. Neither school re-entry nor further education provided tangible benefits for most or any clear progress towards their goal of establishing a viable livelihood. One-fifth tried to return to school, but most of these left again. The further education scene presents a similar picture; 10 per cent undertook vocational training courses, for instance, but again most of these did not complete the courses they entered.

Employment outcomes for the young women in the study had some distinctive features. For example, they aimed to take much more narrow job and training pathways than their male counterparts. Only four of the fifty-one women in the study aimed to go into areas that were non-traditional ones for young women. The others aimed to become hairdressers, to work in the service industry as clerks, childcare workers or social workers, or to become models or air hostesses. Only three of the young women were accepted for apprenticeships, compared with fourteen of the males.

Policy disjunctures

We have now reached a stage where economic planning at a national level has come to dictate to public policy concerning education. One of the worst aspects of this is the reliance on statistical models setting future national targets based on a projection of current trends. Even if we accept that a dramatic change of attitude towards school participation has occurred since the mid-1980s such projections are unrealistic. It is hard to avoid the suspicion that a considerable amount of statistical sleight-of-hand, or at best wishful thinking, is taking place. What that wishful thinking conveniently ignores is the fact that in all Western societies there is still a significant minority who leave school without completing their final years.

It is true that for a majority of students in the early school leavers study, we found that leaving school was a negative choice. However, young people who leave without finishing high school are not necessarily rejecting the notion of education, but rather the relationships and structures that exist within the school system. Many found the teacher/student relationship profoundly negative or found the school environment and work uninteresting and uninspiring. There was a mismatch between their own expectations of schooling and the school's expectations of them. Even if leaving school was a negative choice, the reasons varied from person to person, from school to school, and from locality to locality, in ways that the general statistics and the mainstreaming policies failed to identify or take into account. The interview data reveal a wide degree of diversity that challenges the illusion of uniformity of provision and circumstances which underpins the setting of national goals and participation rate targets.

- I'm glad I left because I was the king clown in the class and everyone was missing out because of me. But, I'm also not glad because if I could have stayed, who knows what I could be doing now.
- I didn't like anything [about school]. I just liked graphics and woodwork [out of the subjects] . . . I didn't bother to tell the school I wasn't coming back.
- In the final year I started going well . . . I really don't know why I left. I lost my confidence. [I felt] I can't do it, I'll fail. Everyone was saying, 'Now you're in final year, you have to work hard.'
- I had trouble at school because I was aboriginal. The teachers left us to last. You put your hand up and they come around to you last. They worried about the others.

What the findings of our study leave no doubt about is that the notion of pathways is illusory for those who leave. Most of the participants did not have a concept of any pathways which might guide them towards their goals. Their ideas for their future were not based on realistic evidence or experiences, and once they left school their lives became chaotic and their options short-lived or foreclosed.

- It's been a really big lesson for me since leaving school. I've learnt that things don't always go your way. School is like a cover. It's like insulation from the big wide world. You don't really know anything until you leave and try and make it on your own.
- Thoughts about going back to school have been destroyed. Now I'm on my own, I'm barely scraping through. I haven't the money to support myself let alone go to school.
- It's been difficult paying the rent and bills. It's my own fault, I should have thought about the rent before I left home.
- I never thought I'd do this kind of crap [stealing and dealing goods]. It started when I went on the dole. It was the kids I hang

around with. First I was watching them doing it, then I was covering up for them. Before long I was doing it too.

Only 49 of the 132 in our study had received any counselling or advice prior to leaving school and most had found it unhelpful, and on leaving school their only institutional contact was with various welfare agencies. They were vague about available training programmes (only three had undertaken a course), confused about apprenticeship requirements, and ignorant of employment rights regarding under-award wages, discrimination and work hours, yet 'other social and welfare services were not accessed'. Holden (1992, p. 39) concluded that:

> Overall, our focus on the pathways taken by early school leavers has indicated a lack of support for young people, both inside and outside of the school. They appear to be making decisions about their futures based on misinformation and myths. It would seem that, at the same time that they are being asked to make decisions which will affect their futures, they are not receiving appropriate information about the options available to them. This lack of support appears to be evident both in the school and in services and organisations in the larger community.

The same issue confronts the early school leavers of Great Britain referred to earlier. Williamson suggests that the element of choice is still present in the attitudes of young people towards leaving school, but he warns that such choice 'is hardly exercised on a level playing field' and that the supposed 'opportunities' provided to them in established policy prove to be illusory when considered alongside their actual personal circumstances.

> In the context of training, all kinds of factors enter into the frame for consideration and evaluation; levels of pay, proximity of the scheme, being with your mates, flexibility around attendance, the prospect of a job at the end, how hard they work you, the perceived quality of the training (the list is not exclusive and is in no particular order). Thus, anticipated 'pay-offs' are traded against the apparent penalties arising from participation. When the pay-off is not obvious, or blindingly elusive, it takes relatively few negative features (real or perceived) to deter young people from participation.
>
> (Williamson, 1996, p. 223)

It might be assumed that the target of universal participation in education and training allows for some early school leaving followed by re-entry into the system at some later stage. The experience of those in our three-year study indicates definite barriers to re-entry. Thus, at the school level, experience in the labour market encouraged some young people to re-enter school as a potential pathway to improve their situation. One-fifth of the young people in the study attempted to return to school, and some of these found difficulties when schools were reluctant to re-enrol them or resorted to past prejudices against them. Others indicated they would like to return to schooling, but only if there was a more adult environment, while some who had left home said that, although they would have liked to return to school, they could not afford to on their available levels of financial support (Holden, 1992).

–   I didn't have anything else to do, so I decided to go back to school. The school said a flat out: No. They didn't think I was fit to go to school.
–   Now I look at it, going back to school was the best thing I could do. Unless I could have found a long-term job, it was the best thing I could have done.
–   When I went back to school I found it hard to get along with the kids there. None of them would sit down and do their work. I got irritated with it so I left.
–   I couldn't get a job in the field I wanted so I went back to school. The second last year wasn't bad. I didn't really like it very much because of the work. I passed, but I thought it was irrelevant.
–   I wouldn't go back to normal school. I'd probably do a college course. At normal school you get a lot of immature brats. Smart alec 15-year-olds who think they're hot shots who hassle you.
–   I tried to do a college computer course. It was good because there weren't a lot of young kids there, I was with adults. I found it too hard. I just sort of left it. I didn't go any more.
–   I'd think about going to a vocational college maybe. It would depend on the course. I'd like to do the new childcare course they've got. I went to see about it at the beginning of the year, but it was full. They had 20 places for 400 applicants. They wouldn't tell me anything about it.

Most of the attempts at school re-entry were unsuccessful, with the young person dropping out of school for a second or third time. Barriers to successfully completing school were: placement in classes

with younger 'less committed' students; troublesome dynamics associated with age discrepancies; the lack of individual autonomy and
responsibility; and finding school and the curriculum even less relevant to them once they had made the attempt to establish themselves
as independent adults. Thus the negative factors which had precipitated the decision to leave early were accentuated on their return.

This highlights what is the most serious policy issue of all. For
many non-completers re-entry becomes an unfortunate return to a
set of negative experiences that had contributed to their non-completion at an earlier age. In the meantime, however, they have matured
and have a new set of experiences in life which lead them to conclude
that re-entry would be well worthwhile. In general however re-entry
is not well planned for in the provision of post-school education.
The special needs of redevelopment of study skills and allowance for
differences in age and experience are only catered for, if at all, in an
haphazard way. The type of programme suited to an uninterrupted
progression is not the most appropriate for those who have a number
of years of post-school experience, who have developed other commitments in the meantime, who are more pragmatic about the usefulness
of any course, who need refresher courses of some kind to renew
their study skills and basic knowledge, and who need to be encouraged to see positive value in resuming the education they have rightly
or wrongly interrupted.

Concluding remarks

The available research on the pathways of young people beyond the
years of compulsory education reveals that for the majority there is
little coherence in their educational and employment experiences
after they have left high school. Unless a much broader understanding
of pathways is adopted at a policy level, and unless the diversity of
young people is taken account of in practice, the needs of a significant
minority of young people will fail to be served by the education and
training system. Currently the standard response to non-completion
begins with a negative premise that defines the non-completers as
essentially a 'problem' group. This premise is due in part to a tendency
to think of non-completers as a homogeneous group. For statistical
purposes they may be, but once we disaggregate the overall figures,
considerable diversity of intent and outcome becomes apparent. To
think of non-completers as a single category gives insufficient weight
for example to the experience of those who do seek to finish their high
school certificate at a later stage, or of those who are successful in

finding employment for themselves, and of those who follow up other legitimate priorities in their lives.

In other words, outcomes for non-completers tend to be artificially limited by mistaken assumptions about 'linear pathways' based on an expectation that young people who are at the same age should all be doing the same thing (Lesko, 1996a). Thus, the reasons why young people make the choices they do, and consequently the explanation for the positive dimensions of the decision to leave, are at times underestimated because they do not fit neatly into the view of linear pathways underlying much policy-making and teaching. Yet we know for example that, within two years of leaving, close to half of American dropouts do complete their GED certificate. Given that, it is shortsighted to assume that dropping out is a final 'No' to education on the part of non-completers. Policies need to be put in place to make effective re-entry within a five-year period a genuine educational option for those who do not complete their schooling. For re-entry to become an effective option greater attention needs to be paid to giving non-completers much clearer access to and guidance through programmes specifically designed to meet their needs. In other words, re-entry needs to be structured in a way that makes it accessible both by being clearly 'signposted' and by being organised to take into account the post-school experience of the participants and the fact that their education has been interrupted during that time.

If we are to explore adequately the fundamental issues raised by this group of young people concerning their adult education and training needs, we need to do so not merely with reference to their schooling as teenagers, or their transition from school to work, but more importantly in the context of the transitions from school to independent adult life. Unfortunately, current schooling practices and education policy settings tend to present an age-based transition for all teenagers as a 'make or break' experience. Dividing teenagers into those who form a student 'mainstream' and those defined as a non-student 'at risk' minority ignores the uncertainties and risks which all teenagers have in common due to the far-reaching social and economic changes affecting their lives. If Western society is really to benefit in the twenty-first century from what this new generation has to offer, it needs to find ways of bridging the gap between policy assumptions derived from the past and the challenges arising from the more flexible and less predictable life-patterns of post-industrial society. Perhaps it is time that the policy-makers themselves learnt something about how young people are already coming to terms with those challenges in the choices they make about their adult futures.

3 The policy gap

The issues raised in the previous chapter highlight the uneasy balance that exists between a concentration on the problems associated with youth and assumptions about what might be considered to be a normal or mainstream experience of growth into adulthood. Often normality is used as a vague unsubstantiated reference point for making negative judgements about other people's children, and at times we are left wondering whether there are any 'normal' young people anyway. As one author puts it, young people of the 1990s are in effect 'the scapegoat generation' (Males, 1998), because of the way distorted or alarmist accounts are given of their lifestyles and the threat they pose to social order. Certainly there is, for example, a well-documented tendency in the media to sensationalise extremes of anti-social behaviour as if they are representative of the generation as a whole, and even at an academic level there is a tradition (Griffin, 1993) derived from the writings of G. S. Hall (1904) which regards adolescence as essentially a problem-stage of 'storm and stress' which if left unchecked lends credence to outbreaks of 'moral panic' (Cohen, 1972) about widespread irresponsibility among the younger generation. Meanwhile, within the fields of developmental psychology, family studies and life-course analysis, norms of personal development are emphasised (Erikson, 1965; Elder, 1985; Heaven, 1994; Holmes, 1995; Graber et al., 1996) which make a clear distinction between the functional and the 'dysfunctional' – between a normal developmental process and problems that need to be dealt with as 'deviant' and exceptional behaviour.

This uneasy balance between the normal and the problematic is reflected in the formation of public policies which shape the lives of young people. For example, changes in policy in the fields of education and employment affect the hopes and fears of young students who could be said to come from comparatively secure and supportive family and school environments (Schneider and Stevenson, 1999), because those changes have also disrupted the traditional expectations about a legitimate transition from school to work for those not contemplating academic or professional careers. Understanding the experience of the post-1970 generation inevitably draws us into a consideration of the part policy plays in determining their progress towards effective participation in adult society. This chapter is concerned with the ways in which policy-makers define the experience of youth.

A 1994 article in the Harvard Education Review drew attention to how in the field of education an arbitrary construction of a mainstream category perpetuates a false image of a disadvantaged minority. It has a double effect: on the one hand it presents the 'mainstream' as a unified and coherent grouping, while on the other it marginalises the 'disadvantaged'.

> Whatever the formulae used to measure disadvantage ... the procedure always involves drawing a cut-off line at some point on a dimension of advantage and disadvantage. Where the cut-off comes is fundamentally arbitrary ... In practice, however, the cut-off point is always placed so as to indicate a modest-sized minority. This demarcation is credible because of the already existing political imagery of poverty, in which the poor are pictured as a minority outside mainstream society. The policy implication is that the other 80 or 90 percent, the mainstream, are all on the same footing.
>
> (Connell, 1994, p. 130)

This double-edged effect has particular relevance to developments in education and youth policy in North America, Australia and the United Kingdom. In Australia, for example, in the early 1990s there was a widely accepted assumption that changes in education and training at the post-compulsory level would establish a coherent and successful mainstream comprising at least three-quarters of the 19-year-old age group. This was expected to extend to as much as 95 per cent of that age group by the year 2001 (Australian Education Council [AEC], 1991). Allied with this was an assertion that those 'outside' the mainstream amount to at most 14 per cent of 19-year-olds (Commonwealth of Australia, 1994, p. 90) and that this proportion would decline to a mere 5 per cent by the turn of the century. The 1994 Working Nation policy statement of the Australian government of the time accepted the target and concerned itself with measures to bridge the remaining gap by addressing the needs of those who still lie outside the mainstream (Commonwealth of Australia, 1994, p. 90).

This emphasis on developing policies for the young based on a reference to a supposed 'mainstream' has become a common and central feature of national policy throughout the world. The specifics of the implementation of those frameworks further indicate that in nations such as the UK and Australia there are parallels also with policy in the US in that there is now a two-tier mainstream/disadvantaged model for youth policy in each of these countries which makes a clear-cut distinction between an 'at risk' minority and the age group as a whole. It is the purpose of this chapter to examine these international parallels with particular emphasis on the policy implications of national planning in the youth sector.

Mainstream: the image of success

The management of projected 'outcomes' is central to current policy formation aimed at prolonging the educational participation of the young in most Western countries well into their twenties. Unfortunately, this means that current policy and planning regarding young people's futures, particularly in English-speaking countries, also has a make-believe quality to it. There is much talk about the coming of the 'knowledge society' of the future and its demand for the highly skilled, even though the official data show that the dominant area of growth is that of the 'service society' and its demand for lower-level skills. Policies are presented with the support of the latest computer packages – projections are made, models are developed, scenarios are outlined, targets are set, reams of statistical data are printed and charted – and the outcomes appear so convincing because they are preordained and programmed in a self-fulfilling way. We have already seen in the opening chapter how the 'misaligned ambitions' of young Americans are directly related to the upheavals that have occurred in employment policy and practices throughout the 1990s. Ainley illustrates this with regard to policies for 'the learning society' in the UK as well. He points to a degree of statistical sleight-of-hand in the way key indicators are conveniently redefined to present a picture of successful outcomes.

> One can even imagine a 'learning society' in which the unemployed are redefined out of existence. Their numbers have already been obscured by the 33 changes made to the way unemployment

figures have been calculated since 1979, but at any one time average around two million, though some definitions of those 'wanting work' range as high as five million – depending on whether part-time workers and those on schemes and in education are included . . . In a similar way compulsory Youth Training supposedly converted unemployed 16– to 18–year-olds into 'trainees' at the stroke of a pen in 1986.

(Ainley, 1998, p. 566)

Evidence such as this indicates that a caution is called for about the claims that are made about the size of the mainstream and what the improved educational retention rates of the recent past actually mean in terms of 'participation'. There is a degree of confusion and even distortion in the figures presented to substantiate the existence of the mainstream at the post-compulsory level with the result that the actual participation rate is at times seriously overestimated. At the same time, within the labour-market figures, the reclassification of the 'unemployed', by forcing them into either short-term 'training programmes' or workfare 'work for the dole' schemes, is combined with euphoric forecasts about the job prospects for the 'highly skilled' to create an impression that within the mainstream employment is blooming.

For example, talk about the learning society or 'the clever country' and the need for a more highly skilled and flexible workforce hides or ignores the fact that a major reason for increased post-compulsory participation is the collapse of the youth labour market along with a major restructuring of adult workplaces, and that therefore higher levels of education and training cannot in themselves provide any guarantee that jobs even for 'more highly skilled' 19-year-olds will be assured by the year 2001. Even if an unemployment rate of 5 per cent across the workforce as a whole was achieved by then in most Western nations, the rate for 19-year-olds in many of those nations is still likely to be around the 15 per cent mark.

Recent developments in the US are informative on this issue. Since the mid-nineties, there has been a remarkable turn-around in US economic indicators. By 2000 it was seen as a low inflation/full employment growth economy which presents a marked contrast to most other nations. Alongside low levels of unemployment, real wages have risen 2.6 per cent annually for the typical American worker since 1996. A closer look at the general statistics, however, indicates growing disparities between different sections of the society and a widening of the gap between rich and poor. Of particular interest is the fact that, despite claims about the importance of higher levels of education to provide for the 'knowledge society', even young graduates in scientific and engineering occupations were worse off in 1997 than their counterparts in 1989, and there had been a sharp reversal for women graduates. In the supposedly bright new 'technology-driven' economy, the proportion of workers in long-term jobs had declined from 41 per cent in 1979 to 35 per cent in 1996, while the 'contingent' (those without regular full-time jobs) workforce had increased to 30 per cent of all workers by 1997 (Mishel *et al.*, 1999). Even those graduates who had found full-time employment were not working in their area of specialisation and were not in jobs that warranted a college degree, as can be seen from Figure 3.1.

Although current unemployment rates are much lower in the US than elsewhere, there is still evidence therefore of a degree of mismatch between qualifications and job outcomes. In fact official projections for the new millennium indicate that 'over the 1996–2006 period, the majority of occupations with the largest expected job growth will require less than an associate degree' (Bureau of Labor Statistics, 1999, p. 61). As with their Australian (Gregory, 1995) and Canadian (Anisef *et al.*, 1996; Livingstone, 1998) counterparts, rather than being 'under-skilled' graduates are more likely to be 'over-qualified'. Even for university graduates seeking employment, at best only three-quarters tend to be successful within six months. A closer examination of the graduate surveys, however, reveals that 'finding a job' is not the same as 'beginning a career' – it is not unusual to find that six months after graduation, of those with jobs less than a third consider their job to be 'a desired career position'.

Evidence such as this suggests a different interpretation of the heavy emphasis that has been given to high levels of 'participation'

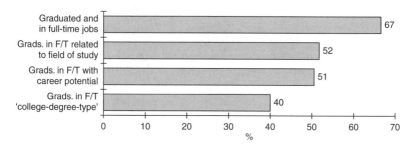

Figure 3.1 US 1992–3 college graduates

Source: US Digest of Education Statistics.

in education and training. What that emphasis conceals is that the participants are in a kind of holding pattern in which their actual 'arrival' within the labour market has been deferred. Eventual under-employment or even unemployment for both completers and non-completers is the external manifestation of the deferred agenda but it is not the full story. The issue at stake is really what are the likely long-term citizenship or livelihood options and outcomes for Youth 2001? Will there ever again be full-time career paths even for the 'highly skilled' 19-year olds of the future? Arbitrary distinctions between a near-universal mainstream and a dwindling disadvantaged minority gloss over what is at stake here and what remains the major concern that the supposed mainstream and the disadvantaged have in common: being at risk in terms of their prospects for the future.

This is a theme that has been explored by the Canadian researchers Côté and Allahar (1994). They describe the post-1970 generation of young people as a Generation on Hold. It is a tempting image in that it captures the uncertainties the generation has grown up with. They have experienced a widening gap between their aspirations as high-achieving, well-credentialled young adults and harsh economic realities. They have had to come to terms with narrowing competi-tive employment markets and the postponed fulfilment of economic and family security which their parents had encouraged them to ambi-tion. The authors claim that

> young people are the biggest losers as the conditions of advanced industrial society have become entrenched. The contradiction between credentialism and occupational disenfranchisement sends many of those attempting to come of age on an extended journey that does not lead them to the independence of adulthood, but rather to the uncertainties of prolonged youth.
>
> (Côté and Allahar, p. 48)

Other Canadian researchers (Redpath, 1994; Trottier *et al.*, 1996) have indicated that this 'extended journey' has affected outcomes for university graduates as well, with many of them after three years in the work force unable to achieve 'vocational integration' or estab-lished careers. This was particularly so for females, with only 33 per cent of them in permanent full-time career jobs by contrast with 47 per cent of males (Trottier *et al.*, 1996, p. 98). On the basis of the available evidence from Australia, North America and the UK, it would appear that the utilitarian link which may have once been assumed between the two markets of labour and education has been severed. In other words, there is now a marked disjuncture between high youth-participation rates within the education market and a decline in long-term career outcomes for them in the employment market. It is therefore ironic that assumptions about one-to-one links between the two markets, and expectations about education as a vehicle for upward social mobility, are being accentuated within policy frameworks at precisely the time that global economic developments have forced a far-reaching reshaping of the nature and conditions of the workplace at a national level.

Masking outsiders

This heavy promotion of an image of success associated with the mainstream serves the purpose of masking continuing inequalities affecting the education and employment outcomes of young people. It is hard to believe that the consistent misuse of the available figures is not a conscious attempt at statistical sleight-of-hand. We have already referred to the ways in which the calculation of unemployment figures in the UK has been repeatedly revised since 1979 to effectively lower the apparent rate. This has happened in Australia also, but perhaps more serious is the official distortion of participation levels. Often the peak national 77 per cent final-school-year retention figure attained in 1992 has continued to be used despite the fact that in every year since then the rate has been in steady decline. By 1998 it had fallen back to the 66 per cent mark. If that is the reality it means that the high school non-completion rate would now be well above the 30 per cent mark.

It would scarcely be necessary to draw attention to this evidence except that this tendency to misuse the available figures on participation even finds a place in official policy statements. The logical slippage from retention, to participation, and then to completion has become so well entrenched that officially a 77 per cent retention rate has been interpreted to mean that 'more than three-quarters now *complete* secondary school' (Commonwealth of Australia, 1994, p. 89, our emphasis). What makes this worse is a concomitant tendency to minimise the extent of non-completion by reducing the numbers of those 'at risk' to a small and 'manageable' minority. Thus, the official report on post-compulsory education in Australia moved quickly from an initial base of 27 per cent 'non-participants' at the post-compulsory level (AEC, 1991, p. 46) to a more stringent assessment of 14 per cent 'at risk' (p. 133), which it then counterbalanced with an alternative estimate of only 6 per cent (p. 134), before finally restricting its focus to 'a very few areas where it appears that greater effort may be warranted' (p. 134).

The most serious implication of this twofold distortion of inflated success rates on the one hand and minimised non-completion numbers on the other is that it becomes written into the goal settings of official policy. Again, this can be illustrated from official planning documents used to promote the knowledge society of the future. Figure 3.2, for example, gives the overall picture relating 1990 actual participation levels in education and training in Australia and the target scenario for the year 2001. There is a noticeable gap with respect to technical and further education college enrolments between the 2001 target (30.5 per cent) in the official report and the 1990 actuals (only 14.9 per cent), as well as between the 'not even completed high school' scenario figure of 5 per cent as against the 1990 actual of 27 per cent. The official report not only claimed that this was 'a realistic and measurable policy objective' but even boldly asserted that the picture this presented was 'related closely to the reality of involvement by young people' (AEC, 1991, p. 48).

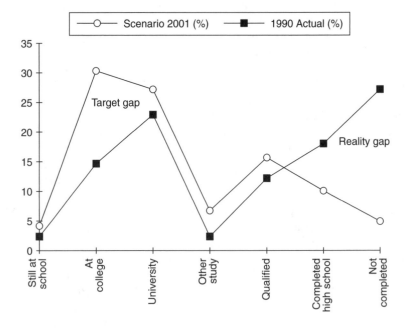

Figure 3.2 Educational outcomes for 19-year-olds
Source: AEC, 1991, p. 171.

As we have seen, similar evidence is available from other countries and highlights a distinct danger that what might have been conceived as a progressive 'all inclusive' education and training policy runs the risk of becoming in effect an exclusive policy because the attainment of a specific post-school education/training 'threshold' has been set up as a normative precondition for adulthood. In effect the claim that the scenario portrays 'the reality of involvement by young people' implies that those who do not fit the picture (including those who legitimately choose to postpone the completion of their education until some later time in their lives) are effectively excluded or disaffiliated. At a policy level, the recourse to a two-tier conceptual model which distinguishes between a successful mainstream in excess of 90 per cent and a small disadvantaged or 'at risk' minority is far from the 'reality' for the year 2000 when only 62 per cent of 17-year-olds were still at school.

This policy myopia has its parallel in a long-standing trend in the United States. Because of the consistently higher school retention rates in the US, both state and federal policy regarding young people has largely been restricted to the provision of programmes for the disadvantaged. Even as far back as 1960 the figure for 14–17-year-olds still in high school was as high as 83 per cent, and by 1987 as many as 22 per cent of all 25–29-year-olds had completed four years of college. There remained many who went straight from school into the workforce but in the past they had been able to find a means of livelihood for themselves fairly quickly – particularly in those periods when labour was scarce and the economy was expanding. Because the skill levels of the available jobs were either of a manual kind or easily acquired 'on the job', the transition from early school leaving to employment was not considered a major policy concern. At the same time, there was a piecemeal accumulation of special-purpose programmes often set up in response to 'problems' which were seen as a threat to society as a whole – crime and drug use, gang conflict, delinquency, urban unrest or racial tensions. Thus, outside the mainstream of college-bound youth, the unmet needs of young Americans were largely subsumed under programmes (Shears and Matthews, 1983; Grant Foundation, 1988) defined in terms of 'remedial action'.

In a brief period from 1978 to 1981 YEDPA (Youth Employment and Demonstration Projects Act) was a notable exception (Levin and Ferman, 1985) – until it was disbanded by the Reagan administration. During its short life it averaged over one billion dollars annually, reaching about 750,000 young people. In the meantime, changes to the American economy and the nature of its labour market had a debilitating impact on those outside the new educational 'mainstream' of university and college entrants. Throughout the 1990s concern began to be expressed about a new class of the 'at risk' – 'non-college-bound youth' (Smith and Rojewski, 1993). As a result there is now a growing movement devoted specifically to the school-to-work transition which has drawn attention to the failure of main-stream provisions to take account of the large numbers of high school graduates who do not go on to college (Hamilton and Hamilton, 1992; Gregson, 1995; Stern *et al.*, 1997). The successful completion of their high school certificate has in effect been devalued in the 1990s and it no longer has the significance for employability that it had in the past.

> In fact, non-college bound youth in our society receive little or no assistance in preparing for and finding employment when they complete their secondary education. Byrne, Constant and Moore (1992) described the transition process as a 'do-it-yourself' system that may affect upwards of 20 million young people who will not go directly from high school to a four-year college or university … The result is that most flounder from one low-paying job to the next until their mid-20s and are never seriously trained for a career.
>
> (Smith and Rojewski, 1993, pp. 224–5)

Training beyond the mainstream

One of the widely promoted policy responses to high levels of youth unemployment in Western societies has been the design of 'training' schemes. Particular groups of young people are specifically targeted for these schemes and their receipt of welfare support is made dependent upon their enrolment in some form of training. The ideological underpinning for this policy response is the promotion of the 'highly skilled' workforce of the future.

In the UK for example a concern developed during the 1980s about its levels of educational attainment by comparison with those of its major trading partners. Emphasis was placed on developing a more highly skilled workforce, with a view to raising levels of participation in post-compulsory education and training.

> The existence of a UK deficit in education and training is now widely accepted by all parties. Participation rates in post-compulsory education and training are amongst the lowest in

Europe . . . The situation with vocational qualifications is equally disturbing.

(Green, 1991, p. 328)

This 'deficit in education' was largely explained by the reliance in the immediate period after the Second World War on training for youth within the labour market in apprenticeships via industrial training boards. By the early 1970s the growth in youth unemployment led to changes of policy based on a 'transition' model. In 1973 a Youth Opportunities Programme was designed around the transition from school to work and was aimed specifically at those young people considered particularly disadvantaged. In 1983 the Youth Training Scheme was formed with, as its title suggests, more of a focus on training almost as an end in itself. This had dubious results and so, as in Australia, in 1988 the provision of unemployment benefits to 16- and 17-year-olds was revoked, and replaced by a 'youth training guarantee' subsequently under the auspices of locally based TECs (Training and Enterprise Councils). After this came the Enterprise Allowance Scheme to encourage individual enterprise and self-employment – promoting a return to 'Victorian values of self-reliance and individual responsibility' as against a culture of dependency 'alleged to be operating in depressed areas of the country' (MacDonald, 1991, p. 256). Some ventures were successful, but other main outcomes were an artificial reduction in the statistics on youth unemployment, high rates of failure of many ventures as well as some inevitable displacement of existing businesses (Williamson, 1996; MacDonald, 1991).

As youth unemployment in Great Britain escalated there were reports of large numbers of young people who were non-participants in either employment, training or education (British Youth Council, 1992). We have already referred in the previous chapter to one study (Istance *et al.*, 1994) which indicated that as many as 16 to 23 per cent of 16- and 17-year-olds lay outside the training and labour markets and were in what was termed 'status zerO' – young people who count for nothing and appear to be going nowhere (Williamson, 1996). These high levels of disaffiliation led to concern about the growth of an 'underclass' in the UK – and accusations that a culture of dependency had taken hold in sections of the population (Murray, 1994). Whatever the explanation, there can be no doubt that prevailing youth policies were proving ineffectual. What is particularly disturbing is the pattern of long-term unemployment and occasional 'recycling' through one work or training position or another.

Similar evidence is available concerning training programmes in Australia. The Department of Employment, Education and Training (DEET) estimated in 1993 that the relevant percentage of non-mainstream 19-year-olds was about 23 per cent. It defined the group as a 'target group' made up of those who 'are aged 19, and left school before Year 12, and not studying and do not have a post-school qualification' (DEET, 1993, p. 1). They were a target group because it is for them that the second-tier youth training programmes and job creation schemes had been designed by the out-going federal government.

With the change of government at the federal level in 1996 a new initiative in the training sector was introduced. This was the system of New Apprenticeships which was a revamp of the existing system giving greater emphasis to links with small business, the broadening of the traditional apprenticeship profile through the provision of apprenticeship places in 'non-traditional' or emerging industries, and greater flexibility in training arrangements. For those who did not even qualify for this new system, and particularly the long-term young unemployed, the provision of ongoing income support was made conditional upon enrolment in a workfare or 'work for the dole' scheme. This was further extended in 1998 in the development of the Common Youth Allowance scheme. This had particular impact on school non-completers, because as from January 1999 young people under the age of 18 years would not even be eligible for the Youth Allowance if they did not engage in full-time study or training. Youth Allowance recipients over the age of 18 years, who had been unemployed for six months were required to undertake additional activities such as engagement in part-time work, voluntary work, education or training, or participation in a government-funded programme such as a literacy or numeracy programme or a work-fare 'work for the dole' scheme.

These new youth training programmes since 1993 have been concentrated particularly on the long-term unemployed, despite a large array of international evidence which demonstrates that training programmes do not by themselves create jobs and that improving the 'skill factor' in the unemployed has only a marginal impact on unemployment numbers (Freeman and Katz, 1994; Nickell and Bell, 1995). In fact, after detailed economic analysis of OECD countries, Nickell and Bell concluded that most of the rise in unemployment has been 'the consequence of factors which have operated neutrally with regard to skill' (Nickell and Bell, 1995, p. 61). Miller expressed the same point in a different way by pointing out that training 'appears to be associated with the job, not the worker' (Miller, 1990, p. 12), and Gregory's more recent detailed study concluded that 'the increased education levels of the young have not protected them from bearing the major adjustment from the lack of job growth' (Gregory, 1995, p. 321). The most plausible assessment is that training policies at present operate as deferral devices which for some are mere time-serving mechanisms, for others recycling programmes, and ultimately for all across the board sorting devices to select the 'flexible' (disposable) workforce of the future.

The heavy reliance at a government level on training programmes serves to perpetuate a false assumption about a one-to-one relationship between being qualified and being employed. In Canada for instance, which has one of the highest participation rates in post-compulsory education in the world, levels of educational participation obscure clear inequalities in terms of employment outcomes. In the late 1980s as many as 50 per cent of community college and university graduates were actually going on to further studies, but in many cases this was precisely because their initial qualification had not proved adequate in the contracting job market.

The myth-making and propaganda about the 'knowledge society of the future' create a false impression concerning this widening gap between credentials and careers. Yet we know from the latest data from the United States that between 1986 and 1996 '2 of every 3 jobs created over this period were in occupations that do not require a degree' (Bureau of Labor Statistics, 1999, p. 55) and that 'over the 1996–2006 period, the majority of occupations with the largest expected job growth will require less than an associate degree' (p. 61). As Allahar and Côté (1998, p. 146) point out with regard to the Canadian data, 'only about 20 per cent of workers will be needed to bring their considerable expertise to design and maintain the technology and to manage complex technical systems'. This contradicts the view that with full participation and the formation of possibly the most highly skilled generation of 19-year-olds in the world, the new century would see a new educational agenda of success to replace the agenda of failure that had preoccupied the researchers and policy-makers of the 1970s. There is an element of double-speak in this. Given that these policies encourage the high status and aspiration associated with the university pathways by comparison with vocational education, for example, actual outcomes of higher participation rates are likely to display clear contrasts of success and failure in terms of adult livelihoods and careers.

Because of the technical skills it imparts, what remains of the higher education system after government retrenchment will likely be increasingly important in determining who has access to the relatively small number of lucrative high-tech jobs. But social class advantage will likely come into play, as parents already positioned in the lucrative sector give special guidance to their children and provide 'social capital' for them. Thus, we may see a situation where education is an uncontested means of reproduction of social classes, as it was before governments attempted to correct class-based injustices.

(Allahar and Côté, 1998, p. 146)

Continuing inequalities

Prior to the dramatic increases in post-compulsory participation rates from the mid-1980s onwards, it was common for educational outcomes in Western nations to be analysed in terms of inequalities associated with factors such as class, gender and ethnicity. Studies by Jencks (1973) and Coleman (1974) in the United States, for example, demonstrated the degree to which opportunities for effective participation by the disadvantaged were severely restricted, and official reports in Australia such as those published by the Poverty Inquiry (Wright, Headlam and Ozolins, 1978) and the Commonwealth Schools Commission (1980, 1984) drew attention to continuing inequalities and the need to formulate policies to overcome them.

One of the effects of the recent development of the 'mainstream' image has been a shift in attention away from earlier concerns of educators about significant levels of inequality. Post-compulsory education participation will supposedly open up rewarding futures for all. Yet recent studies from the US (Smith and Rojewski, 1993), the UK (Furlong and Cartmel, 1997), Canada (Allahar and Côté, 1998) and Australia (Teese, 2000) suggest otherwise. Despite higher levels of participation in all these countries, the evidence suggests that it is still important to examine the agenda of post-compulsory educational participation from the standpoint of inequality. Is inequality of outcomes in education a dead issue, or are there definite continuities with the past that are being ignored or masked by the apparent improvement in participation?

It must be acknowledged that the increased emphasis on extending the educational participation of the young has resulted in a significant decline in the numbers of those who leave school without completing an initial qualification. For OECD nations as a whole, by 1995 only one in four 20–24-year-olds lacked such a qualification – although there were significant national and regional variations. The proportion of non-completers for Portugal and Turkey was as high as one in two, while for Norway, the Czech Republic and Korea it was as low as one in ten. Within countries there were also variations of some magnitude, so that in both Australia and the United States rural students were more likely not to complete, while in Portugal 9th-grade non-completion rates were more than twice as high in the poorer regions by comparison with the rate for Lisbon. Also, in many OECD nations, youth unemployment rates remain high (in some nations the rate is three times that for adult workers).

The experience of rural youth perhaps best illustrates the continued existence of inequalities. Thus our recent comparative study of rural youth in both Canada and Australia found that:

> fewer rural than urban young people go on beyond high school ... Rural respondents who did pursue post-secondary education were more likely, in both studies, to opt for a non-university programme. Urban youth were more likely to opt for the higher status university path ... unlike their urban counterparts, most of the rural youth do not have a post-secondary institution in or near their community. Most say they would have to leave their community, which also means leaving the parental home, to pursue their education beyond high school. This means that the decision about pursuing post-secondary education is a very different one for rural as compared to urban youth. Their educational decisions involve different costs, both financial and social.
> (Looker and Dwyer, 1998a, p. 14)

With perhaps the rare exception of Norway (Heggen and Dwyer, 1999), it remains true that rural participation is generally lower than urban, so that in Australia, for example, 'participation in higher education among people from remote areas per head of population was roughly half that of people from urban areas' (Department of Education, Employment and Training [DEET], 1990, p. 1).

The international trends (Furlong and Cartmel, 1997; Allahar and Côté, 1998) suggest that there is still a discernible link between social class and the make-up of the one-quarter or more who do not complete their schooling. Students from families with lower-status occupations are more likely to discontinue their schooling, and detailed research on retention rates at a school by school and region by region level has documented the extent to which early school leaving is associated with working-class areas. Retention rates, curriculum access and successful participation in post-compulsory education display distinct patterns directly related to locality. 'Living in lower status areas ... is associated with poorer access to the curriculum and weaker results. Young people living in the upper status areas of the city have a secure expectation of educational success' (Teese, Polesel and McLean, 1993, p. 1).

As we shall see in a later chapter, a clear demonstration of the deceptive nature of the current outcomes from post-compulsory participation is the way in which the improved participation rates of young women have led to claims that, if anything, girls now surpass boys in terms of successful educational outcomes. It is true that from the early 1980s in countries such as Australia and Canada female participation rates for post-compulsory schooling and higher education began to exceed those of their male counterparts. Whereas prior to 1978 males outnumbered females at the post-compulsory levels of schooling, since then the situation has reversed – the female rate in Australia being 82 per cent in 1992 as against 73 per cent for males (Women's Bureau, 1993, p. 14). Similarly, since 1987 females have come to outnumber males in the field of higher education, with an increase in their share of enrolments in Australia from 20 per cent in the 1950s to 53 per cent in 1992, or from 43 per cent in Canada in 1972–3 to 53 per cent in 1992–3 (Allahar and Côté, 1998, p. 111). At first sight this evidence suggests that the genders are now virtually on an even footing in terms of educational participation.

There is, however, another aspect to the statistics. First, final school year retention rates for males need to be counterbalanced by the fact that many males do not continue through to the final year because they transfer across into an apprenticeship or vocational education alternative. Females are less likely to do so. Once we allow for this a different picture begins to emerge, so that for example when vocational courses are included in the participation rates for 15–19-year-olds the ratio changes and the male rate becomes 69 per cent as against that for females of 67 per cent (Ainley, 1998, p. 63). Similarly the rates for higher education only tell part of the story.

Some of the increase in female university participation rates is partly due to changes which have taken place within the teaching and nursing professions which led to a conflation of the rates as a result of the transfer of their courses into the higher education arena. It must also be noted that female higher education participation is confined to a narrower band of courses, with females still largely concentrated in what are seen as their 'traditional' fields of study – arts, education and nursing.

This narrow 'participation' also mirrors gender divisions within the labour market. In many countries women make up about 70 per cent of the part-time workforce and are restricted to a narrow band of jobs. In Canada in 1994, for example, as many as 70 per cent of women's jobs were in the five categories of clerical, sales, service work, teaching and nursing (Allahar and Côté, 1998, p. 108), while in Australia over half of all female employees were restricted to the two occupational categories of clerks (30 per cent) and sales/personal service (24 per cent). It is not surprising therefore that this labour market segmentation is mirrored in a clear gender imbalance in educational choices, and that female secondary students withdraw from continuing enrolment in high-level mathematics and physical sciences, which has a flow-on effect with regard to their selection into tertiary courses. Thus, at the school level males continue to dominate in the physical sciences, mathematics and technical studies with females strongly represented in languages, biological sciences and home science, so it is not surprising that even in the late nineties in Australia

> gender segregation by field of study is still discernible and 28 per cent of males in the Graduate Careers Council figures for 1997 were in the five highest paying fields of dentistry, medicine, optometry, earth science and engineering by comparison with only 7 per cent of females.
>
> (Marginson, 1999, p. 174)

A comprehensive analysis of data on school non-completers in Australia (Lamb *et al.*, 2000) does show that the incidence of non-completion is higher for boys than for girls. It also shows that – as in the United States – there has been very little change in the overall social and class profile of non-completers since the increase in school retention rates. By the mid-nineties the 'non-completers' still came from the same types of family and schooling background that characterised educational inequality before the changes in policy. In America, one recent study concluded that 'the child who grows up in a neighbourhood that has a high proportion of youth who are high-school dropouts will have a higher probability of dropping out of high school' (Haveman and Wolfe, 1994, p. 156), and that 'the number of years in poverty appears to affect adversely and significantly the number of years of schooling completed' (p. 160).

Furthermore, the same kinds of gender imbalances in aspirations and employment opportunities persist despite the public attention given to equal opportunity issues over the past twenty years. There is a definite divergence between the reasons males or females give for leaving school, and that divergence is reflected in the employment outcomes for each gender. As many as 41% of males but only 12% of females in the Australian sample had left school to enter apprenticeships, and for those who found jobs 53% of females and only 9% of males ended up as sales assistants while 38% of males (but 6% of females) found labouring jobs (Lamb, 1994, pp. 211, 215).

The policy gap

If we look back over the evidence presented in this chapter, it is clear that within Western societies there are currently substantial numbers of young people who are considered to lie outside the mainstream but for whom policy provisions are failing to bring about lasting outcomes. At best what these outsiders have been confronted with is a deferred agenda which subordinates their futures to the cost-cutting exercises of the successful generation that preceded them. At first sight, the link between credentials and employability appears self-evident, but it is deceptive if it leads to the conclusion that education and training remove the threat of underemployment or the risk of unemployment. In most OECD countries, while continuing high levels of unemployment have been felt by the younger age groups, this has been counteracted to some extent by the increasing proportion of those who are extending their educational participation well into their twenties. This then poses the problem that on completion of their studies these young adults are now beginning to experience the kind of 'study-to-work transition' uncertainties previously associated with the end of high school.

The heavy policy emphasis on the preparation of a future workforce for the 'knowledge society' conveniently glosses over the fact that the main growth area in Western societies is in the labour market for the 'service society', for which contingent and casualised labour is most in demand. The shifts that have taken place in employment sectors for a range of OECD countries since 1986 are shown in table 3.1.

There is a clear policy gap between the ideology of increased educational participation and the persistent uncertainties of outcomes for the post-1970 generation. False assumptions about a one-to-one relationship between being qualified and having a lasting adult professional career continue to be made despite the far-reaching

Table 3.1 Industry distribution of employment: 1986 and 1996 (%)

	Australia	Austria	Canada	Czech Rep.	Norway	Portugal
1986 Industry	27	38	25	48	27	34
1996 Industry	23	33	23	42	23	31
1986 Services	67	54	70	40	66	44
1996 Services	72	60	73	52	72	56

Source: Organisation for Economic Cooperation and Development (OECD).

changes that have affected labour markets in the global economy. When will the post-1970 generation and their supportive parents receive a genuine return on the very heavy investment they have made in terms of educational participation and promised career outcomes? The investment has been heavy in sheer dollar terms, but there are personal costs too – their hopes and fears, their personal growth and relationships, and the judgements made against them in terms of the success and failure that they are expected to bear. This has been the formative context of their lives but, as we shall see in the next chapter, they have not only learnt how to come to terms with the uncertainties it gives rise to, but are now as young adults drawing their own conclusions about it.

4 Coping with change

The evidence examined in the previous chapters illustrates the extent to which the lives of the current generation of young people in Western societies have been disrupted by change. They are having to cope with degrees of uncertainty that in many ways constitute a new kind of experience. This uncertainty can pose a problem for those who as parents, teachers, youth workers, or researchers are shaping young people's lives. They have their own experience of youth behind them and it is likely that their interest in and goals for the young have been influenced by their own experience.

On the positive side there is the possibility of establishing some 'common ground' or insights into youth as both an individual and social process which enables concerned adults to identify what is worthwhile and what is likely to be significant in the experience of the next generation. On the negative side there is the danger of a predetermined agenda that has been shaped by past understandings about 'growing up' and what are the established markers of achievement of adult status. Youth has been accepted primarily as an age category in the established model of human development in Western thought, and this approach has been reinforced by traditions in Western and non-Western cultures whereby identifiable markers or 'rites of passage' were seen as time-honoured indicators of transitions from one stage of life to another. The upheavals of the past quarter century have posed a dilemma which challenges these prevailing understandings of youth.

In seeking a better understanding of the lives of the post-1970 generation, therefore, we must take these upheavals into account. We cannot ignore the far-reaching changes that have occurred since the seventies in the organisation and operation of modern society, in its formal institutions, its family and labour market structures, in its social norms, attitudes and behaviour, and in the impact of international forces and trends on the lifestyles, cultural traditions or social priorities of individual nations. Some simple social indicators contrasting aspects of society in the 1970s and the 1990s display some of the ways in which personal experience has changed (table 4.1).

These particular figures are Australian, but they present a picture that is common to other countries as well (Anisef *et al.*, 2000, pp. 14–15). Someone born in the early 1970s in most Western nations would have faced the increased likelihood of growing up in either a double-income or else a single-parent family, would have had the clear prospect of a parental separation affecting themselves or their friends by the time they had reached their teens, would have come to the end of their compulsory years of schooling in the mid-1980s at a time when the youth labour market was in a state of collapse, and thus would have stayed on at school as a member of the first generation in nations such as Britain and Australia in which the majority actually completed their secondary schooling. At the age of 17 or 18 they would have been confronted with a shift in public attitudes and government policy which carried with it an expectation that they needed further education and training. By the time they were completing these further studies and juggling a part-time job at the same time they, and their younger siblings, would be faced with the prospect of paying increasing university fees to escape continuing high and long-term unemployment rates for young adults with only

Table 4.1 Changing social indicators

		1970s (%)	1990s (%)
Women married			
	aged 20	33	6
	aged 25	83	42
Women mothers			
	aged 25	66	25
Men in full-time work			
	aged 15–19	49	22
	aged 20–24	86	64
	aged 25–34	95	81
Women in full-time work			
	aged 15–19	46	13
	aged 20–24	52	48
	aged 25–34	27	41

Source: McDonald, 1997.

a high school qualification. Even university graduates with jobs would be experiencing uncertainty about their longer-term career prospects in a more 'flexible' restructured workforce. Many of the certainties and much of the predictability of the 'transitions into adulthood' that their parents' generation had enjoyed were now items of history and not part of their 'living memory'.

Relying on our own past can lead us to assume that it represents a 'normative' experience of youth. This establishes a predetermined expectation about what happens in the lives of the next generation. It takes for granted a linear model of development which assumes that young people progress through a pre-set series of separate 'stages' in their lives which involve innate processes of maturation and normative forms of socialisation within stable families and an age-based education system, leading at the proper time to a movement from dependence to independence, from school to work, from young people's status as adolescents to their eventual achievement of a stable and secure adulthood. This linear model has been reinforced in formulations of policy with regard to young people's education and training and has led to the adoption of a metaphor of 'pathways' in international reports in the mid-eighties (OECD/CERI, 1983; Henry, 1996; Green, 1991) and in national planning strategies concerned with the relation between educational attainment and employment outcomes (Commission on the Skills of the American Workforce, 1990; Department of Employment/Department of Education and Science, 1991; Canadian Labour Force Development Board, 1994; Commonwealth of Australia, 1994).

The linear model has also had a significant impact on the organisation of schools and classrooms, their rules and their curriculum, and on the way young people react to these. Lesko has commented that in many American studies and much teacher practice teenagers ' are massed together on the single criterion of age' (1996a, p. 156). Despite what they might be doing and achieving in their lives outside of school (working, acting as surrogate parents to their siblings, making adult decisions and achievements in sporting or religious organisations) as students they are accorded nothing more than pre-adult status. Because they are pre-adult and presumably not yet in proper control of their drives and hormones, subjecting them to the surveillance of adults becomes a major preoccupation in schools.

> Only those youths who demonstrate how reason, rather than hormones, rules their lives (e.g., youths who are compliant with *and* successful in meeting educators' demands for how, when,

and what to learn and accept as important) are deemed mature and given some small measure of freedom and responsibility.

(Lesko, 1996a, p. 157)

Even discussions of the philosophy of education or planning documents which allow for a diversity of educational outcomes maintain the linear model as a subtext. They assume that while individual pathways might display considerable variety in practice, the overall process of 'growing up' follows a predictable route between separate and sequential stages in life. The problem with this is that it over-simplifies the process of transition. It tends to trivialise young people's lives, by applying the pre-adulthood status of studenthood to young people who are already in their adult years and carrying out adult responsibilities. This produces some strange anomalies that have tended to be overlooked.

> For example, because the assumed separation of these two worlds – school and work – has shaped expectations and definitions of childhood and adulthood, being a young student and having full adult status have been seen as separate realities, even though the established literature provides evidence of a mixture of commitments in young people's lives that do not fit the sequential pattern. Thus, although full-time involvement in the workforce is often taken as a marker of adulthood, this status is often not extended to young students who also work, perhaps on the grounds that they have not yet moved beyond the world of education. Young students are seen as having 'not-yet-adult' status, despite their age, until they have completed their transition through education. Similarly, there are problems for the lineal model arising from the commonalities in experience and status between young workers who are married and married people of the same age who are 'still' students.
>
> (Looker and Dwyer, 1998a, p. 7)

Apart from these anomalies the main problem with the linear model is that it now misrepresents the actual transitions that are being made by the post-1970 generation. Recent European and North American books (Ball *et al.*, 2000; Côté, 2000; Evans and Heinz, 1994; Côté and Allahar, 1994; Cohen, 1997; Furlong and Cartmel, 1997;) and articles (Looker and Dwyer, 1998b; Rudd and Evans, 1998; du Bois-Reymond, 1998; Chisholm, 1997; Lesko, 1996b) manifest a growing concern about the need for new models and definitions of transition for the current generation of young people in Western societies. The evidence in these studies indicates that many in the younger generation are developing new ways of their own for dealing with risk and uncertainty of outcomes, and are making pragmatic choices for themselves which enable them to maintain their aspirations despite the persistence of more impersonal or 'structural' influences on their lives.

This convergence of evidence from different countries and continents points to a need to re-examine established understandings of the transition to adulthood and the frameworks which have been adopted in the past to explain the experience of the young. The remainder of this chapter is concerned with this convergence of evidence and also some of the unresolved issues it raises. It begins with a discussion of similarities in changing trends affecting youth transitions, and then examines the problems of definition and analysis which arise in taking these new directions seriously.

Elements of convergence

As we have seen in the opening chapter, there are some definite parallels between a study of young people in the United States (Schneider and Stevenson, 1999) and our own ten-year longitudinal study of young Australians. One of the themes the two studies have in common is the disparity between the aspirations of college students and their actual employment prospects and outcomes. A detailed comparison with a comparable Canadian study presented a similar picture (Looker and Dwyer, 1998a), which also appeared to be confirmed by some other studies from the Netherlands and the United Kingdom. The study from the Netherlands (du Bois-Reymond, 1998) was begun in 1988 and was concerned with the transition to adulthood of 120 adolescents. One article which reported on the study concentrated particularly on those participants who are by now in their twenties and who could be defined as belonging to a cultural elite within their generation. It presented four case studies to illustrate the ways in which transitions to adulthood have changed in recent years. One British study (Rudd and Evans, 1998) of interest was concerned with school-to-work transitions, and was based on 223 respondents from two samples of 16–19-year-old college students in the UK in contrasting labour markets.

All of these studies from different countries are concerned with elements of choice in young people's responses to the increasing contingency and risk which characterise transitions to adulthood and future careers in the contemporary world. For example, the title of the Dutch study ('I Don't Want to Commit Myself Yet'), conveys an impression of an open-ended choice on the part of the participants, and much of the evidence is concerned with changes in the life-course of young people and the complex ways in which they negotiate and balance a range of personal, occupational and educational commitments in their lives. The British study is explicitly devoted to an investigation of the extent to which personal autonomy and control counterbalance or reinforce more impersonal or structural factors in the economy and social variables such as gender, social class and ethnicity. The Canadian and Australian studies questioned established assumptions about youth transitions and education pathways, and explored how they endeavour to define their own educational and life commitments and construct futures for themselves.

Evidence of this increased pressure on young people to negotiate their own way into adult life can be found in their 'blending' of different aspects of their lives. They now combine both study and work (Stern *et al.*, 1990) in ways that challenge the sequential pattern of movement from study to work which was part of the established approach to transition. Schneider and Stevenson report (1999, p. 170) that in their United States study as many as 80 per cent of the students in the sample had jobs. In our Canadian and Australian study (Looker and Dwyer 1998a, pp. 11–12), at least half in both countries 'report a mix of school and work', while only 20 per cent in the Australian sample had 'rarely' or 'never' combined the two. Comparatively similar evidence is available for other countries. Chisholm (1997, p. 14) reports that the study/work combination is 'a significant activity pattern' in a number of European countries, and Rudd and Evans indicated in their study that 'over 60 per cent of the sample had a part-time job … at the time of the survey, though this figure masks local labour market differences' (Rudd and Evans, 1998, p. 54). The Dutch study noted that the blending of areas of life has become increasingly common. 'What used to be arranged in series – learning, and then work – is currently becoming a *double field* and a *double life* for adolescents and young adults: learning and work, work and learning, alternately' (du Bois-Reymond, 1998, p. 67, italics in original).

It seems likely that there is an element of constraint in this blending of study and work commitments due to changed economic and social circumstances, but there is also evidence that a significant number of young people now express a preference for it. Thus, Chisholm (1997, p. 14) notes that in Europe 'Labour Force Survey data suggest that a third of 15–29-year-olds in the Community are positively choosing part-time employment in order to be able to pursue a qualification alongside or in connection with their work'. This evidence matches up with the data we have from our Australian participants. There is considerable variation in their assessments of the combination, but less than a third indicate that they 'would prefer study without work'.

Another aspect of change that is introduced by the Canadian and Australian material concerns variations and changes of direction in the students' courses of study. One of the shortcomings of many quantitative studies on educational transitions is that the general trends of enrolments and outcomes neglect the internal transfers within and across courses and institutions that are part of those trends. The Dutch study under consideration here makes reference to a 'variety of options' which allows the choice of training and profession to take on 'a temporary or even arbitrary character insofar as it is always possible to revise a decision' (du Bois-Reymond, 1998, p. 69), and the four case studies also allude to changes of decision about courses of study and career aspirations. The Canadian and Australian data are more definite, and provide evidence (table 4.2) concerning widespread variations over time, including interruption and deferral of courses, which indicates significant numbers had not followed a single or uninterrupted pathway.

The interview material from both countries points to an element of trial and error involved in these changes and that overall 'pragmatic choice' is a fair description of how the participants are weighing up their options.

These figures raise questions about the idea of young people following a set trajectory, based on their high school performance and the expectations held by themselves and their significant

Table 4.2 Multiple transitions

	Rural (%)	Urban (%)
Canada		
Changed institutions	12	12
Changed courses	13	15
Discontinued studies	14	12
Australia		
Changed institutions	18	22
Changed courses	22	26
Discontinued studies	20	13

others. The young people do not experience their pathways as preset or linear. Rather they report them as complex and interconnected, as involving false starts and redefined possibilities, as requiring negotiation and redefinitions. Research and policy that assume linearity and that focus on one dominant mainstream will miss many of the complexities that the young people say are important to their decisions about how much and what type of education to pursue.

(Looker and Dwyer, 1998a, p. 17)

The evidence on pragmatic choice in the face of increased uncertainty about eventual outcomes points to an increasing complexity in the life-patterns of different groups of young people. Rudd and Evans (1998, p. 61) draw attention to young people's attempts to find a balance between the influence of social structure and their own agency in a way that would allow much more for young people's 'perceived feelings of autonomy and control' (p. 60). The Dutch study (du Bois-Reymond, 1998, p. 65) makes use of the distinction, derived from Beck's Risk Society (1992), between 'choice' and 'normal' biographies which has become quite influential in recent studies. The distinction is one between the traditional understanding of the various determined and sequential stages of development from adolescence to adulthood – taken as part of a 'normal biography' – and a possibly more problematic sequence of the choice biography where much more is left to the individual and which involves negotiation of a diversity of options and even a degree of 'tension between option/freedom and legitimation/coercion'.

The link between these independent studies from a range of countries adds further weight to the need to examine a diversity of patterns in the choices that young people are currently making in their transitions into adulthood. While this does not imply the rejection of the customary 'vocational' and 'occupational' trajectories associated with the established model, it calls for an acknowledgement that in both our policy and practice we need to add to those trajectories in ways which allow increasingly for other life-patterns which reflect more truly the experience and choices of the young generation of today.

A perplexing optimism

One of the puzzling issues raised by current studies of 'growing up' is the degree of positivity in the responses of the participants despite the uncertainties they face in current social and economic circumstances. The British study in particular pays considerable attention to this and teases out some of the possible explanations. The authors link it to the theme of individual choice because this belief in

> the importance of individual effort was often accompanied by a degree of optimism on the part of the students in terms of their own job prospects, whatever the state of their local labour market: this was one of the most interesting (and in some ways perplexing) findings of the research.
>
> (Rudd and Evans, 1998, p. 53)

Like their American counterparts in the 'ambitious generation' (Schneider and Stevenson, 1999), more than 90 per cent saw the link between qualifications and employment prospects as very or quite important (p. 52). Only about 4 per cent thought it unlikely or impossible that they would find suitable employment on completion of their studies and most were confident (p. 53) that they would avoid unemployment.

Similar evidence is available from other nations. In our Life-Patterns Project the participants shared high expectations about future careers that displayed little divergence between what they 'would like' and what they 'realistically expect' – with about two-thirds expecting to achieve professional careers. In the Dutch study we have already referred to, the theme of optimism was also commented on (du Bois-Reymond, 1998, p. 71). 'Like young people with a 'normal biography', post-adolescents do not fear becoming unemployed (they too are optimistic and prepare themselves for all eventualities)'. By contrast with their British, Canadian and Australian peers, the Dutch respondents are less at risk with regard to unemployment. Given this, one of the puzzling aspects of the other studies is that actual outcomes are likely to be at odds with participant expectations.

Thus, the British research draws attention to the fact that even students in the East London region, 'who were by all accounts in a relatively depressed labour market at the time of the fieldwork, continued to be at least as optimistic as their Westdown counterparts' (Rudd and Evans, 1998, p. 57). With regard to the Australian data actual employment outcomes for the total sample indicated that even of those who had already graduated only 40 per cent were able to claim that they had found a job in their 'preferred career area' despite what they had seen as 'realistic' expectations. The American data indicated that the ambitions of almost 60 per cent of the participants were 'misaligned' with their likely outcomes, and many of them were categorised as 'drifting dreamers' (Schneider and Stevenson, 1999).

A further perplexity is added, however, by evidence from studies of other young people who have not gone on to further study on leaving school. For example, in attempting to explain the degree of optimism expressed in their sample, Rudd and Evans examined two other British studies concerning non-students that indicate levels of optimism even among school leavers or dropouts. While some (Wallace 1989, pp. 361–2) modified their aspirations downwards after five years of trying to find work, others (Church and Ainley, 1987, p. 83) displayed continuing high levels of aspirations despite increasing unemployment. This is true of other European countries (Chisholm 1997, p. 13) and

> we know from a range of qualitative studies that young people can be proactive and sometimes ingenious in negotiating their way into the labour market (including its grey sectors), and that these behaviours are by no means confined to the better qualified and those with more social and cultural capital. On the contrary, the survival skills of the young disadvantaged and marginalised can be singularly impressive, even if largely unrecognised in the formal qualifications system.

It is perhaps more difficult to form some comprehensive picture of the impact of social change at a generational level in the case of the United States, because of some clear-cut social divisions that are part of its traditions. At a very general level, to the outsider there is a clear divergence of approach and understanding related to a well-established distinction between 'mainstream' young Americans and those categorised as 'at risk'. This is obvious when we see how books such as *Succeeding Generations* (Haveman and Wolfe, 1994), and *The Ambitious Generation* (Schneider and Stevenson, 1999) on the one hand, and *America's Youth in Crisis* (Lerner, 1995), *Fugitive Cultures* (Giroux, 1996), and *Cold New World* (Finnegan, 1998) on the other, present such diametrically opposed pictures of American youth. Even the titles are at odds with each other. It is not simply a matter of distinctions between 'success' and 'failure', or even that the United States has very serious social divisions that are too easily glossed over, but that the assumptions behind the two strands of interpretation are so different that they focus the attention of the reader on different types of evidence and different forms of conclusions. Mainstream young Americans tend to be pictured and studied with reference to the established institutional frameworks of American society, and so we are told much about their varying levels of educational attainment, employment outcomes and family relationships. What is seen as distinctive about those 'at risk' is what is dysfunctional in their lives – and, unfortunately, even those who are in a sense 'on their side' and concerned about their futures tend to highlight failure, alienation and family breakdown, so that young people with problems come across as 'problem kids'.

A likely explanation for the divorce between these two assessments of American youth is offered by Lerner (1995, p. 38) in his analysis of the professional literature on young people in the United States. The major journals display a heavy preoccupation with those sections of youth who are seen as representative of the 'mainstream' in American society. As a consequence, those who challenge the representativeness of the evidence that is offered are almost inevitably forced to concentrate on the supposedly 'non-mainstream' groups and the evidence about them that has been excluded or overlooked. The 'other America' becomes the focus (Ayman-Nolley and Taira, 2000). For example, as the authors of *Studying Minority Adolescents* point out

> leading journals in adolescent development continue to show a conspicuous paucity of research in this area. The little research that does include ethnic minority youth focuses disproportionately on problematic aspects of adolescence, such as delinquency, academic failure, and teen pregnancy. As a result of this bias, our understanding of normative adolescent development in diverse populations is exceedingly limited. Given the changed and changing demography of adolescence, this situation must change.
> (McLoyd and Steinberg, 1998, p. vii)

Choice biographies

Because of the disruptions that have taken place since the early 1970s in the processes of transition from youth to adulthood, some youth researchers have begun to draw some clear contrasts between industrial and 'post-industrial' societies. In referring to the experience of the young in contemporary Western societies, they draw upon the work of the German scholar, Ulrich Beck (1992), and make use of his theme of 'choice biographies'. Beck was concerned with the emergence of the 'risk society' in the last part of the twentieth century, which gave rise to his distinction between the 'normal' biographies of the industrial era and the 'choice' biographies of the risk society. The 'normal' biographies of the industrial era presented a linear, and largely predictable, sequence of developmental stages whereby young people moved from dependence to independence, from school to work, and from adolescence into an adulthood (defined in terms of marriage, family and lifetime career or occupation) similar to that of their parents. The biographies were 'normal' because they developed within a social context shaped by the predictability and assumed permanence, over any one lifetime, of the established institutional structures of the family, education, industry and the labour market. Most of the 'markers' of transition (the age of consent, voting age, adult wage, marriage and parenthood, home ownership, and at the end of the term the age of retirement and pension entitlements) reflected this twofold assumption about linear and predictable norms.

Increasingly adults of all ages now find themselves negotiating changes that have affected established institutions and expectations – marriage break-ups, retrenchment, new workplace agreements, single parenthood, retraining, flexitime, outsourcing, or intermittent unemployment. Theirs are now 'choice' biographies:

> the proportion of the biography which is open and must be constructed personally is increasing ... Decisions on education, profession, job, place of residence, spouse, number of children and so forth, with all the secondary decisions implied, no longer can be, they must be made. Even where the word 'decisions' is too grandiose, because neither consciousness nor alternatives are present, the individual will have to 'pay for' the consequences of decisions not taken.
>
> (Beck, 1992, p. 135)

Other authors (Furlong and Cartmel, 1997, p. 6) compare this distinction between 'normal' and 'choice' biographies to the contrast between train and car travel.

> Unlike the railway passenger, the individual car driver is constantly faced with a series of decisions relating to routes which will take them from their point of origin to their destination. They can take the motorway, follow A roads, stick to minor roads, scenic routes, or can follow any combination of these routes. At many junctions, they can switch routes and may decide to change roads due to difficulties in making progress on roads previously selected.

There is a further dimension to the emergence of 'choice' biographies, however, that is important to mention here. Apart from changes in the study and work dimensions of young people's lives, there are other aspects which have also changed significantly in recent years. Those aspects are sometimes examined under the theme of lifestyle (Chaney 1996), but whatever term is used, it would include people's personal commitments, interests and 'leisure-time' pursuits (Hendry *et al.*, 1993; Mommaas, *et al.*, 1996; Haworth, 1997). All of these have been subjected to considerable social and economic change during the second half of the twentieth century: changes to the status and roles of women; new styles of family formation; the increasing commercialisation and promotion of different forms of leisure and entertainment – much of it directed specifically at the young; and an emphasis on fulfilment in the 'private' aspects of life that until recently was not given equal prominence in research into young people's identity formation (see Featherstone, 1991; Lunt and Livingstone, 1992). As Chaney (1996, p. 112) has pointed out,

> whereas traditionally work or occupation determined social class and thus an individual's way of life, in the second half of the century leisure activities and/or consumer habits are being increasingly experienced by individuals as the basis of their social identity.

If therefore 'choice' biographies are becoming a dominant feature of the life-patterns of emerging generations this further dimension of their lives is also likely to be affected. Among young people in the Netherlands, for example, the tendency to combine study and work is associated with a corresponding tendency to 'combine work and leisure time' – a 'further step on the way to increasingly more complex concepts of life'. We need to uncover the ongoing significance of this growing trend and, as the Netherlands study indicated (du Bois-Reymond, 1998, p. 76), it would be 'of great interest, especially in view of life-long learning and further 'flexibility' of jobs, to find out if this is becoming a general tendency or if it will remain restricted to specific groups of people'.

It is important to note that this emphasis on 'choice' does not deny the continuing influence of factors such as class, gender or ethnicity on the range of options available to particular people. Proponents of choice biographies recognise the inherent inequalities associated with concepts of 'risk'. Beck, for example, draws attention to individuals who lack real alternatives in their lives, but who nevertheless will have to 'pay for' the consequences of decisions not taken (Beck, 1992, p. 135). Structural constraints continue to affect the range of choices available to young people from different social backgrounds, even if they appear to subscribe to prevailing notions of choice and personal autonomy (Rudd and Evans, 1998, p. 60). Furlong and Cartmel (1997) have examined evidence from the UK which indicates that young people's experiences are still 'strongly affected by gender divisions', and that 'there is little evidence to suggest that the effect of social class on life chances is diminishing' (Furlong and Cartmel, 1997, p. 112). While they concede that the influence of structural constraints has become more obscure, and that a shift has taken place 'promoting individual responsibilities and weakening collectivist traditions', they nevertheless contend that life chances remain highly structured. They argue that there is a deceptive element or 'epistemological fallacy' in the recent emphasis on 'choice biographies' which leads young people to discount the influence of the structural factors which still determine many of their choices.

Participant research

One way of testing the theme of 'choice' is to involve young people directly in the shaping of research questions and methods and to extend the practice of 'participant research' in studies about their choices. One outcome of our comparative analysis of Canadian and Australian data was a recognition of the need not merely to combine quantitative and qualitative research much more closely but also to develop ways that would make us better 'equipped to measure and describe multiple activities and complex relationships' (Looker and Dwyer, 1998a, p. 18). We need to develop new types of questions which can uncover some of the uncertainties and mixed priorities hidden within the emphasis on choice. 'A focus on outcomes and linear patterns misses much of the complexity that young people say they experience as they move beyond high school' (p. 17).

The need for a more interactive research process that enables the participants to articulate their own meanings and experiences is recognised by other authors as well. For example, some British authors argue that many studies of youth transitions

> underestimate the degree of choice or agency evident in such processes and there have been few attempts to explain the apparent incompatibility between young people's perceived feelings of autonomy and control and the alleged over-arching often

unmediated, influence of 'deterministic' social structures on their lives.

(Rudd and Evans, 1998, pp. 60–1)

If, for the young people involved, the influence of social structures such as class, gender and ethnicity are no longer being read as taken-for-granted truths, those involved in youth research need to develop ways of investigating what this shift in their understanding – and sense of agency – implies with regard to the researcher's own understandings and predetermined agendas regarding their transitions (Ball *et al.*, 2000; Côté, 2000).

There has always been an alternative tradition in youth research which has made considerable use of qualitative and ethnographic methods. Much of the best Scandinavian or Nordic research is notable for this (Gudmundsson, 2000), and studies of this kind have been effective in giving 'active voice' to the participants and bringing out in some detail the complexities involved in growing up. Contextual issues related to race, gender and class in the US, Canada and the UK have been treated in this way and the work of the Birmingham Centre for Contemporary Cultural Studies in the UK was important in this regard, particularly because of the emphasis it placed on notions of resistance and cultural identity (Willis, 1977). Some more recent examples of this type of research in the US have dealt with how issues of social identity, gender, class and schooling are intertwined (Wexler, 1992) and how teenage workers are negotiating a way of life for themselves in the new working conditions of the service society (Willis, 1998). Some good examples from Australia are a study of 150 young people from a variety of ethnic and cultural backgrounds (McDonald, 1999), another on the impact of ethnicity and leisure interests on different subgroups of students in an all-male school (Walker, 1986), and a detailed study devoted to examining young adult's self-perceptions and life contexts (Evans and Poole, 1991). That study was deliberately designed to move beyond a narrow preoccupation with economic and vocational definitions of youth transitions by placing equal emphasis on the concerns and interests that the participants regarded as most important to themselves: 'the major life settings "action contexts" in which young people lead their lives – work, study, leisure and personal relationships'. From a research point of view there is a need for more studies of this kind that would provide more detailed evidence about the lasting significance of these other dimensions of young people's lives.

There are other studies which support this type of approach to young people's lives (Miles, 1995; Lunt and Livingstone, 1992; Redhead *et al.*, 1997; MacDonald, 1997) but, within the UK in particular, questions continue to be raised about whether these are still subordinate or 'subcultural' concerns or whether they can be explained as a misreading of the ongoing importance of structural constraints on young people's identity formation. One of the aspects of youth research that is often seen to justify this type of criticism is a concern about the ways in which factors such as class, gender and ethnicity place particular groups 'at risk'. This is a legitimate concern and an important warning against exaggerating or romanticising elements of 'choice' in the life circumstances of a generation that is faced with the twofold pressures of a collapsed youth labour market and increasing demands from educational credentialism. However, it is equally important to note the ways in which those considered 'at risk' come to terms with their own circumstances. In commenting on the situation of young unemployed working-class men in the Teesside area of England, MacDonald makes a significant point about the need to broaden research agendas.

> The connections between changing cultures of employment, emergent youth leisure forms, illicit drug use and criminal activities have not, as yet, been fully unravelled. What is clear, though, is that there are connections between these social developments and that sociologists might usefully go beyond their recent fascination with just the labour market of jobs and training schemes to consider more broadly the variety of vibrant cultures and careers – mainstream and alternative, licit and illicit, work-based and leisure-based – that young adults are establishing in the 1990s.
> (MacDonald, 1998, p. 171)

Furlong and Cartmel (1997) argue that this sense of being able to cope with risk at an individual level is, however, often deceptive. They suggest that there is an underlying 'epistemological fallacy' in assertions about the significance of choice biographies – young people may be overestimating the degree to which they are shaping their own life-patterns and underestimating the extent to which they are still constrained by persistent structural factors of class, gender and ethnicity which continue to define their educational opportunities and occupational outcomes. The authors concede that there is an increasing emphasis on individual choice in young people's outlook

on life, but they also contend that 'although the collective foundations of social life have become more obscure, they continue to
provide powerful frameworks which constrain young people's experiences and life chances' (Furlong and Cartmel, 1997, p. 109).

Evidence about the growing importance of choice is often taken
from the comparatively 'successful' or achieving members of the generation. This can give a misleading picture of young people's capacity
to cope with the challenges of contingency and risk to the extent that
it underestimates that for many of the generation 'risk' is much more
of a threat than a challenge. Certainly, further detailed study of the
constraints affecting eventual career and life-course outcomes needs
to be pursued, and not only regarding those gaining some educational position of advantage but across the generation as a whole.
We have already drawn attention to the way in which in the American
research into the mainstream and that concerned with the disadvantaged tend to be in two separate compartments, so that it is often difficult to compare effectively the findings in the two different strands
of research. It is clear, however, that there is considerable evidence in
the United States 'at risk' research literature that extremes of advantage and disadvantage have if anything grown worse over the course
of the past decade (Giroux, 1996), with the result that for those at risk
the tightening of welfare provisions makes the renewed emphasis on
choice a matter of selecting between basically unpleasant options.
Notions of contingency and risk have negative implications as well
and so must be counterbalanced by a continuing investigation of the
impact of structural constraints and advantages.

There are definite tensions which affect the relationship between
personal choice and impersonal forces, and these manifest themselves
in the development of choice biographies. Perhaps the factor which
sharpens the tension for the purpose of analysis is the link mentioned
earlier between individual agency and a 'perplexing' optimism about
eventual outcomes of life-choices. Rudd and Evans (1998, pp. 56–9)
discuss this issue at some length and offer four possible explanations
for it: either it is because the young people have been socialised into
a belief in choice and the results of individual effort; or there is a
time-lag affecting the gap between aspirations and commensurate
outcomes; or it is a feature of the psychological make-up of these
young people at this particular stage; or finally, locality may be an
influence in that urban labour market opportunities are still considerable, even though actual levels of youth unemployment remain high.

What is important here is that for young people their own sense
of agency carries a degree of personal investment that looks forward

to – even insists on – positive outcomes. Their expectations may appear to be over-optimistic, and the almost total rejection of the possibility of unemployment may appear unrealistic, but what is clear is that their chances of establishing a livelihood in the terms they value will depend on the extent to which they can work with the complexity they currently face. Agency implies that they will construct positive links and experiences where, on the face of it, none may be apparent. In other words, where structured pathways do not exist, or are rapidly being eroded, individual agency is increasingly important in establishing patterns for themselves which give positive meaning to their lives.

However, this evidence should not be taken to underestimate the seriousness of the circumstances faced by the post-1970 generation. The crumbling of 'bridges' between childhood and adulthood (Land, 1996), remains an issue. In most industrialised societies, there has been a withdrawal of support provided to young people and their families during the time that young people are making the transitions to adulthood, and an increase in the costs associated with education and training borne by students or their families. Individual success in the labour market and in education is inevitably at the expense of others who are not as fortunate. The success of a minority serves to reinforce the idea that gaining credentials through education and training provides a pathway to employment. Here too the experience of marginalised young people in the United States (Finnegan, 1998) adds a cautionary note to the heavy emphasis on individual growth and achievement that is so evident in the mainstream literature and suggests the need to be more critical about the frameworks of that literature. For example, we know that half the dropouts in the US come from white middle-class families (Ianni and Orr, 1996, p. 290), and even studies such as *Succeeding Generations* (Haveman and Wolfe, 1994), and *The Ambitious Generation* (Schneider and Stevenson, 1999), contain evidence that demonstrates that there are considerable numbers of 'mainstream' young Americans whose credentials have not led to the hoped-for outcomes – in fact in the Schneider and Stevenson study over half the sample had been unsuccessful in achieving 'aligned ambitions' for themselves.

If we are to pay more attention to young people's own voices, it is important to ask whether the 'epistemological fallacy' that Furlong and Cartmel refer to has its own research implications. Does it so to speak have a 'mirror-image' in the inability of research practices derived from the industrial era to account for the more diffuse post-industrial experience of an emerging generation that has grown up in a very different kind of world from that of its predecessors? One of the central assumptions of many of the established research approaches was the relatively clear-cut approach that could be adopted regarding distinctions between the public and private dimensions of life. The problem now is that if we perpetuate those distinctions in our research frameworks and modes of analysis we may well find apparent confirmation of them, but at the expense of ignoring the ways in which changes in the labour market, in patterns of social mobility and occupational security, in gender relations and consumer styles have called into question the clear-cut categories the research model assumes. As Chaney (1996, p. 159) puts it,

> lifestyles have acted to significantly blur, and thus transform, established distinctions between public and private spheres – and in so doing they have acted to inform and constitute new understandings of the relationships between individual and collective forms of social existence.

If then the relationship between structural constraints and individual perceptions of choice has become 'obscure', we must not only seek to clarify the continuing importance of structural factors, but also allow that some of the obscurity might be due to blindspots in the established assumptions of structural analysis. There may well be a caution needed here about the tendency for policy and research agendas regarding a younger generation to become predetermined by the life experience and intellectual preoccupations of their predecessors. The caution emerged sharply in the attitude of the participants in the study by du Bois-Reymond. She comments that one of the 'most disturbing' findings was that these 'young people do not like adulthood' (du Bois-Reymond, 1998, p. 74). What she was referring to was their preference for blending different aspects of their lives – study, work, personal relationships and leisure interests, in contrast to their parents whose lives were dominated by narrow, time-consuming or debt-ridden responsibilities.

> If there is one thing (post)-adolescents do not want, it is the idea of 'nothing but work' until they are 65 by which time they will be 'old and knackered'. Now already, before they have started their professional life properly, they are thinking about *mixed models* where work and leisure time complement each other profitably – and leisure time is certainly not the part they want to lose out on.
> (du Bois-Reymond, 1998, p. 74, italics in original)

The point at issue here is that while many researchers at least acknowledge changes in the links between study and work they still have difficulty giving equal attention to other aspects of young people's lives. This is a criticism that has been made of some of the contributions to a recent collection of articles on young people and social change in Europe. While some articles in the collection (Bynner, Chisholm and Furlong, 1997) take up the kinds of issues discussed in this chapter, the reviewer nevertheless contends that it falls short of being 'a genuinely holistic study of young people's progress towards adult status across the social spectrum' (Catan, 1998, p. 350). It tends still to be preoccupied with elements from the 'old' agenda of British youth research regarding economic transitions and structural determinants of young people's life-chances, and so

> the new agenda consciously reflects concerns of UK policy-makers facing European integration and global competition, not primarily concerns of young people themselves. Indeed, many issues that interest and motivate young people, e.g. empowerment, youth culture, sexuality, consumerism, leisure are only briefly mentioned, not developed.
>
> (Catan, 1998, p. 351)

If, however, these issues are of increasing importance for young people today and an emerging trend of 'mixed patterns' is becoming more widespread, there is a clear need to build on a more flexible understanding of people's study, work and lifestyle commitments. If these mixed life-patterns amount to more than only a short-term manifestation of youth, and are instead a shaping of life-long identities and possibilities, then a new form of adulthood is taking shape in their lives, and both policy and research need to provide a forward-looking response to these multi-dimensional lives.

Concluding comment

In the course of their lifetime young people of today have found themselves confronted with a new set of life challenges which are in significant ways unique to their generation – changes not only encompassing the dimensions of education and employment but which also extend to other dimensions of their personal lives. Much of the ongoing parental advice, teaching practice, careers information, policy formation and research activity regarding their processes of transition still operates within well-established preconceptions that make it difficult to incorporate new perspectives into our understanding of young people and our assessment of future developments.

What is particularly surprising about this is that the fundamental shifts in social and economic relations occurring over the past quarter century have affected both young people and older people (Côté, 2000). Changes in labour markets, in the relationship between education and employment, in workplace relations, in family formations and consumer lifestyles have not only altered the significance of the traditional 'markers' of adult status for the young in industrialised countries but have also affected the established relationships of family and dependency between the different generations involved. The mixed responses of the new generation to a mixed future therefore pose a challenge for us to think beyond the preconceptions which still influence much of our understanding and writing about youth and which lead to misreadings of the impact of change in their lives. We need not only to explore the extent to which this generation is affected by the contingency and risk of late modernity but also to examine the ways in which they are entering upon a new form of adulthood.

Part II
Problems of transition

5 Student hopes and outcomes

As we saw in Part I, by the late 1980s in Western societies there was a marked change in public attitudes and official policies towards school participation rates, reflected in a substantial shift in the proportion of young people continuing through to the final years and contemplating enrolling in university or college. In their attitudes towards education, an 'ambitious generation' had been formed.

There is, however, another side to this story. American authors (Schneider and Stevenson, 1999) draw attention to a gap between ambition and outcomes which indicates that the majority of students have misaligned ambitions. Other research studies suggest that a number of extraneous or non-educational factors have influenced the increased participation, and that much of the increase is due to a lack of sufficient or suitable jobs; students who would otherwise have left school are filling in time by staying at school until they do find a job. There is greater pressure for students to stay on at school longer and to develop their personal abilities further, but the extent to which they themselves see this positively depends on how supportive the 'school culture' is. The promotion of effective pathways into adult life for those still at school is not simply an issue of successful levels of achievement at a subject level, but also involves the types of social relationships and 'sense of belonging' manifested within the school. The following extract from a review of participation in post-compulsory education illustrates a common finding.

> There is also evidence that positive attitudes towards school are associated with continuing at school and that favourable views of school life are not necessarily dependent on high achievement. A general satisfaction with school and a sense among young people that school work is relevant to their future are important influences on the decision to stay at school. Therefore programs

aimed at raising achievement but which have the unintended consequence of reducing students' satisfaction might prove counterproductive ... A number of submissions to this review made the point that school culture and, in particular, teacher attitudes have a significant influence on the willingness of disadvantaged young people to remain at school ... Interpersonal support and the expectations of 'significant others' play a crucial role in shaping educational participation.

> (Australian Education Council [AEC], 1991, p. 135)

If part of the improvement in educational participation has resulted from the foreclosing of alternatives outside school for a number of students, it is perhaps not surprising that the American research reveals that many of those who have continued have poorly aligned ambitions about the links between education and future employment. It is likely that there were students who had continued with their schooling but who would have preferred to leave if the economic circumstances had been different. Nevertheless, in the framing of policy little attention had been given to determining the consequences, on the lives and outlook of students themselves, of this change in retention, even though increasing concern was being expressed both within policy formulations and public debate about the uncertainties and risks facing the next generation of students.

If the more negative effects of contemporary social change were having a far-reaching impact on young people's lives, and if it was true that some of the increased participation in education was the direct result of a lack of employment opportunities for those who wanted to leave, to what extent was this beginning to colour the outlook of students and reshape their hopes and fears regarding their own outcomes? Were these concerns that lay in the future and which therefore were not yet taken into account, or did they already have an impact on student attitudes and levels of personal satisfaction in the early nineties even before their post-compulsory education was complete? The purpose of this chapter is to examine this issue of student hopes and fears in the face of new labour-market realities.

Future prospects

The heightening of ambition among high school students in America has not been a unique experience isolated to the young of a single nation, but something that is shared in other parts of the world. One of the central themes of this book is the need to look beyond national boundaries in order to realise that this is a generational experience resulting from a process of worldwide changes in social, educational and economic circumstances that has posed a new kind of future to the coming generation. This becomes clear when we examine some of the comparative evidence; it extends our understanding of the converging impact of global change on young people's future prospects and aspirations. We begin this chapter with an illustration of this provided in a Canadian study (Andres Bellamy, 1993) based on two sets of interviews with British Columbia final-year school students in 1989 and 1990. The findings show how the heightened emphasis on educational credentials was influencing the ways in which young people near the end of high school were coming to assess their schooling with reference to their own future prospects.

The study was concerned with the students' plans for what they wanted to do after they had completed high school and to explore 'in depth their perceptions of the processes underlying their decisions regarding post-high school destinations' (Andres Bellamy, 1993, p. 141). Three schools were selected – one metropolitan, one urban/rural and one remote – and fifteen to twenty students from each were part of the interview programme. The first interview was held six months before their high school graduation and the second took place a year later and after they had graduated. The responses of the participants regarding their future study plans indicated that there were effectively four different categories of students.

First, there were those who had always planned to go on with post-secondary studies (mainly university), and many of these were either following in their parents' footsteps or at least fulfilling their expectations. Thus as one of them put it (p. 145):

> they want me to go to [university]. Both of them have gone there before . . . My mom and dad have brainwashed me sort of thing. But I know that's the best way to go.

Another student saw their parents' expectations as arising from their lack of post-school qualifications and desire for the student to do better:

> I guess that's kind of sunk in and stayed there . . . She expects me to do things that she couldn't do like because her family was poor.

Secondly, there were those who were aware of the increasing importance placed on further qualifications but who had decided against it. Again, parental expectations had something to do with this, either because the parents themselves had not done further studies or suspected that their offspring were not that way inclined (p. 146).

> Dad doesn't even think I'm going to graduate, so he hasn't really put much into my education ... It's my choice what I want to do, they really don't get in the way of what I want to do.

A third type of response was ambivalent – perhaps including some vague plan to go to a community college rather than to university, while the final category included students who were deciding very much on their own regardless of what the parental expectations might be. A typical response here was:

> it's totally up to me. Like, [my parents] would prefer it ... but if I don't want to, I don't have to.

Despite this obvious variation in responses across the whole group, there was however a shared recognition, 'held as strongly by the young women' as by the young men, about the increasing emphasis on and importance of post-secondary qualifications for perceived success in the adult world.

> For the most part, regardless of intended post-high school destination, almost all students expressed the belief that without a post-secondary qualification their lives – in terms of employment, quality of life, and future careers advancement – would be compromised.
>
> (Andres Bellamy, 1993, p. 151)

The only major reservation expressed came from those who did not go on to further study after graduation and who thought that unless there was a real purpose or goal at stake, 'post-secondary participation would be a futile exercise', 'another way to drift' and a 'postponement of the inevitable' (p. 153).

> Yet they appeared well aware of the consequences. They held few pretences about the life that awaited them. Limited job opportunities, monotonous work, and bleak futures were anticipated. Escalating credentialism would continue to limit their futures.
>
> (1993, p. 157)

What was particularly informative for us about this Canadian research was that it demonstrated how the increased emphasis on post-school education was already by the end of the eighties beginning to influence young people's own thinking about their futures. It not only confirmed the evidence from the United States but also a range of independent studies conducted by different researchers in other nations which suggested that there were now new influences emerging in the lives of members of the post-1970 generation that transcended national boundaries. A new transition into adulthood was taking hold and becoming common currency throughout Western societies even amongst high school students. Some of these commonalities emerged in one of our own projects conducted in early 1991, which sampled 2,500 students in seventeen schools at a national level. The study was much broader in scope than the Canadian one, and it therefore brings out in greater detail some of the uncertainties involved in students' attitudes towards the future. The schools were very different from each other in terms of size, locality, family and ethnic background of the students, and on a range of socio-economic indicators the final survey sample was comparatively representative of the generation as a whole. Because the sample was drawn from a group of Catholic schools the student population belonged to particularly 'intact' family groupings, and in the light of this the findings regarding students' apprehensions about their own futures were particularly revealing. Of particular interest was the relationship between the positive and negative elements in the data and what this revealed about the impact of change on the lives of the participants.

At first sight, the results of the survey appeared to present a positive picture of the lives of the students. If anything, it seemed likely that these students had a higher than average level of family support and security and also high levels of satisfaction with school. The dominant indicators are shown in table 5.1.

Table 5.1 Positive indicators (n = 2393)

	%
Living in two-parent household	85
Satisfied or very satisfied with school	82
Want to develop their abilities to the fullest	86
Satisfied or very satisfied with their friends	96
Very close or close families	92
Look forward to a good and happy family life	89

Two of the main aspects to the findings of the survey were the consistency of responses about basic experiences across all schools, at each year-level, and for both gender-groupings and secondly, the high level of positive evidence concerning those experiences. It is likely that both aspects reflected the school cultures and family backgrounds associated with the fact that these were students of Catholic parents who had chosen to send their offspring to these particular schools. The positive experience of school can be seen from the 82 per cent level of satisfaction with school; and the positive outlook on family life is shown by the claim by 92 per cent that theirs is a close or very close family and the view by 89 per cent that they themselves can 'look forward to a good and happy family life'.

This very positive (and conventional) outlook was reflected in some remarkably conventional differences between the responses of males and females, particularly evident in the questions related to students' values and priorities (Figure 5.1).

Thus, in the question which asked about career values, males were much more likely to ambition riches – 41 per cent favouring that item as against only 17 per cent of females. Males also placed more

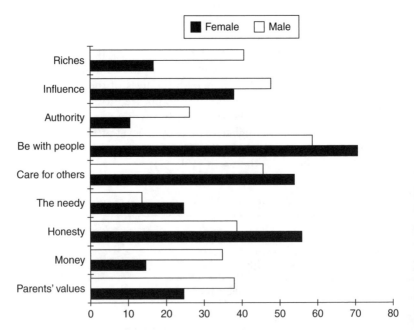

Figure 5.1 Priority contrasts

emphasis on having influence (48 per cent versus 38 per cent) and authority (27 per cent versus 11 per cent), while females favoured self-fulfilment (76 per cent versus 68 per cent), spending time with people (71 per cent versus 59 per cent) and making a contribution to society (35 per cent versus 29 per cent).

In the questions about their personal values and priorities females also favoured 'other-directed' options: caring for others (54 per cent versus 46 per cent); contributing to society (33 per cent versus 26 per cent); being generous (36 per cent versus 31 per cent); helping the needy (25 per cent versus 14 per cent); and being honest and fair (56 per cent versus 39 per cent). Males gave higher priority to their parents' values (38 per cent versus 25 per cent) and making money (35 per cent versus 15 per cent). In the question about their personal troubles females were more concerned about: their relationships with family (34 per cent versus 21 per cent); relationships with friends (43 per cent versus 31 per cent); and also their appearance (46 per cent versus 27 per cent). In the question concerning the future, males were more often very hopeful (40 per cent) than females (29 per cent).

A number of questions about the students' social attitudes and values had been included, as were questions directly concerned with spiritual and religious ideals (Figure 5.2).

The values that were given clear majority support – family, friendship, financial security, and self-fulfilment – once again indicated how conventional their outlook was in that their values reflected what might be expected to be given pre-eminence in the secular milieu of

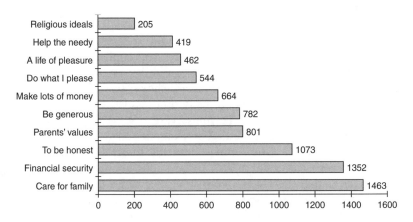

Figure 5.2 Lifetime priorities

society as a whole. The responses of the females in the sample were perhaps more in line with a concern about spiritual values, as can be seen from their leaning towards 'caring for others' (54 per cent), being 'honest and fair' (56 per cent), and their lack of preference for the more materialist options of becoming 'really rich' (17 per cent) or making 'a lot of money' (15 per cent).

Given their high levels of satisfaction with regard to their home and school life, and given their seemingly conventional outlooks on life, it came as a surprise to discover that once the survey turned to the students' social expectations and their future lives as adults a different picture emerged.

The change in responses was dramatic. A high degree of insecurity and uncertainty about future prospects emerged from questions about personal troubles and hopes. The lack of jobs dominated the thinking of most students and they displayed an awareness of the difficulties confronting their own generation. This became particularly evident in their responses to a question concerning their own feelings when they think about the future. They were asked to indicate how frequently (often, sometimes or rarely) they experienced feelings ranging from being 'very hopeful' to being 'hopeless'.

There were the 'optimists' among them who 'rarely' felt pessimistic or hopeless, but who were 'often' either very hopeful or hopeful. They contrasted clearly with those who were 'often' uncertain, less hopeful or pessimistic (the 'pessimists'). Their responses led to a fairly even division of the total sample – 47 per cent Optimists and 53 per cent in the Pessimist category. The Pessimist grouping proved to be larger for the 16-year-olds, and this group registered only a 17 per cent response in terms of feeling 'often' very hopeful, or hopeful, about the future.

The break-up of the total sample (see table 5.2) indicates that this division operated across all of the schools and applied to a series of subgroupings such as age level, gender, and day or boarding pupils.

The contrasts for the 16-year-olds are shown in table 5.3.

Despite the positive results on many other issues, the majority fell into what was termed the Pessimist category once the question about expectations was raised. A re-examination of the data indicated that this pessimistic feeling about the future was reflected in degrees of negative response also to questions about the present. It became clear that there was a consistent divergence in the responses of the two groupings on important items in key questions. For example, with regard to their experience of school, the responses from the two groupings at both year levels presented clear contrasts.

Table 5.2 Optimist/pessimist break-down of total sample

		Total	Optimist	Pessimist
		2393	1134	1259
Age level	14	1308	668	640
	16	1085	466	619
School status	Day pupil	2205	1020	1185
	Boarder	147	74	73
Sex	Male	1529	769	760
	Female	864	365	499

In their relationships with teachers the Optimist grouping received – or perceived – much more positive treatment from teachers. Thus, those in that group were more inclined to say that their teachers: 'take a personal interest' in them (41 per cent versus 34 per cent); give them 'enough encouragement' (45 per cent versus 38 per cent); and give 'helpful classes' (37 per cent versus 29 per cent). Those in the Pessimist grouping were more likely to say that their teachers: 'insist too much on rules' (45 per cent versus 38 per cent); and give classes that are 'often boring' (46 per cent versus 27 per cent). Again, in terms of their views about society in general, those in the Pessimist group were more likely to agree that 'the future for young people is grim' (39 per cent versus 31 per cent), and in a final question about preparing for the future they repeatedly raised the issue of 'relevance' particularly with regard to the world of work.

Why did the majority fit the 'pessimist' mould? Why was it, for example, that when asked about their attitudes at a more general level the majority (57 per cent) of students were dissatisfied with the state of society at present? The answer presented itself when we asked our respondents to identify their personal troubles at *present*. The

Table 5.3 Contrasts: 16-year-old optimists and pessimists

	Optimist (%) (n = 466)	Pessimist (%) (n = 619)
Very hopeful	41	8
Hopeful	48	9
Uncertain or less hopeful	11	83

issue of jobs was paramount and outweighed the issues their teachers were most anxious about (sex, alcohol, drugs, or family violence). As many as two-thirds identified 'getting a good job in the future' as their major 'trouble' (table 5.4).

What was even more revealing was that, while 64 per cent of the students said they were personally troubled about getting a good job, the response rate rose as high as 77 per cent when they considered the fate of their age group as a whole (Figure 5.3). Furthermore, the consistency of results which had characterised their overall responses to the questionnaire was even more noticeable as they identified the concerns confronting their own generation. The question on the main issues facing young people drew the most thoroughly consistent response of the whole survey. Not only were the Optimist and the Pessimist groupings in agreement on what the main issues were, but they consistently agreed with each other in terms of their percentage support for each item. As might be expected the lack of jobs topped their concern. The agreement between both groups is remarkable.

It is worth emphasising here that, while on socio-economic indicators this was a representative sample, in terms of their positive experience of schooling, friendships and close family relationships, these students might have been much more secure and less vulnerable than many of their contemporaries, above all than those who could be identified without doubt as casualties of change. This was certainly true of the Optimist group, and yet even they felt that as future adults in the 1990s their generation faced an uncertain future – and they were part of it.

Table 5.4 Personal troubles

	Order	*Persons*
Getting a good job in the future	1	1539
Lack of money	2	920
Relationships with friends	3	842
Personal appearance	4	817
Family relationships	5	616
Relationships with teachers	6	500
Lack of popularity	7	461
Sexuality	8	348
Peer pressure to use alcohol	9	235
Pressure to use other drugs	10	225
Violence in the home	11	132

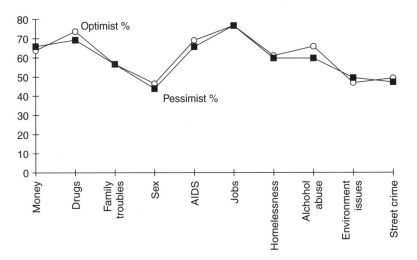

Figure 5.3 Main youth issues

This concern about the uncertainty of jobs for their generation became even more evident in the responses of those students who were already contemplating leaving school. One of the most informative aspects of the survey data was that degrees of negativity increased significantly for those who were reluctant to continue their education up to the end of schooling or beyond. On further analysis, it became evident that particularly the 16-year-olds who were 'reluctant stayers' displayed higher levels of uncertainty and dissatisfaction in a variety of areas of their lives.

We identified a Reluctant Stayer subgroup of the 16-year-olds who showed a marked increase in negative responses across the questionnaire as a whole. The subgroup was established on the basis of the responses on their future intentions with regard to continuing their education. Those in the Pessimist grouping who did not want to continue were termed Reluctant Stayers for the purposes of analysis. They represented a substantial 25 per cent of the 16-year-old student population in the schools.

The actual responses of all the students to the options offered on this issue are shown in table 5.5. The majority of students indicated that they wanted to continue, although the percentage (60 per cent) was not as high as might be expected given the increased emphasis on the importance of school completion in the 1990s. As might be expected, as many as 64 per cent, or about two-thirds, of the Optimist

Table 5.5 Views of 16-year-olds about continuing with education

	Optimist (n = 464)	Pessimist (n = 615)	Reluctant stayers (n = 267)
I want to continue	297	348	
Other options (as below):	167	267	267
I don't want to but feel it's necessary	83		133
I don't want to but my parents insist	8		20
I'd leave if I could get a job	26		47
I'll finish school and then get a job	30		67

grouping said they wanted to continue on with their education, whereas only 56 per cent in the Pessimist category gave that response.

What was revealing, when attitudes towards continuing with their education were taken into account, was the fact that amongst those who were less eager about continuing there was a clear increase in signs of negativity in response to a range of other questions in the survey. This was particularly true of the Reluctant Stayer subgroup. Thus, in re-examining responses across the other items in the survey a clear trend emerged in terms of negative reactions, ranging from the Optimist grouping, to the Pessimist category as a whole, and then to the Reluctant Stayers.

The degree of consistency in the patterns of response of the three groups was unexpected. Given this recurrent aspect of the data, the high levels of negativity amongst the Reluctant Stayer subgroup became a cause for concern. Not only is it evident that the closer students were to considering quitting their education the higher the scores on the negative indicators became, but also it was precisely on the issue of job troubles (despite the fact that this was the most negative indicator) that the three groups, the Optimists included, came closest to agreement with each other (table 5.6).

The impact of change

What this evidence indicates is that the changes that were being orchestrated in both education and the labour market in Western nations at the beginning of the nineties were already having a decidedly negative impact on the outlook of those in the process of completing their schooling. In this regard the Australian evidence confirms what we saw in the Canadian study. The Canadians were close to the

Table 5.6 Percentage responses on negative indicators (n = 2393)

	Optimist (n = 1134) %	Pessimist (n = 1259) %	16-year-old reluctant stayers (n = 267) %
School dissatisfied (Q3)	14	20	48
Boring classes (Q7)	27	46	64
Home dissatisfied (Q22)	8	14	32
Grim future (Q27)	31	39	44
Anti-church (Q28)	12	16	32
Job troubles (Q31)	60	68	73
Family troubles (Q31)	21	30	41
Lack of money (Q31)	34	43	52
Uncertain future (Q34)	13	41	48

end of their secondary schooling and thus were more likely to be finalising their plans and intentions about what they would be moving on to next. Also it is likely that if they had been successful thus far they had already resolved for themselves the uncertainties of staying on till the end of their schooling. For the Australians, and particularly for the 'reluctant stayers' among them, those uncertainties would be more noticeable because even the 16-year-olds at the time of the survey still had a year and a half at school before their final graduation. Yet, despite the contrasts it is clear that both sets of participants were very conscious of the increasing difficulties that they would confront on leaving school because of the increasing importance of post-school qualifications allied to changes within the labour market.

Those in the Canadian study who had already decided not to go on to further study were nevertheless ready to admit that this was likely to make life harder for them. Although at the time of the Australian survey there was a definite shift towards high rates of educational participation, there was still a substantial minority who were 'reluctant stayers' and whose pessimism about their own post-school economic prospects was associated with degrees of negativity in other aspects of their lives. For the 'reluctant stayers', staying on at school was associated with a range of negative indicators. Their personal vulnerability would seem to be accentuated, and if an element of 'forced retention' was partly responsible for their continued participation, it pointed to some hidden negative consequences. There were three in particular that were of major concern: an inability of schools and teachers to cope with 'reluctant stayers'; a change of attitude towards dropouts or early school leavers; and a widening gap between apparent improvements in educational participation levels and actual outcomes.

Firstly, one of the conveniences of lower retention rates in the past, as far as teachers were concerned, was that to a degree it saved teachers and schools from having to cope with student dissatisfaction about the gap between schooling and 'the real world'. Students who found schooling irrelevant left or were encouraged to leave, and this in turn also saved teachers and schools from having to cope with too many of those who were likely to be reluctant participants in the schooling process. If, however, the improvement in rates was due to job uncertainty and thus only partly due to educational reasons, it was unlikely that changes in school curricula would help alleviate levels of dissatisfaction among the less academically inclined students. Alternatively, it remained questionable whether teachers would respond positively to these 'reluctant stayers' in their classrooms, rather than being tempted to ignore, or marginalise them, because the teachers think they should not really be there (Batten and Russell, 1995).

It is important to remember that prior to the recent rise in retention, in nations such as the UK and Australia leaving school early was not necessarily viewed as a disadvantage. This contrasted with the outlook in the United States, for example, where the term dropout has commonly been used in both the popular and professional literature to refer to young people who did not 'complete' their schooling. In Australia, by contrast, the much more neutral term early school leaver was used, and it was common for young people to be advised to leave school in their early teens and establish themselves in life.

This raises the second issue of a likely change of attitude towards such early school leavers. Now, with the changes in government policy regarding post-compulsory education in both Australia and Britain, and the decline in the youth labour market, the situation is much closer to that of the United States. Already at a policy level these countries are beginning to regard their early school leavers as 'dropouts', with all the negative connotations that this has had in the United States. In other words, the shift towards mainstreaming policy now accentuates the risk of marginalising that significant minority of young people who will continue to leave school early.

There is a third consequence, however, that is in our view even more serious. It relates to many of the issues discussed in earlier chapters concerning misleading assumptions underlying 'mainstream' experience and a widening gap between the policy and research literature about changes in young people's transitions and their actual experience and outcomes. Increased participation in education through completion of schooling and beyond is now being interpreted as a defining factor of young people's lives, and is producing misleading and distorted analyses of what is actually taking place. This not only means that those who do not fit the mould of extensive ongoing educational participation well beyond their teenage years are automatically assumed to be 'at risk', but it also leads to a false assumption that those who do prolong their years of pursuing educational credentials are also automatically on the road to 'success'. This narrowed view of what 'transition' means in the lives of contemporary youth both ignores what is happening in the other dimensions of their lives as well as the growing gap between their educational achievements and what in reality is on offer to them in terms of 'careers'.

The following section examines this third issue in considerable detail by making use of key elements of the longitudinal study we discussed in the opening chapter. The participants were young students who were completing high school in 1991. The study is following them through to the year 2001. By that time we shall have built up a ten-year record of what they have done since leaving school and what career outcomes they have achieved. Our discussion in this chapter will be mainly concerned with their post-school studies from 1991 to 1996 and their initial career outcomes after that.

The Life-Patterns Project

– It's like one of those ... you know ... fun park horror halls ... when you go in it's all dark and there are lots of doors but you're not sure where they go ... and they're all locked, and you need to know the passwords ... but they're secret ... and nobody will tell us what they are.

– I trusted them when they [teachers, parents, advertising] told me that a ticket would open doors for me ... I did the course straight through without taking a year off [even though I wanted to], and now I'm finished I can't get a job because I have no practical work experience in the area.

– It's harder these days for young people to follow a dream.

– I feel I am the trunk of a tree, a tree of opportunities, with thousands of branches beginning to grow.

- If an employer sees you as self-motivated and you have made a significant commitment by furthering your education you are a much better candidate from the start.
- I feel the pressure of being unemployed, of being an individual failure, or of having done the wrong course when neither is really true – even though I am tempted to think it.
- Millions of people go to work everyday and hate their job, I don't want to be like that. I will chop and change and do whatever I can to be happy.
- It is nice to know when looking back that you've made it this far (and most of it due to yourself) and you've proven that you can take charge of your life: financial, emotional, social.
- The future is vague and uninviting . . . I don't want to think in the long term because it seems to be simply an exercise in futility. It's a self-fulfilling prophecy.
- My values are gradually changing. I enjoy working but now try to live a more balanced life and to separate work from home/ social life. I think that I will be less likely to 'burn out' at work if I do this – I like the notion that we are continually learning and no longer have one job for life.
- I have grown from being very career-focused when I was at university to now valuing family/homelife, friends and leisure activities much more. I would no longer consider sacrificing time with my partner, family and friends for career opportunities.

All of these are personal comments from young people in their mid- to late twenties at the turn of the millennium. They are coping, each in their own way, with a series of changes and upheavals that have affected their transitions from youth into adulthood. Some of them are achieving success for themselves; others are not. They are all participants in our Life-Patterns Project.

The study began with a survey of about 30,000 students leaving school in 1991, which was followed in 1992 with a further survey and the development of a consistent data-set for 11,000 of the original participants. In this first year after finishing school, the pathways of the total group were already beginning to display considerable diversity. Figure 5.4 provides the relative proportions in the various 1992 study and work outcomes. About 19 per cent had gone directly into the workforce without doing any further study, 23 per cent were working but were combining that with further study, 44 per cent were fully involved with study and were not currently employed, and 13 per cent were unemployed and looking for work.

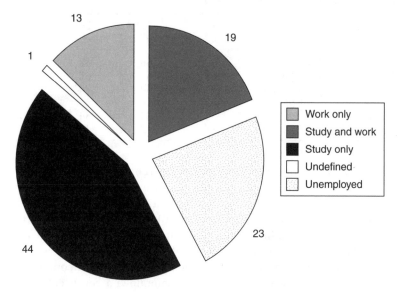

Figure 5.4 Outcomes in first year after school

The most marked difference between intentions and outcomes arises with regard to the subcategory of 'study'. There was some divergence for the group as a whole between overall study intentions before leaving school and the actual outcomes, but as table 5.7 indicates this was overwhelmingly due to outcomes for the females in the sample. Although 80 per cent of them had intended to continue their involvement in study of some kind, only 71 per cent indicated that this was the actual outcome for them. By contrast there was an almost perfect match between study intentions and outcomes for the males in the sample.

In 1996, the data-set of 11,000 was narrowed down to concentrate mainly on those who had undertaken further study on leaving school, but we also re-surveyed those who had not gone on to further

Table 5.7 Study intentions and outcomes

	Females (%)	Males (%)	Total (%)
Intended study	80	65	73
Study as outcome	71	64	66

Table 5.8 Sample compatibility: 1996–2000 (%)

Indicator	1996 n = 1926	1998 n = 977	2000 n = 965
Government school	60	56	58
Australian-born mother	65	65	67
Father: professional/managerial	33	34	34
Mother: uni. qualified	13	14	15
Rural	33	31	34
Interrupted studies	15	12	12

studies, because since then some may have reconsidered their options and decided to enter upon a study pathway. The 1996 follow-up sample of 2000 included students from both urban and rural areas, covering a representative range of school (60 per cent from government schools) and ethnic (with one-third of parents born outside Australia) backgrounds, and a variety of parental educational attainment (close to half not having completed high school). In comparing the annual surveys since then we have maintained a consistent 1996 core sample as shown in table 5.8.

Of the respondents, 90 per cent had undertaken courses since 1992, with two-thirds spending at least three years. Nearly 80 per cent had made the university their first preference, but initially only 64 per cent gained entry. Although only 11 per cent had sought entry into vocational education and training (VET) colleges, 24 per cent actually enrolled directly on leaving school. The differences between preferences and initial enrolments are shown in table 5.9.

In general the respondents to the 1996 survey indicated that they had high expectations about their own futures. Most of their parents had not participated in much post-compulsory education of a formal kind. For the male parents, 19 per cent had university degrees, 15

Table 5.9 Enrolment

	Preference (%)	Outcome (%)
University	78	64
VET	11	24
Apprenticeship	4	3
Traineeship	1	1
Other	6	8

Table 5.10   Career expectation contrasts (%)

Job type	Would like	Expect	Father's job	1992 workforce
Professional/management/etc.	66	61	33	31
Tradesperson	3	4	14	15
Factory worker or labourer	0	1	11	22

per cent had trade qualifications, but 44 per cent had not even completed high school. As many as 54 per cent of the female parents did not have a high school certificate, while 13 per cent had university degrees. How much higher their offspring were aiming is clear from the major occupational categories given in table 5.10.

Since leaving school in the early nineties the vast majority had continued to live with their parents – 72 per cent gave that as their place of residence during these years and even by 1996 (aged about 22) 63 per cent were still living in the family home. This was more likely in the case of males, for whom the total was as high as 70 per cent.

Gender representation in study fields was especially strong. Males were more likely than females to take up: apprenticeships (14 per cent of males compared to 1 per cent of females); engineering and surveying (14 per cent of males compared to 2 per cent of females); and information technology courses (12 per cent compared to 4 per cent). Females were more likely than males to enrol in: nursing or health (13 per cent of females compared to 2 per cent of males); arts and social sciences (14 per cent compared to 5 per cent); and education (9 per cent compared to 2 per cent). Workforce participation rates were much the same for both genders, the main difference being that in 1997 there was a higher proportion of females in the part-time workforce (23 per cent compared to 16 per cent of males).

In terms of secondary schooling, almost three-quarters of those who came from private or independent schools went into university courses, whereas at most 41 per cent of government school students enrolled in a university course. In contrast, government school students were more likely to try both university and vocational college courses than their private school counterparts.

In our 1998 report, Harwood provided evidence that confirms some of the findings of a recent report from Canadian research on educational aspirations and expectations (Andres *et al.*, 1999). Parental background had an influence on respondents' pathways through post-compulsory education and the workforce. The offspring of fathers with a professional or managerial occupation were more likely to enter university and less likely to take up vocational college studies. Those whose mother had some post-compulsory training were more likely to try college options than other groups, while offspring of mothers with a university qualification also tended to focus on university study, 69 per cent of their number doing so. Metropolitan-based respondents were the most likely to enter university, while rural respondents were the least likely, less than one-third of them going on to a tertiary institution.

However, the similarities with this particular set of Canadian findings about the social background factors influencing movements from schools into further study have not carried across evenly into the further stage where the survey respondents were entering the workforce and looking to establish careers (table 5.11).

Males had in general been more successful than females, so gender was still a factor and, while there is a slightly higher career success rate by those from a professional/managerial family background, there is an under-representation of those whose female parent had a university qualification. Similarly, while there are variations related to particular fields of study undertaken, in general those participants who had completed their studies at a university did not yet appear to have been as successful in gaining successful career outcomes as those with a college qualification.

We shall discuss these outcomes in greater detail in a later chapter, but for the present it is important to note that even after eight years of post-school training and experience only a minority (47 per cent) of our sample had achieved ongoing careers for themselves. The career expectations of the majority of participants had not yet been realised,

Table 5.11 Permanent full-time career outcomes: 1999

	%
Males	51
Females	46
Professional/managerial father	49
University-educated mother	42
University qualified	47
College qualification	53
Total sample	47

and many of them were beginning to have second thoughts about the supposed one-to-one link between being qualified and having a career. The transition was not proving to be as straightforward and predictable as they had been led to believe. Some serious questioning of policy was under way.

Uncertain outcomes

As we have seen in earlier chapters these uncertain outcomes are becoming a common feature in the experience of the post-1970 generation in many Western nations. They are related to the fact that changes to the labour markets in these nations, linked to the themes of globalisation and the deregulation of the economy, are not necessarily consistent with the changes being implemented within the field of education. Our concern in this chapter has been the ways in which from the early 1990s this inconsistency – and the subsequent uncertainty of outcomes – had begun to influence young people's own hopes and assessment of their future chances.

It would, however, be misleading to suggest that young people in each of these nations experience uncertainty of outcomes all in the same way. One of the problems with the process of globalisation is that it impacts on different nations very differently. The contrasts between new world countries like Canada and Australia and European societies with different cultural traditions, economic priorities and educational structures caution against reading global trends in a univocal or homogeneous fashion. As we have noted in a study of youth transitions in both Australia and Norway:

> That the youth of two such contrasting countries as Norway and Australia, with very different demographic, historical and geographical circumstances, and tenuous mutual ties, are confronting markedly similar options regarding educational participation and outcomes provides some justification for the themes of globalisation . . . and re-definition of life-courses . . . that are part of the new agenda. On the other hand, the persistence of structural constraints such as class and locality, and the ways in which young people in both countries are coming to terms with new forms of those constraints, lend similar justification to the themes of risk . . . and individualisation . . . that are also included in analyses of changing student transitions.
>
> (Heggen and Dwyer, 1998, p. 270)

One of the clear differences that emerged from that study was that in Norway, unlike most other Western nations, both the rate of increase and the overall participation rates were actually greater in the rural, and not in the urban, areas. The reasons for this were complex but were at least partly related to the growing uncertainty of employment outcomes for rural youth (e.g. in primary industries like fisheries) in contrast with a rapid growth of jobs in urban areas as a result of changes in government policy. What the young in both Australia and Norway were facing in common, though, was that the 'increasing emphasis that has been placed on the economic importance of improving participation rates in post-compulsory education has been translated into formal policy provisions' and that 'their education has been sharply redefined with reference to national economic goals, and the completion of some form of post-compulsory education or training is being demanded as a prerequisite for active adult life' (Heggen and Dwyer, 1998, pp. 270–1).

Thus the differences between the educational participation rates of the rural youth in each country are much less a function of educational policy and owe much more to the differential impact of economic changes at particular regional locations. At a general level, however, it remains true that during the 1990s across the whole of the Western world 'employment was becoming increasingly fluid, occupational boundaries were changing or dissolving, and more jobs were temporary' (Stern *et al.*, 1997). Given that this was the case, it made it all the more important for individuals to 'negotiate' their own outcomes – to weigh up for themselves whether they should give priority to job 'stabilisation' rather than pursuing further educational specialisation; whether they should delay their entry into the labour market by being more selective about their career paths; or whether they should change their study or career orientations to fit the emerging realities of the labour market.

> The net result was that these political and economic circumstances sent very different signals to youth in central and peripheral areas in Norway. The signal to many urban youth could be: 'You can easily get a job and have a good life without any longer education', while the signal to rural youth could be another: it underlined the need of a solid education.
>
> (Heggen and Dwyer, 1998, p. 265)

Depending on local circumstances young people in different nations or different regions will make their own assessments of how best to respond to a discernible mismatch between educational levels and job-market realities. The evidence suggests that 'the increased education levels of the young have not protected them from bearing the major adjustment from the lack of job growth' (Gregory, 1995, p. 321). What we do find now in many countries is an increased tendency for students to pursue post-graduate study because of the difficulty of access to 'career' jobs. And what they then find is that the career on which they then settle may not necessarily bear a one-to-one relationship to their actual qualifications or original intent. Graduates may eventually find a stable job, but it may not correspond 'to the one that the graduate hoped to hold based on his or her initial plans for the future and on the training that he or she acquired' (Trottier *et al.*, 1996, p. 94).

In an earlier review of European studies, Teichler (1989, p. 235) similarly cautioned about the need to pay attention to 'the diversity of the links between higher education and work'. This is particularly true for the post-1970 generation because they are entering into a radically restructured labour market in which greater flexibility and contingency are at play, and for whom a dilemma arises because the meaning of career has changed. Unfortunately, the images (and advice) they are offered with regard to transitions between study and work still promise a world of predictability of outcomes, permanence of career, and security in future prospects. Thus, in reporting on the impact of 'the clever society' policies adopted in the UK, Ainley notes that

> many graduates, for example, enter jobs for which they are 'overqualified'. They therefore feel dissatisfied, do a bad job and leave at the first better opportunity. So, while educational investment may sometimes be an enabling factor for productivity growth, the assertion that economic development necessarily follows from educational investment is a statement of pure faith.
>
> (Ainley, 1998, p. 562)

When we look back at the concerns of high school students in nations like Canada and Australia at the beginning of the nineties and compare them with the outcomes for their generation at the end of the decade, their fears and uncertainties prove to have been well justified. They were aware of the pressures upon them to perform educationally in ways not asked of their parents' generation, but they were also aware of changes taking place in the labour market that cast doubt on their likely outcomes. Still, like their parents and teachers they too placed an inordinate degree of faith in the prospects that they thought would flow almost automatically from an investment in the education of the young. In truth, some of that faith seemed to be confirmed by two significant emerging trends – one positive and one negative – common to many Western nations. On the positive side there was the impact that increased educational participation was having on the lives of young women in these societies. They achieved educational and employment opportunities that previous generations of women had been denied. At the same time, there was also a more negative trend related to a growing concern that those whose education had been disrupted or discontinued were in serious danger of becoming an 'underclass' of 'at risk' young people – they were seen not only as casualties of change but as a potential threat to the stability of society and a burden on public funds. These two trends raised new questions about the challenges of transition in the nineties. The following chapters look at some of the issues raised.

6 The gender factor

Despite the faith invested in education as a means of social mobility and the increasing emphasis on personal choice, young people's lives remain strongly influenced by the social divisions of gender and class. At the level of macro-analysis, gender and class patterns suggest strong continuities with previous decades. Large-scale statistical studies of young people in the UK and the US provide evidence that both gender and class have a strong influence on young people's educational aspirations and on their employment outcomes (Furlong and Biggart, 1999; Mortimer and Finch, 1996). Other studies show that young people's identities are still shaped through class and gender structures in significant ways (Rattansi and Phoenix, 1997; Finnegan, 1998).

Alongside the continued presence of structural factors, there is a strong theme running through much of the contemporary youth research literature which identifies a paradoxical response of youth to their circumstances. Young people, whose opportunities to gain a livelihood are limited by high rates of regional unemployment, for example, tend nonetheless to have a strong belief in the capacity of individuals to negotiate and shape a future for themselves (Rudd and Evans, 1998; MacDonald, 1998; Looker and Dwyer, 1998a; du Bois-Reymond, 1998). This is also true of some of their attitudes towards the impact of gender on their life-chances. Despite the evidence at a structural level of its continuing influence, there is also a marked tendency in contemporary society for young people to play down its effects on their lives (Roberts and Sachdev, 1996), and to insist that making the most of your available choices is what really counts (Willis, 1998). Thus, a comparison of the experiences of learning and work of Australian and Canadian youth found that young people tend to hold strong personal responsibility for their outcomes and to be optimistic about their own job prospects (MacLaughlin, 1999).

This is despite the strong and continuing trend for men and women to study within different areas, to enter gender-segmented labour markets and for women to earn less than their male counterparts (Marginson, 1999).

In order to understand young people's paradoxical optimism and sense of their own power to shape their lives, we need to explore the conditions under which different groups of young people are living and to understand the meanings they attach to life-events. We need to look at particular changes in the labour market and in education that create the conditions which make it a necessity for all young people to be able to 'write their own scripts' in the absence of institutional supports. We also need to ask, What implications do these changed circumstances have for the formation of gendered identities?

In exploring these themes, this chapter inevitably touches on the question of how 'the facts' about young people and gender are constructed and reconstructed through different theoretical and ideological approaches. By exploring the relationships between schooling, the labour market and gender, we are able to see how different understandings about gender relations and social divisions lead to conflicting and contradictory views on what is happening. For example, there is widespread debate on whether schooling serves boys' or girls' interests to the detriment of one or the other group, and whether this has changed over the last twenty years. In the section that follows, we look at research on youth labour markets and education. We then reflect on the construction of facts, mysteries and paradoxes about gender and youth through research processes. Finally, we consider the implications of life in the 1990s for the construction of gendered identities.

Gender and work

Discussions of youth and change inevitably return to two notable features of the labour market. One is the tendency (particularly in the US, Australia and the UK) to mix work and study from an early age, blurring the distinction between child, youth and adult labour. The other is the increase in levels of participation of young women in education and in the labour market. Both have implications for gender relations and the construction of gendered identities.

It is now commonplace for young women to have paid jobs while they are still at school. As we have seen in earlier chapters, many begin a pattern of combining work and study which lasts for a decade or more after leaving school. The proportion of young people who do this varies across different countries and also, within countries, by region. However, the pattern is strong enough to be called 'normative' in the US and in the UK (Mortimer and Finch, 1996; Mizen *et al.*, 1999). The US Department of Labor found that

> More than a third of 14- to-16-year-olds who were enrolled in school also worked at an 'employee' job (defined as having an ongoing relationship with a particular employer) at some point while school was in session during 1996. Even at these young ages, many of these student workers had a fairly strong attachment to the formal labor market: most worked while school was in session as well as during the summer.
>
> (US Department of Labor, 1999)

A review of school-age workers in the UK found that young people were a significant component of the labour force, doing jobs that are usually associated with adult employment (Mizen *et al.*, 1999). The study found that young people and children were doing 'washing up, serving in shops and waiting at tables, doing door to door selling, working as carers, cleaners and in offices' – the same kinds of jobs that their counterparts in the US and Australia are doing. They hold part-time, contract and often short-term positions, predominantly in the service sector, juggling work and study. The work is a real – and even for some an equal – part of their lives, but in much of the literature the work experiences of young people are still predominantly seen as part of a developmental process, or as a stage of formation which precedes their 'real' engagement with the labour market as older youth or adults (e.g. Mortimer and Finch, 1996).

> The treatment of childhood phenomena as notable primarily in terms of what children are supposed to become, rather than what they actually are, positions children as a passive or deficient social group, being relentlessly pushed towards full adult (and therefore social) status. Thus children's work becomes significant primarily as a marker of adolescent development.
>
> (Mizen *et al.*, 1999, p. 426)

This approach to young people's experiences is also noted in the comprehensive review of thinking about youth identities by Rattansi and Phoenix (1997). They point out that research and writing from both a sociological and psychological perspective has tended to reproduce the notion that youth only has 'meaning' as a preparation for adult life.

If, however, school-age work experience is now the norm in many societies, we need to ask what impact this has on young people. There are some interesting parallels emerging across different countries. Mizen *et al.* make the observation that children in the UK are keen to work because 'as more and more of children's leisure worlds are reconstituted according to the dictates of money and the market, large numbers of children are pressured to look for work simply to enjoy what many take to be common childhood practices' (1999, p. 435). This point strikes a surprisingly similar chord with a study of young people in the US.

> 'I can't wait 'til I can work because then I'll have something to do all day.' Charlotte's comment knocked me for a loop. We were in the bank where her older sister, who had a summer job, was opening an account. In the context of the bank and her sister's income, I expected Charlotte to say 'I can't wait 'til I can work because then I'll have money to spend.' Granted, Charlotte is young, nine years old, and likely to regard work as one more thing that teens 'get' to do and therefore something to be desired.
> (Willis, 1998, p. 347)

Willis's study shows how understandings of occupation and success and of the individual's relationship to work have changed dramatically among some young people, and perhaps particularly among women. Her findings add support to an emerging sense that young people are developing a very different perspective on what work means. She found that young people held strong views about work as a process of 'horizontal mobility' through a range of jobs, in which the particulars of the jobs matter less than their own ability to move across jobs. This 'autonomy' was highly valued. She comments that for these young people, 'independence is having a pointless job I can quit any day' so that autonomy exists 'in the loopholes between jobs' (1998, p. 352). For young women, then, the situation offers opportunities to 'make a life' on what they see as 'their own terms'. Vickie, one of the young women in Willis's study exemplifies this:

> Vickie, an eighteen-year-old who recently graduated from high school, demonstrates how the philosophy of 'take this job and shove it' underscores a contradictory relationship between the

possibility of being free and not free. When I met Vickie, she had a full-time job as a salesperson/counselor at a fitness gym. She also worked afternoons and some evenings as a drugstore clerk. She topped off her employment with a weekend job at Blockbuster Video. In describing her employment, Vickie expresses a curious blend of pride in the fact that she had three jobs and worked close to sixty hours a week and a desperate appeal for sympathy for her inhuman schedule. She complained of fatigue and accentuated her victimization by wearing a vampire hue of makeup and a deep mauve lipstick.

(1998, p. 353)

If we take these young women's experiences and point of view as a starting point, the frame changes. For example, from the point of view of the young workers themselves, the distinction between school-age and post-school-age workers becomes less significant. Both groups are working in the same labour market, and a substantial proportion of post-school young people in Australia, the US and the UK are managing both study and work. In other words, there are important commonalities within child/youth/adult labour markets that are masked by the assumption that schooling precedes work in a developmental and 'lockstep' process. Schooling does not necessarily lead to work, and in many cases, the opposite is true – work 'leads to' schooling – as young people make decisions about what they need to know and what qualifications they believe will help them to get the jobs they want. Young people's participation in the labour force is significant, not only because they are future workers, but because the experiences have meaning, in their own terms, in the present. A focus on young people's identities and on their subjective assessments of their situation provides a mechanism for acknowledging the complex ways in which young people themselves shape and change their world. The question we need to explore in this chapter is what implications this has for the construction of identities, especially in relation to gender.

The collapsing of child/youth/adult labour markets means that young people are entering 'adult' work practices at an early age. This will inevitably have implications for gender identities and gender relations. Rattansi and Phoenix suggest that the increased participation of young women in the labour market has meant that young women have evolved cultures of 'greater independence and self-confidence', which are reflected in consumption patterns as well as patterns of work or production (1997, p. 139).

Many studies report on the steady increase in the participation of women in the labour market over the last decade. For example, the US Department of Labor reports that in 1950, only one-third of women in the United States worked outside the home, whereas in the late 1990s, 60 per cent of women were in the labour force (1999). This is now true of approximately 70 per cent of Australian women between the ages of 20 to 50 (Kenway and Willis, 1995). Related to this is the fact that women are also increasing their participation in education in most industrialised countries, right through to postgraduate study. In Canada, for example, women are enrolling in traditional male areas (such as engineering and applied sciences) with the likely outcome that more women will get the jobs in these areas in the future (MacLaughlin, 1999). The evidence shows that the occupational aspirations of young Canadian women have increased significantly over the last decade (e.g. Andres *et al.*, 1999), and these trends would seem to point to a significantly changed labour-market position for young women.

However, we would suggest a note of caution. Given the changes to the nature of work which have been apparent for at least twenty years, it is pertinent to ask what level of correspondence there is between the notion of 'occupation' which was current in the early 1970s and the meaning that young people in the 1990s attribute to this word. If young women are more ambitious than their counterparts of the pre-1970s generation, how do they express this? Ironically, few researchers have asked them. One of the few studies to do this is by du Bois-Reymond in the Netherlands, to which we have previously referred. She reported that young women were ambitious for themselves in terms of having a good level of material comfort and being happy, but they were explicit about not wanting to have an 'occupation' in the way their parents had. Willis's research on young people in the US suggests an eagerness to engage with the labour market, but at the same time a reshaping of the traditional notions of autonomy and career (Willis, 1998).

Some of the evidence from our own studies suggests that there are some gender differences in the way the necessity to blend study and work is assessed. One of the findings is that the young women tended to be more flexible in their approach to their lives, placing a high emphasis on achieving satisfaction and happiness even if that included changes in courses and institutions in the pursuit of their goals. Another finding was that, in combining study and work, young women were more likely to take the 'transferability of skills' into account in assessing the value of their part-time jobs. For example, one young woman wanted to be a teacher, but she did not initially get entry into teacher education. She retained her long-term goal of becoming a teacher, however, while exploring other options that could in her opinion be seen as compatible with her goal: 'I was quite happy to do things in my own time – I was willing to do things related to teaching if I couldn't teach'. She had a sense of continuity and focus, pursuing what she judged to be the best path for now, and changing options if necessary with the goal of 'life satisfaction' as the underlying factor (Dwyer *et al.*, 1997, p. 26).

One of the major differences between this type of outlook and that adopted by the young men in the study was that the latter were more likely to rely on their study programme to provide clarity and focus of direction. Young men were more likely to assume that the key to success was to 'stick' to the initial option chosen, as a formula for achieving a successful outcome. As one of the young men commented: 'You've got to stay on with what you're doing. You have to keep on with what you've got'.

This suggests that the orientation of many of the young women, towards 'life satisfaction', provides them with the possibility of developing their own narrative or script in which changes of direction, disappointments and setbacks are placed in the context of wider life-concerns. In one sense, the fragmented nature of the processes to which they are subjected is less problematic to the construction and maintenance of their identities than to the young men, whose identities have traditionally been constructed through their involvement in the full-time workforce and the pursuit of a defined career choice.

Even though there has been a significant increase in young women's workforce participation, the enduring nature of gender division at a structural level is evident in the extent to which work is still segregated. Analyses of large data-sets on labour-force participation in Australia, the UK, the US and Canada reveal that, while the detail may differ, the overall pattern of gender segregation persists. Mortimer and Finch (1996) report that there is a gender difference in the jobs taken up by young people in the US. Mizen *et al.* (1999) found that even amongst school children in the UK, the labour market was gender-differentiated. Some researchers claim that Australia has one of the most gender-segregated labour markets in the OECD. The great majority of women in Australia are employed within five main industries and two occupational groups and it has been noted that gender segregation has increased both industry-wide and within specific occupations (Kenway and Willis, 1995, p. 5).

Other researchers have noted that there has been a trend for new industries to reinvent gender segregation even though the use of new technologies, in theory, has made gender distinctions irrelevant. Examples of this in Australia are found in the whitegoods and banking industries (Probert and Wilson, 1993). The links between women's relatively low rates of pay and gender discrimination in workplaces is explored comprehensively in Adkins's study of the hospitality and tourism industries in the UK (Adkins, 1995). She found that one of the factors limiting women's participation in these occupational areas was the sexualisation of women's work. Based on this evidence, young women entering the labour market are facing entrenched patterns of gender-based practices of discrimination. Certainly, despite apparent improvements in women's educational levels over the last two decades, women's earnings are consistently less than those of their male counterparts.

> If the position of women in the workforce is better than it was, gender power still works against women. In a review of human capital theory in Australia, Preston (1997, pp. 72–3) finds that there is a 'raw' gender gap of 19.9 per cent between male and female earnings.
>
> (Marginson, 1999, p. 173)

Furthermore, there is a continuing interplay between gender and social class which serves to perpetuate inequalities between members of the same gender with regard to their participation in the labour market. This is illustrated by recent research which reveals that there is an extreme polarisation of women's employment patterns:

> By 1991 the probability that a woman would be employed if she lived in the top 5 per cent of SES [socio-economic status] neighbourhoods was 78 per cent more than if she lived in the lowest 5 per cent SES areas.
>
> (Probert and MacDonald, 1999, p. 150)

Gender therefore remains powerful in structuring the conditions under which young people form and negotiate their identities. However, as young men and young women begin to construct working lives in which 'horizontal mobility' and autonomy are prized above loyalty to any one employer, it is likely that these changes will have very significant implications for the future. A new approach to work, already apparent in the thinking and actions of the young people in a number of countries, has significant implications for the relationship between work and gender identity.

The increased contingency of work, even for those with a university education, and the increasing demand for women's labour in the expanding service sector means that the notion of the 'male breadwinner' is becoming less appropriate. The privileged place of paid work in the construction of male identities is seriously under challenge. At the same time, women's engagement with the labour market means that, as in the case of Vickie (referred to above), although they may now feel that they are independent they are still highly constrained. In the highly polarised labour market that is emerging, gender and class are intertwined. Vickie's work experiences, despite gender, will most likely have more in common with the young men who also work in the low-skill labour market, than with her female counterparts who are preparing for elite careers in the new, highly paid, professions which draw on the human capital of law degrees, accountancy, engineering and computer science.

Gender and education

One of the paradoxes of the increased participation of young women in education is that women have not transformed their educational achievements into labour-force advantage to nearly the same extent. As one US commentator has put it, in this respect, 'schools shortchange girls' (Bank, 1999). The gendered outcomes from education raise many questions about what is happening in workplaces to create the patterns described in the previous section. Young people's work experiences also raise questions about education processes in the 1990s and their relationship to young people's lives. The collapsing of the distinction between child/youth/adult labour for example has repercussions on how people experience 'growing up'. If young people who work while they are still at school are already 'part-time adults', this has implications for their gender identity too and what are read as the traditional 'markers' of social status.

Evidence from a large number of research studies displays the shifts that have taken place in thinking about the relationship between education and gender over the last twenty years. The most significant of these relates to the question of which gender is privileged and which is disadvantaged through schooling. For most of the last twenty-five years, educational reform has been focused on improving the educational outcomes of girls compared with boys. In the 1990s, however, coincident with changes in the labour market, the problematic relationship of boys to schooling has come to the fore in educational discourses.

During the 1980s and 1990s, there has been a clear tendency for increasing proportions of young women to complete secondary education and to enter post-compulsory education and training (Yates and Leder, 1996). The increase has been noted in the UK, the US, Australia, Canada and many other countries. In response to the new opportunities that school completion offered, young women have steadily increased their participation in university courses. In part, this change could be seen to be the result of the constraints imposed by the collapse of the teenage job market. In Australia, the jobs that young women traditionally took up were amongst the first to go (Sweet, 1992). Many young women who would have preferred to leave school and get a job remained at school to gain the educational credential of school completion. However, a further factor was the increasing reliance that young women were placing on education as a means of securing a future. Over the late 1980s and 1990s then, school-leaving certificates became sought after by a majority of young people, both young men and young women, rather than by only the traditional minority who were destined for university or other formal post-school training.

Hence, for this generation completion of secondary education is regarded as the norm. It was widely seen as a crucial first step in an orderly progression of steps which would lead to a possible work career, either because of the opportunities a school certificate offers in terms of access to higher education or because it is seen as a necessary credential for getting a job. However, for both young women and young men who complete secondary school, academic achievement does not necessarily reap the desired rewards. Gaining the school-leaving certificate does not gain automatic entry to higher education, so students are often pitted in a competition for too few places. The increased participation of young women in secondary schooling meant that, in the early 1990s, for the first time, a visible minority of girls competed successfully against boys in the traditional masculine areas of physics and chemistry. This pattern is now common. MacLaughlin comments that in Canada the largest increase in female graduates is in engineering and applied sciences (1999, p. 79).

This increased participation of young women in post-compulsory education, and in subject areas that were once regarded as predominantly male preserves, has led in the 1990s to the widespread claim that boys now constitute the new disadvantaged in education. Media reports convey the impression that the increased educational performance of girls is evidence that they have been advantaged to the detriment of boys, and competing theoretical analyses are made use of to explain how this has come about.

On the one hand, it is argued that, because of their different mental developmental processes, boys' and girls' brains are structured differently by the time they are adult. The consequence of this, according to the argument, is that the 'male brain' finds it 'hard to deal with reflective emotional-centred tasks and hence boys have a preference for speculative thinking and action' (Reed, 1999, p. 99). This approach supports the argument that educational programmes need to be refocused in order to pay more attention to these inevitable biomedical and physical differences between all males and females. In an overview of debates about masculinity and education, Gilbert and Gilbert (1998) conclude that this type of biomedical or 'essentialist' argument for gender differences has 'little regard for evidence or theoretical consistency' and is used to 'justify rather than explain behaviour' (1998, p. 32). Nonetheless, arguments based on these ideas have gained enormous currency.

On the other hand, there is a view that 'the boys issue' has been a largely unacknowledged problem in education for many years (Yates, 1997; Teese *et al.*, 1995). Studies of school-leaving patterns show that boys from low socio-economic backgrounds have traditionally made up the numbers of early school leavers and there is considerable evidence that working-class boys are the least likely to benefit from education (Lamb *et al.*, 2000). The group who have most increased their participation in education are girls from high socio-economic backgrounds, and these are the girls who have, in the 1990s, made headlines for their outstanding examination performance in the traditional 'male' areas of mathematics and sciences and precipitated the call for more attention to boys' education.

In general, where there is evidence that girls and young women are 'outperforming' boys in education the evidence is based on aggregations of figures of achievement in subjects. Once the figures are disaggregated, a different picture emerges. There are two findings that are relatively consistent across the different databases. These are that young men and young women continue to take up subjects in very different areas of the curriculum and that young people's results differ consistently according to socio-economic status and ethnicity.

A recent study of schooling outcomes from different localities in Australia has analysed the disaggregated data on performance in subjects according to gender and socio-economic background (Teese,

2000). One of its most important findings is that it is inappropriate to regard girls (or boys) as a single category. It is girls and young women from the higher status groups who are most likely to be represented amongst those who are seen to be 'outperforming' boys. What we find is that

> as we descend the social scale, the gender gap widens. The lower the social status of girls, the less likely they are to take maths and the more likely to fail when they do. Working class girls have higher rates of failure in English than other girls and are more likely not to take it when they can or to take school-assessed options instead of externally-assessed subjects.
>
> (Teese *et al.*, 1995, p. 109)

What this suggests is that the very success by a small group of girls in examinations highlights the fact that little else has changed and that in the past, as now, schooling has always presented problems for boys – that they were the ones who were falling behind in school rather than teenage girls. Thus, while there have been some gains for girls in terms of increased participation at the post-compulsory level, the continuities with the past remain significant. Paradoxically, boys' low levels of literacy do not appear to disadvantage them when it comes to earning money (Gilbert and Gilbert, 1998, p. 12), and the advantages gained by some girls need to be put in the larger context of broader social systems and discourses.

> Documenting such research explodes the myth that all girls are winners at school and that all boys are losers. It demonstrates how such simplistic renderings of educational disadvantage with regard to boys and its corollary of privilege for girls fail to take into consideration broader social systems and discourses that intersect with gender, such as ethnicity, rurality, class and poverty.
>
> (Martino, 1999, p290)

Perhaps the question about boys' education should be rephrased to ask, Which boys? The evidence suggests that it is middle-class boys whose interests have been most threatened by the changes in educational participation (Yates, 1997). Thus an unforeseen consequence of the feminist strategy of improving girls' educational outcomes – so wholeheartedly taken up by middle-class interests – was that middle-class girls would ultimately be placed in competition with middle-class boys. If this is so, it is not appropriate to see gender as offering a simple binary category system for analysis, because the circumstances and outcomes of girls differs *within* as well as across gender. Similarly, all subjects in the curriculum are not of the same value. The other real question might be Which subjects?, because there is a hierarchy of subjects in the curriculum. In Australia, a competitive advantage is enjoyed by students who take maths, physics and chemistry. The disaggregation of the data on school outcomes also reveals that girls consistently take subjects in the humanities curriculum, including languages, literature and history, which offer a narrower range of options for further education. For example, a study of enrolments by Year 12 (final-year) students across Australia found that:

> Gender accounted for a considerable variation in Year 12 subject enrolments, with males dominating in the physical sciences, mathematics and in technical studies, while languages other than English, home economics and to a lesser extent the biological and other sciences were the subject areas in which females predominated.
>
> (Yates and Leder, 1996, p. 101)

Asking Which boys? implies, however, that some of them are disadvantaged in a variety of ways too. Clearly, the way in which the curriculum operates discriminates against boys from low socioeconomic backgrounds, as well as girls from these backgrounds This point is well made by Connell (1994) when he states that the 'mystery in broad daylight' is that it is young people in poverty who fail at school, and this is confirmed by data which also suggest (Teese *et al.*, 1995) that it is often boys who tend to be less positive about school, to be less integrated into school and to have a narrow view of what school is about.

It is, therefore, misleading to see gender simply as composed of two oppositional and universal categories. Yet the 'boys issue' also raises questions about the indicators that we use to measure disadvantage and how we assess educational outcomes. Examination results on their own can be misleading and therefore need to be seen in their broader context, but taking a broader approach to gender relations also means going beyond the category of 'boys' to place masculinity itself under scrutiny. This means re-examining some of the gender-based processes in schools that have previously been ignored. The under-representation of boys in the arts and humanities, for example, can be seen as a trend which denies a large group of boys access to the important areas of literature, history, philosophy and studies of society. As a result many boys are failing school because they are being inappropriately guided into narrow studies in mathematics and the sciences. The focus on mathematics and sciences is at the expense of developing an understanding of the way in which social change affects individuals, or how novels, movies and other forms of contemporary culture both reflect and shape social life. Students who exclusively study the 'hard sciences' do not experience a curriculum which encourages them to reflect on their values, to listen to other perspectives, and to express their views cogently. But it also has the effect of excluding others – males and females – and of reinforcing a narrow, singular view of what masculinity, essentially, 'is'.

Gender and identity

The 'modern girl', argues Lesley Johnson (1993), was a construct of the 1950s. Her study of 'girlhood and growing up' explores how the particular social, economic and political conditions present in Western societies at that time resulted in the construction of particular feminine identities. Her study provides a valuable insight into the significance of the role played by developmental psychology in providing the rationale and conceptual framework in support of the construction of particular femininities and masculinities.

We have argued elsewhere that there was a close congruence between the social conditions of the 1950s and the highly deterministic conceptual framework within which femininity was constructed (Wyn and White, 1997). For example, the growing economy of the 1950s sustained the notion that 'young people' were a relatively homogeneous category. The youth labour market provided options for young men and women who wanted to leave school, leaving the elite to continue their education and go to university. Working-class women, as always, were engaged in the labour market, but the proportion of women who were employed, especially after marriage, was very low. In other words, there did seem to be a social reality to back up the idea that youth was a period of establishment of identity, of progressing through maturational stages and that childhood, youth and adulthood were discrete stages of life.

It would be more difficult to describe the construction of the 'post-1970 girl' in the same way that Johnson has described 'the modern girl'. But this is not only because the 'gender factor' has become much more complex and difficult to analyse in the two areas of education and employment. One of the persistent themes emerging from our dialogue with members of the post-1970 generation is that we need to look beyond such a two-dimensional understanding of their lives. For them the relational and lifestyle dimension of life has also undergone change and upheaval involving new ways of seeing themselves and of shaping their personal identities.

This became clear in our 1991 study of sexually transmitted diseases (STDs). The study involved interviews with a sample of 95 young women aged between 16 and 18 (Wyn, 1994). The sample was stratified to include young women from sectors of the population which have particular relevance for health service provision. The key categories were rural, outer urban, inner urban, homeless, and indigenous groups. Within these categories, other categories were included, such as non-English-speaking background, single-sex and co-educational schools, and sex workers. Just under half of the young women (42) were currently or had been sexually active. Of the total sample, only 16 had a good knowledge of safer sex practices, and more than half of the group who were sexually active had engaged in unsafe sexual practices at some time.

Despite the diversity in the social and geographical contexts of the young women in the sample, it was found that the key issue determining young women's likelihood of employing safer sexual practices was their attitude to heterosexuality and the symbolic significance of penetrative sex. For example, a number of the young women felt that condom-free sex signified a level of trust appropriate to a loving relationship. To be prepared to not use a condom was a way of indicating something important about the relationship. There was also a strong tendency to define 'a relationship' in terms of a narrow view of sexuality, consistent with culturally defined masculine needs for sexual expression. Their comments were revealing about the extent to which desire, fantasy and power(lessness) influence their actions. Asked if she would ask a boy out, a young women from an outer urban area said:

> No, not usually, because guys get called studs and girls get called a slut. A guy can go to school on Monday and say 'I got on with six sheilas' and then a girl can go in and she'll be like this [indicating shame] because people will be saying 'you dumb scrag'. It happens all the time.

One of the young women preferred to take the risk of pregnancy or infection rather than buy or insist on the use of a condom by her partner because of a fear of being judged. She said, 'I'd be too embarrassed to go and buy a condom. Anyway, he's going to think I'm a real slut if I ask him to use one. I've been OK so far'.

Karen was becoming aware that intimacy, sensuality and pleasure for her may have a different meaning than for her partners, but she was unable to redefine the relationship as the following illustrates:

> A lot of my boyfriends I didn't have sex with. I know it sounds stupid but I found I've been hurt a lot by it. This time, he was a guy I really liked, I'd been with him for like two or three months, it doesn't sound like a lot, it was quite a surprise when it happened. We had a shower together after it and I thought it was absolutely brilliant. To me, the sex was *nothing*, but the shower afterwards was brilliant – it was just the romance of it all that I liked. The nakedness, the closeness, but not the actual act [emphasis in the original].

As Karen describes the scenario, it becomes clear that she is regarding 'sex' as the act of penetration. Whatever intimacy or sensuality was shared in the first two or three months was not seen as sex. The 'actual act' she hadn't liked, but the real focus of their mutual experience remained limited to penetration by and ejaculation of her man.

Karen's experience highlights the complex ways in which powerlessness for women in general can be translated into a personal experience of vulnerability and lack of power. The intimate relationships, which she seeks with men, are precisely those in which the assertion of feminine power is the most difficult for her. For her and other young women, the fear of being judged a slut is effectively a barrier to taking a measure of control over their relationships with their men. In this context even to ask for the use of a condom may seem too risky to a young woman.

In contrast to the experience of vulnerability and powerlessness, some young women had constructed an alternative understanding of their relationships with men. This was generally a conscious position they had taken up in opposition to the messages about femininity and constraint identified above. For example Trish, from an outer urban area, was prepared to insist on the use of a condom, even in the face of resistance from her partner. When he refused to use a condom (which she supplied), she said:

> I walked away. He got pretty pissed off though. He was really abusive. Yeah. I told him to go and fuck himself. He was pretty

drunk, though, so I wasn't too worried. He might have stood his ground if he hadn't been drunk. I had a condom, but he just didn't want to use it. He said 'no way', so I said fine, 'no way'.

Another young woman said that she carried condoms with her, in her purse. When asked what guys thought of that she commented:

That's their problem. If they can't handle it then there's not much point having sex. If they're too immature for that then they're too immature for sex, so, I mean, if they can't handle me being open enough to say 'in case you haven't brought it' sort of thing, that's tough luck.

The contrasting attitudes that this group of young women had to sex, sexuality and relationships underlines the importance of employing strategies of research that enable young people to speak for themselves. Their views revealed how complex decisions about identity and unconscious desires have an impact on their behaviour. To simply characterise the behaviour of some of these young women as risk-taking behaviour, would be to impose an adult-driven agenda that objectifies their experience.

This point is as true for research on young men as it is for young women, because, for the present generation as a whole, the comfortable congruence between life-patterns and a single, dominant theory of youth has been shattered. Rather than the meaning of youth residing within individuals as an essential, pre-social quality, the meaning of being a young woman or a young man is tied to historical and culturally specific circumstances.

'Youth' then, is an historical construct, which gives certain aspects of the biological and social experience of growing up their meaning. To put this another way, everyone 'grows up', but 'youth' is a specific process in which young people engage with institutions such as schools, the family, the police, welfare and many others. The outcomes are shaped by the relations of power inherent in the social divisions of society.

(Wyn and White, 1997)

There are many examples of research on young people and gender, which draw on this approach (Gilbert and Gilbert, 1998; Davies, 1993; Blackman, 1998; and McRobbie, 1997, for example). Many of these authors have concentrated on the complexity of young women's lives but what they have in common is their portrayal of the constantly changing and critical nature of their negotiations with institutions such as schools, the family, the workplace and in other sites. These studies of young people offer insights into social practices through which young women and young men construct identities, negotiate their spaces and are in turn defined in an ongoing struggle which has many dimensions. They reveal how identities and identifications are context-dependent. They also raise questions about the relationship of young people's identities to institutions and social structures.

As is evident from our discussion of the changes and continuities in both education and labour markets for the post-1970 generation, we would agree that:

> Gender identities are subject to transformation with the increase of women's participation in work outside the home, a trend accompanied by much higher levels of male unemployment especially in manual work in formerly dominant manufacturing industries. Together with the increasing significance of consumption in identity construction and the rise of the women's gay and lesbian movements and their impact on lifestyles, there is considerable discussion of an emergent crisis of conventional forms of masculinity and femininity.
>
> (Rattansi and Phoenix 1997, p. 124)

In particular, schools have become increasingly acknowledged as sites where sexualities are contested and negotiated. Davies's research, for example, reports the processes involved in the construction of gendered identities, based on the experiences and views of different groups of girls (one at an elite girls's school and another at a state secondary school). Her study offers insights into the extent to which these young women are aware of how they are positioned through institutional and personal processes and how they attempt to assert their own place. The picture that emerges is one of complexity.

> The powerful visions of images that the girls have of themselves are broken up. Like the wind blowing on the puddle of water, the words they speak involve exclusion, difference, violence. These words, and the knowledge of the social structures which discriminate against women break up the powerful images they see so clearly with such pleasure.
>
> (Davies, 1993, pp. 87–8)

Epstein (1997) argues that until recently it has not been acknowledged how much schools are 'sexualised sites'. She makes an explicit link between sexism and heterosexism, arguing that homophobia and misogyny are 'so closely intertwined as to be inseparable' (1997, p. 113). In other words, the joking, fighting, 'dissing' and 'mucking about' behaviours that help to keep people 'in line' are directed at boys as much as girls.

The dynamic is revealed in the reflections of a gay teacher on the impact of the question a student asked him: 'Are you gay, Sir?' (Crowhurst, 1999). It was, at the time, a shocking question to ask a teacher. The student who asked the question was transgressing the 'code of silence' about sexuality, and in doing so was exercising the power that accrues, automatically, to those who conform to the 'norm'. It was not a sympathetic question. Having been asked, the teacher was already positioned as less powerful, however he responded. The laughter from the other students that accompanied the question was an acknowledgement of the double-bind the teacher had just been placed in. To say 'yes' would have been to be forced to 'come out'. To say 'no' would reinforce the oppressive silence about sexual identity.

Through these schoolyard and classroom conversations, a particular 'normative' or 'mainstream' view of heterosexual masculinity is being imposed – and contested and the boundaries redefined. For example, a description of the experiences of young people in a British school shows how a group of girls (the 'New Wave Girls') emphasised their intimacy in order to 'exclude others, promote group unity and to strengthen close relations between pairs of girls' (Blackman, 1998). As the author points out, the girls' physicality and 'lesbian' displays frighten the boys because they render their masculine sexual bravado pointless.

Despite their stand, however, Blackman suggests that they nonetheless made their confrontation on male terms, because they are forced to defend their right to be 'different' against the boys' definitions of gender. In other words, the boys still controlled the discourses about what is 'mainstream' and what is 'other' or different. In this way, Blackman's research shows how notions of 'mainstream' and 'other' (normal/deviant) are maintained and perpetuated in everyday interactions. He has also revealed how gendered identities are being actively shaped and confined at school.

This readiness to listen to young people's explanations of what is happening, but to pay attention also to the ways in which their interpersonal relations shape the discourse, pushes the boundaries of established research procedures. The complexities revealed introduce elements of 'variance' that challenge the preconceptions which are so often written into research designs. An informative example in this context is a recent report on an impressive large-scale longitudinal study of young people in the United States. The study covered a twenty-one-year period from 1968 to 1988 and followed the lives of about 1,700 children from early childhood through to adulthood. The report, *Succeeding Generations* (Haveman and Wolfe, 1994), was concerned with the changing status of America's children and 'aspects of success in young adulthood'. One of the issues examined in the research which is of particular relevance here was 'teenage non-marital births' – young unmarried mothers.

The basic approach adopted in the research is 'the presumption that the state of unmarried teenage motherhood represents lack of success' (p. 188). The researchers' goal was to examine the teenagers' decisions with reference to a 'focus on the parental choices and community environment in which girls grow up', using an economic perspective which 'views people as rational individual decision makers seeking to make themselves as well off as possible' (p. 193). Attention is paid to the various considerations likely to pass through a young woman's mind prior to choosing to give birth. In the opinion of the authors 'there would seem to be little doubt that the reliability of these individual calculations depends on the characteristics of the girl's parents and the investments that her parents and community have made in her' (p. 194). They then go on to conduct a rather sophisticated series of statistical procedures (pp. 197–209) before coming to the conclusions that 'being African-American is positively associated with the probability of a teenage nonmarital birth' and that the 'decision is associated with the economic resources that are available to the family' (p. 209).

These are not very surprising findings but, in the light of the material presented in this section and in particular the findings concerning our own research on young women's sexual experiences, it is quite surprising to discover the factors that were not examined in drawing those conclusions – because of limitations in the particular data-set.

> Although our approach is rather full-bodied, incorporating a wide variety of potential determinants of the choice of teenage girls regarding nonmarital childbearing, we have omitted a number of potentially [sic!] important factors. We have not mentioned the male partners of teenage girls, and they clearly play a role in determining the level of sexual activity in which the girl

engages, the contraceptive practices prevalent in this activity, whether the girl marries either prior to or after pregnancy occurs, or whether she chooses to carry to term any pregnancy. We have excluded them from our analysis because the data set that we have available has no information on them. Similarly, the availability and accessibility of family planning services that are present in the girl's community are not included in our framework: although they are relevant to the outcome that we are observing, our data contain no information of these community-based factors.

(Haveman and Wolfe, 1994, p. 196)

In offering this type of explanation before undertaking their 'rather full-bodied' twelve pages of statistical analysis, the authors have told us a lot more than they realise about what their research material has forced them to ignore.

Conclusion

This chapter began with the question of whether even in the 1990s young people's lives remain strongly influenced by social divisions such as class and gender. Our aim was to explore both the continuities and the challenges that gender issues present in the field of youth research by concentrating in particular on the increased educational and workforce participation of women since the 1970s. At the centre of this discussion about young women is the notion of agency. It is argued that the circumstances that young women of the post-1970 generation face constitute a clear challenge to researchers to abandon outdated conceptual approaches and to undertake theoretically informed analysis of social action. Rather than simply universalising young women or young men, specific studies of young people within their social, political and economic environment are vital. Most importantly, research can contribute an understanding of the varied meanings of agency in young women's actions, writing and stories, and which young women and which young men we are talking about.

We have looked at particular changes in the labour market and in education that create the conditions which make it a necessity for all young people to be able to 'write their own scripts' in the absence of institutional supports. Some young women, especially those from families with higher socio-economic status, have demonstrated that they can engage with the traditional male domains of education and work. More importantly, there is evidence that other young women are successful in negotiating the difficult terrain of 'youth' through their orientation to multiple goals, which integrate their priority on personal relationships with their vocational goals.

Finally, we have raised questions about relationships of power, which affect young people's identity formation. In particular the experience of young women in their sexual relations with young men indicate the extent to which the prevailing messages many young women receive about femininity continue to emphasise and reinforce their vulnerability and powerlessness. At the same time we have seen how already in school settings those messages are being subjected to a different kind of relational discourse. The different levels of agency that young women or young men exercise can only be grasped through studies which give greater visibility to their own understandings of their lives. By placing an emphasis on young people's own perspectives and experiences, the extent of diversity of circumstances, responses and outcomes can begin to be understood and not only carry us beyond simplistic generalisations about the 'typical' male or female, but also inform policies that respect the diversity of their experience and thus meet their real needs.

7 'At risk'

One of the major consequences of a global insistence on the importance of education for the future of human society is a growing concern about the failure of 'students at risk' to complete their schooling. This concern reinforces other elements of public debate which has become increasingly focused on the threat that those 'at risk' pose to the rest of society. The very term 'at risk' becomes increasingly identified with youth as a whole. Particular problems become identified as young people's problems (school failure, homelessness, suicide, unemployment, drugs, crime, single parenthood) and particular groups of young people (the unemployed, rural youth, ethnic minorities, school dropouts, single parents or their offspring) become identified as forming a potential underclass that needs to be targeted and subjected to remedial programmes. Research money is provided to determine the empirical 'indicators' of these anti-social groups and also for devising strategies of intervention to integrate the 'at risk' back into the mainstream.

While there may be a genuine concern for the fate of young people underlying this type of effort, that very concern gives rise to an 'at-risk' paradox. The intention appears to be one of re-engagement of those categorised and targeted, but the tendency to identify the problems as youth problems (and thus to identify particular sections of the generation as problem youth) has the effect of further alienating and stigmatising them as outsiders. They become defined as a potential underclass, and are then treated as an underclass.

At a professional level this paradox inevitably has a double effect. Because of the stigma associated with definitions of 'at-risk', those who attempt to take an assumed problem seriously by identifying its real causes can be read as giving a degree of academic credibility to public scare campaigns on particular issues. Others resist this type of outcome, but often their attempts to play down public alarm about the assumed problem are tantamount to a denial of the problem itself, thus undermining the credibility of the professional attempts others are making to find genuine solutions to real problems. Thus, just as the preoccupation with mainstreaming policy gives rise to the 'at risk' paradox, so that paradox in its turn results in a professional dilemma. How do professionals confront the problem issues affecting young people's lives and yet avoid either exaggerating or downplaying the 'risks' involved? The purpose of this chapter is to find answers to this question.

Whose problem?

A major subject of debate in the United States and Britain in recent years has centred on the supposed emergence of an 'underclass'. Its focus is mainly young unmarried, unemployed, unhoused people living in run-down suburbs in the US, or in localities such as Teesside in the north-east of England which had suffered severe cutbacks in manufacturing industries during the Thatcher period. To an outsider, there are two significant elements to this debate. One is the fact that those who seemed most ready to relegate particular groups of young people to an underclass were commentators who had little first-hand knowledge of them. They were making assessments about the objective circumstances of people's lives and then proceeding to a series of value judgements about their personal inadequacies and anti-social behaviour. The other significant element in the debate was that, while those who did have some first-hand knowledge had a similar assessment of the objective circumstances, they had a very different reading of the personal attitudes, motivations and behaviour involved.

Thus a leading American conservative commentator (Murray, 1984, 1990) has persistently drawn attention to the growing problems in poor communities and mounted an attack on what he sees as a 'culture of dependency' among the young underclass (Murray, 1994; see also MacDonald, 1991, 1997). Murray offered moralistic explanations for the 'failure' of youth, tied to the need for a return to 'Victorian values of self-reliance and individual responsibility' and blamed the emergence of this underclass on a soft welfare state which encouraged people to opt out of their responsibilities. The extent to which the closure of large manufacturing industries in the north-east of England (and thus the escalation of long-term unemployment affecting the younger generation and also their parents) had contributed directly to their increased 'welfare dependency' was disregarded.

Those professionals working in the area acknowledged the magnitude of the problems and the dramatic increase of unemployment and single parenthood, but they found little evidence to justify Murray's moralistic assertions. As MacDonald, for example, has reported

> young adults excluded from jobs do not necessarily fall into this wasteful, wasting underclass where benefit dependency and crime are encouraged and work discouraged, as Murray would claim. On the contrary, interviews with over 300 working-class young people and adults in Teesside suggest that those locked out of the formal labour market are remarkably persistent, enterprising and resilient in their search for work and attempt to establish new working lives (which are, as well, marginal and insecure) through more informal economic activity.
>
> (MacDonald, 1998, p. 168)

This underclass debate highlights a fundamental issue to do with our understanding of young people's lives. When a youth 'problem' is presented to professionals for their response the agenda is already pre-set and adult-driven. Governments, policy-makers, community leaders, religious and welfare organisations, parents, teachers, academics, the media and research units all play a part in identifying what are the particular threats or risks emerging within the younger generation and what are the issues that demand attention. As a result the funds available for research and the types of solutions that are sought are often tied to pre-set agendas which make young people the 'objects' of inquiry and which rarely allow much scope to involve them in any active ways in shaping the terms of reference and the process of inquiry. Both the problem and its solution are decided on from outside the lives of those most directly affected.

An example of this can be found in a study published in 1993 dealing with the impact of unemployment on young people.

> The project was long and complex. It began in 1980, with a questionnaire to 3000 students attending high schools in Adelaide, and attempted to ascertain their status year by year thereafter until 1989.
>
> Despite the mass of information collected over nine years, the study is as notable for what it leaves out as for what is included. It tells us very little about how these adolescents lived as they became adults, what they did, with whom and for what purposes,

as tertiary students, workers and unemployed, what they hoped for, what they found, and what they thought about it all. We meet individuals only once, on page 130, when two are described briefly to illustrate complexities that escaped the mailed questionnaires and statistical analysis. The omissions were deliberate because, as implied by the subtitle, the focus of inquiry was the young people's states of mind – the psychopathology of unemployment – and the method of choice was the psychometric instrument. Several of them. The first data collection included responses to a Negative Mood Scale, Rosenberg's Self-Esteem Scale and Depressive Effect Scale, the Nowicki-Strickland Internal-External Control Scale . . . [and] the Hopelessness Scale.

(Jordan, 1995, pp. 167–70)

The only effective follow-up at anything that might be called a 'personal' level was some psychiatric interview and further psychometric testing of 100 or so participants who were identified as 'probable psychiatric cases'. Cases is probably the correct term to use in connection with this type of research.

What is at issue here is not the validity of psychometric analysis as such but a research perspective whereby the insistence on positivistic methodology and a particular type of research instrument become ends in themselves, with the result that the subjects of the research actually become the objects of study. Young people are no longer active participants in the research but passive recipients of it. The complex realities of their lives fall into the background, and the dictates of test instruments become paramount.

Some of our own work has focused on issues of social division and inequality and has involved groups of young people who would normally be categorised as 'at risk'. Our work with early school leavers and with young women at risk of contracting sexually transmitted diseases are examples discussed in the course of this book, but others would be projects related to alienation among students in the middle years of schooling (Australian Curriculum Studies Association [ACSA], 1996), disadvantaged youth in rural communities (Wyn *et al.*, 1998), and school re-entry programmes for the 16- and 17-year-old unemployed (Dwyer *et al.*, 1998b). In each of these projects we have found it necessary to challenge the initial brief and move beyond the assumptions being made by adults about these young people and their attitudes and needs. The project on alienation is a good example of this.

Members of the project steering committee were surprised when we questioned the use of the term 'alienation' to characterise the attitudes or behaviour of students and the difficulties they might be experiencing in their schooling. We took issue with the use of the term for two reasons. It was an extremely negative label for the difficulties, challenges or uncertainties that are confronted almost on a day-to-day basis within schools. On top of this, in the professional literature and often in the minds of teachers it was associated with stereotypes about personal deficit, low achievement, disruptive behaviour, poor upbringing, rebelliousness, hostility and rejection. It prejudged the situation, and created the impression that alienation manifests itself through overt signs of 'deviant' or unacceptable behaviour. As a result this not only tends to 'lay blame' on the individual considered deviant but also tends to overlook or underestimate hidden or 'passive' reactions of resignation or withdrawal which may be even more serious indications of an unbearable situation.

We were also particularly concerned that the term might be misappropriated and used to categorise those students who prior to the 1980s might have been expected to become early school leavers or dropouts. The new policy insistence on improved school retention rates was likely to have the effect of forcing potential leavers to stay on at school as 'reluctant stayers' likely to receive lower levels of encouragement from their teachers, and likely to be regarded as an added burden in an already stressful job. In this project therefore, rather than seeking to identify forms of alienation, what we were more interested in were signs of various degrees of disengagement from school and its demands.

Taking this type of approach also led us to question whether we as the researchers or 'experts' are the ones who 'know'. Given our cautions about the use of the term 'alienation', we were aware that whatever meaning we would uncover would depend on the perceptions of the students themselves (enabling them to 'open up' about their experiences to uncover the extent to which alienation was an appropriate description of what was at stake), the perceptions of the teachers (to uncover and distinguish for themselves both the positive and negative aspects of their school practice), and the distinctive context of each school (if there were indeed some signs of alienation, they might turn out to be 'site-specific'). We soon discovered that if the purpose of the project was to identify large numbers of alienated students within the middle years it was sadly mistaken. The overwhelming outcome of our interviews with students at all year levels and at all schools was that the students as a whole, and even those students who might be considered at risk, spoke of their schooling in mainly positive terms and expressed an intention (or at least a hope) of continuing through to the final senior year. This does not mean that no indications of disengagement or even alienation were present, but that these were limited in both their nature and extent.

It is important to emphasise that avoiding a pre-set adult-driven agenda – and giving young people active voice in the process – does not mean that all problems can simply be explained away and notions of 'at risk' can be abandoned. Because of the stigma involved, some would argue that the very use of the term effectively casts young people in a negative light, but it would be difficult to claim that the types of problems faced by young people in Teesside and associated with the underclass debate – or the signs of disengagement that were definitely identified in the course of the alienation project – do not place certain young people at risk, if only because of the lack of responsiveness on the part of the adults in their lives or a failure to see the significance of what is occurring. How do we take risk factors seriously without demonising those affected, but also how do we avoid demonising them without belittling the difficulties they are trying to face?

Nothing brings out more clearly how difficult it is to chart a course between these extremes than the way the 'at-risk' issue is analysed in the United States. Even if we put to one side the alarmist media stereotypes and the moralistic fervour of fundamentalist religious groups, those social scientists who express a serious concern about the problems confronting young Americans often tend to base their arguments on the accumulation of negative statistics and indicators of 'risk behaviours' or social ills that in a paradoxical way serve to reinforce the alarmist stereotypes and moralistic judgements about the threat that young people pose to social stability. This type of dilemma is well illustrated by two recent publications on American youth: *America's Youth in Crisis* (Lerner, 1995) and *Fugitive Cultures* (Giroux, 1996).

The authors share a common concern about the failure of American society to take seriously its obligations towards the well-being and rights of its younger generation, but they approach that concern from different theoretical perspectives. Lerner adopts an approach based on developmental psychology, but one which insists on a respect for the wide diversity of American society and the different contexts in which particular individuals lead their lives. Giroux is concerned about the cultural contexts which influence people's lives and the need for a critical pedagogy which would expose the distorted and destructive values accepted as common fare within American media and films. Both present strong evidence about the problems affecting young Americans, but the evidence is so overwhelming that it is in effect counter-productive. Lerner, for example, begins his analysis with an assertion that in fact all of America's children are at risk – if not because of their own risk behaviours at least because of the threat these pose to others:

> even if one believes that his or her own children are not engaged directly in high-risk behaviors, and even if one's own family is not poor, few people consider themselves or their children immune from such dangers as random violence; few believe that their communities or businesses can continue to prosper if the economic competitiveness of the American economy rests on cohorts of youth wherein drug and alcohol use and abuse, school failure and dropout, delinquency and crime, and teenage pregnancy and parenting are increasingly more prototypic occurrences. As such, it is not just *some* youth that are at risk, or just *some* communities that face the problems of losing much of their next generation. It is all of America's children, all our children, that are at risk.
>
> (Lerner, 1995, p. xiv)

He begins his first chapter with a protracted series of damning statistics about how widespread the risk behaviours of young Americans have become, covering the four major categories of: drug and alcohol use and abuse; unsafe sex, teenage pregnancy and teenage parenting; school failure, underachievement and dropout; and delinquency, crime and violence. In summary he says that of America's 28 million children 'about 50% of these youth engage in *two or more* of the above noted categories' (1995, p. 2).

What is disquieting about this catalogue is how undifferentiated the categories are – almost as if they are interchangeable (use *and* abuse); how all-inclusive the list is – so that his 50 per cent figure is hardly surprising; and supposedly how youth-specific it seems – yet drop the term 'teenage' and his 50 per cent figure might even prove to be an adult figure as well. Perhaps it is not intended, but the impression created is that of a hit-list of personal failure and blame which distracts the reader from the more constructive elements of the book. Once we get over the initial shock we find a worthwhile discussion of positive programmes of support and active involvement which take the actual context and diversity of people's lives into account.

from a developmental contextual perspective, research that 'para-chutes' into the community from the heights of the academy (i.e., that is done in a community without collaboration with the members of the community) is flawed fatally in regard to its ability to understand the process of human development. This is the case because human development does not happen at the general level . . . it does not occur in a manner necessarily gener-alizable across diverse people and contexts. Development happens in particular communities, and it involves the attempts of specific children and families to relate to the physical, personal, social, and institutional situations found in their communities. Without bringing the perspective of the community into the plan for research, then, the scholar may very likely fail to address the correct problems of human development – the ones involved in the actual lives of the people he or she is studying. And if the wrong problem is being addressed, any 'answers' that are found are not likely to be relevant to the actual lives of people. Not surprising, these answers will be seen all too often (and quite appropriately) as irrelevant by the community.

(1995, p. 55)

Giroux adopts a more confrontational approach to the prevailing norms of American society and is much less concerned with risk behaviours than with the social, cultural and economic disenfran-chisement of America's young. Even in his case, however, the impression conveyed is that to be concerned about those 'at risk' calls for a degree of missionary zeal, which leads to a chapter of faults even if in his analysis the blame lies elsewhere:

the dominant media do not talk about the social conditions producing a new generation of youth steeped in despair, violence, crime, poverty, and apathy. For instance, to talk about black crime without mentioning that the unemployment rate for black youth exceeds forty percent in many urban cities, serves primarily to conceal a major cause of youth unrest. Or to talk about apathy among black and white youth without analyzing the junk culture, poverty, social disenfranchisement, drugs, lack of educational opportunity, and commodification that shape daily life removes responsibility from a social system that often sees youth as simply another market niche.

(Giroux, 1996, pp. 28–9)

Again, the dilemma intrudes. Like Lerner, Giroux is writing in favour of young Americans who in his view have been put at risk by the false cultural values promoted throughout society. There is, however, a sense in which, by presenting as convincing a case as possible, he confirms the alarmism and moralistic outrage he is fighting against. It is hard to read his analysis and end with anything other than a sense of stunned dismay.

> Instead of helping children overcome the despair, hopelessness, and isolation that permeates youth culture, many adults appear to blame youth for the problems they face. One measure of the despair and alienation youth experience can be seen in the streets of our urban centers. The murder rate among young adults eighteen to twenty-four years old increased sixty-five percent from 1985 to 1993 ... Coupled with an increase in poverty among children, a changing world economy that provides fewer jobs for the poor, and a rise in fractured families, one of the most notable features about the crisis of democratic public life in the United States is that youth appear to be one of its main causalities. And yet, the assault on youth is happening without the benefit of adequate rights, fair representation, or even public outcry.
>
> (Giroux, 1996, p. 118)

Yet, as with Lerner's book, there is positive intent, and constructive content as well. At various points Giroux demonstrates how the negative imagery in films and media coverage can be made use of in education programmes to enable young people to reflect on their own lives and develop their own assessments and images. Empowerment and a sense of agency can be a creative outcome in the process and, in this sense, a means of resolving the dilemma.

> In part, engaging youth around questions of their own agency in relation to the world they will inherit means using films about youth that capture the complexity, sense of struggle, and diversity that marks different segments of the current generation of young people. In this instance, reading popular cultural texts becomes part of a broader pedagogical effort to develop a sense of agency in students based on a commitment to change oppressive contexts by understanding the relations of power that inform them.
>
> (Giroux, 1996, p. 46)

A very different approach is adopted by other American authors (Swadener and Lubeck, 1995) who directly challenge much of the 'at-risk' literature and the pretentious misuse of supposedly scientific procedures. Without denying the seriousness of the problems faced by young Americans and their families, these authors show up how 'at-risk' categories are used to stigmatise and mistreat particular segments of the population as if the problems were unique to them and entirely their own fault. The false distinction between the mainstream and those 'at risk' glosses over the social and personal problems that they have in common, and reinforces a 'blaming the victim' mentality. The increasing medicalisation of children (the 7 million Ritalin and Prozac kids) and attitudes of 'zero tolerance' bear all the hallmarks of a 'revolt of the elites' (Lasch, 1995) in their pursuit of a 'culture of contentment' (Galbraith, 1992).

> Questions such as how problems are defined, under what circumstances particular 'vulnerabilities' are problematic, and matters of 'degree' to which potential or real problems put children 'at risk' all deserve further reflection and critique. What is particularly troubling and problematic is the degree to which children's race, gender, class, first language, family makeup, and environment all target them for this 'at risk' label and associated interventions.
>
> (Swadener and Lubeck, 1995, p. 25)

Sometimes the 'at-risk' dilemma is expressed in a more obvious and less dramatic form through an ongoing debate between competing perspectives on the problems confronting young people in contemporary society. An example here would be current debates about youth crime rates in the United States (Males, 1998) and also the incidence of youth suicide and depression and what this means at a societal level. Some authors (White, 1994; Eckersley, 1998), for example, highlight the problems at a personal and psychological level that affect some young people's sense of belonging within society. Others (Bessant and Watts, 1998) argue that this is a misreading of the evidence which exaggerates its social significance. In effect, the two approaches represent the two sides of the 'at-risk' research dilemma.

The first approach comes at the issue of risk from a perspective that suggests that young people themselves are threatened and have been placed 'at risk' by recent social and economic trends in society. Eckersley suggests that far from being the main beneficiaries of 'progress' as we currently pursue it, young people today are paying most of the price of progress. We are not in a stable situation where only a small and static number of young *individuals* are suffering, while for the rest – the vast majority – life is good and getting better. This is an uncomfortable truth to face. But there is more hope to be found in admitting to a problem than in denying it.

(Eckersley, 1998, p. 52, italics in original)

The critics categorise this as 'cultural pessimism' and are critical of his attempt to relate specific issues (such as youth suicide and crime rates) to broader social concerns. They argue that

such contemporary dirges are part of a long tradition of repeated 'discovery' that our young are either threats to civilisation or victims of change. Such representations indicate that these 'discoveries' are not empirical discoveries. Contemporary representations of youthful disorder, lawlessness and misrule as novel responses to change, newness and discontinuity, we argue, are better understood as part of a tradition of myth-making.

(Bessant and Watts, 1998, p. 6)

There are two levels to this critique. At one level, the authors are providing an explanatory context which reminds us of a long-standing tendency in youth studies to 'problematise' young people and define them in terms of disorder and threat – what the authors refer to as 'a tradition of myth-making'. This is an important reminder. It seems as if little has changed since the time of G. Stanley Hall (1904) whose influential two-volume work on adolescence drew together the threads of much of the nineteenth-century pseudoscience about human development and set the tone for discussions of adolescence as a stage of 'storm and stress', immaturity, delinquency and 'faults and vices'. The tradition has been a strong one supported by leading scholars in the fields of psychology (e.g. Erikson, Bettelheim) and sociology (Parsons) and has regularly come alive in periods of social upheaval such as the 1930s and the 1960s and now again in the 1990s (Males, 1999). The essentially negative categorisation of young people has derived from or fed into outbreaks of 'moral panic' (Cohen, 1972) about the threat they pose to society, and specific instances of anti-social, disruptive and even criminal behaviour are made use of to lend substance to the sense of panic. Increasingly the media have played a major role in branding 'youth' as lawless and personally irresponsible (Bessant and Hil, 1997) – a simplistic play upon negative stereotypes. There is, however, another level to the critique of this tradition that is in its own way equally simplistic.

At this level, the critique is a virtual denial of any shortcomings on the part of young people – instead of being 'demonised' they are in effect 'romanticised'. The critique of the tradition of negativity is used to buttress a protestation of positivity, and every effort is made to discredit any evidence to the contrary. But there are problems associated with youth and there are lives that can genuinely be described as 'at risk'. In our work with early school leavers discussed in an earlier chapter the key researcher met up with young people who were making a living from various forms of illegal or criminal behaviour (breaking and entering, trafficking in stolen goods, drug trading) and whose lifestyles were putting them and others at risk. In the early part of our study the most successful participant in income terms was a male prostitute; by the end of the study only two participants had been 'lost' and he was one of them, having died from a drug overdose which was possibly suicide. Even though this type of evidence was not widespread in our sample, we cannot deny that it happens. Similarly, when MacDonald reports on the situation of young people in Teesside and defends them against the simplistic charges of commentators like Murray, he does not feel a need to romanticise them.

> For instance, in Teesside, as elsewhere, young working-class men are the most likely social group to be involved in offending and the most prone to becoming unemployed. Whilst precise figures are difficult to substantiate, in Teesside senior police officers report that as much as 80 per cent of acquisitive crime may be drug-related.
>
> (MacDonald, 1998, p. 171)

The difficulty with the tendency to over-react to negative myth-making about young people is that the substance of the issues in contention gets lost. At times this is tantamount to a denial that any substantial problems exist. The discussion can become a theoretical one short on first-hand research findings that might help us make up our own minds. For example, a discussion of the marginalisation of young people is reduced ultimately to the fact that being different 'can lead to some young people being treated badly' (Bessant *et al.*, 1998, p. 206); concerns about youth crime rates are seen to be unwarranted because 'young people are more likely to be victims of crime or violence than they are to be perpetrators' (p. 220); and as far as youth suicide is concerned it remains a 'personal trouble' and not a 'public issue' – after all, 'accounts of the youth suicide rate fail to identify why the great majority of young people do not commit suicide' (p. 117).

What this type of argument ignores is that there are problems at an individual level that do have a wider social dimension to them even though they do not have the magnitude of the large-scale unemployment which Mills offered as an example of a 'public issue' (Mills, 1959). Some of the students in our alienation study illustrated this for us in direct personal terms (Dwyer, 1996a). The cases appear small scale, but there are broader issues at stake which force us to look beyond a merely 'personal trouble'.

Jessie is an example of someone with a reputation as a 'trouble-maker' at school, but for whom this type of label had become a self-fulfilling prophecy and was reinforced by personal problems at home. Any serious attempt to assist her needed also to pay attention to the ways in which her family situation and the school culture were also part of the problem. When Jessie arrived at the start of the high school year she was immediately disruptive and argumentative, and quickly gained a reputation among the staff as being difficult. She was the younger sister of the infamous Michael who, during his time at school, had truanted often, been a discipline problem and been caught dabbling in petty crimes. The family was well known in the local area; the mother and father were separated, and, although the father was living far away in a country town, he still showed a concern with Jessie's progress. Her reputation had helped to make her the centre of attention in the lower grades, but as she moved on to the higher grades the demands of the curriculum had brought her into increasing conflict with teachers and led to further conflict at home. Her mother feared Jessie would start truanting and eventually drop out as her brother Michael had done. Jessie said that she hated school and thought that all teachers disliked her and she saw no future for herself at school.

Her problems could be viewed simply at an individual level as hardly meriting consideration in a study of possible alienation amongst students in their middle school years. Individual they might be, but it was also obvious that a solution to her 'personal trouble' could not be found without attending to the other broader 'social' factors that had contributed to it: her family situation, the ways in which her (and her brother's) reputation as a 'trouble-maker' had become entrenched in teachers' attitudes, and their consequent reluctance to adapt the curriculum in ways that would provide her with some positive incentives and feeling of 'success'. Fortunately, a programme was worked out with her which had wider implications for the organisation of the school curriculum. The new approach included: group work with peers and friendship groups; maintaining ongoing communications between the school and the family; counselling sessions in anger management and interpersonal skills; and participation in an after-school study programme on a regular basis – and, simple as it might sound, an eyesight test which explained the real cause of a lot of her reading problems. Her father also agreed to pay for a private tutor to work with her once a week after school. After this, Jessie still had emotional outbursts but had also learnt to reason and to talk through her problems. She seemed relieved that an answer had been found and that the problem lay with her lack of skills rather than with her problem being simply that teachers didn't like her. As her teachers later reported: 'she readily admits if the work is too hard for her and there have been only a few complaints about her behaviour as compared to the almost constant stream of complaints and endless detentions resulting from her behaviour the previous year. She genuinely enjoys coming to school and has built up a good, honest rapport with students and staff.' A more flexible institutional response became an important ingredient for the resolution of an individual problem.

In Peter's case, the links between a 'personal trouble' and wider social causes and consequences were more dramatic. In 1995 Peter was an 11-year-old with a history of trouble. He had lived with his mother and half sister in the country until his mother overdosed on drugs and died in 1989. Peter took his mother's death badly. His grandmother became sole guardian of him and his half sister, and they moved to the city to start over. Teachers expressed grave concerns about Peter when he first arrived: he was totally out of control, abusive, disruptive, and he refused to do any class-work. Varieties of strategies were used to try to cope with his difficult behaviour patterns, but these only made him more determined to continue with them. Slowly he did improve but only minimally. Then, when he was about nine, his school acquired more computers and situated them in classrooms. Peter suddenly took an interest in learning and spent most of his days on the computer.

In about the middle of that year, however, Peter's half sister was raped. Peter became outlandish with his behaviour. Although teachers were very sympathetic it did not deter his aggressive behaviour and he began regressing – but then he was given extra time on the computers and his self-confidence began to return.

Many outside influences affected Peter's mood swings and unfortunately he brought those moods to school. Some of his mood changes could be pinpointed to concrete happenings in his life – e.g., his uncle getting out of gaol and living with Peter's family, sibling jealousies and rivalries. A lot of time was consumed in trying to come up with a workable formula for both Peter and the teachers. This formula was reviewed weekly and adjusted if necessary – each successfully completed day's attendance was seen as a bonus. Again, we see in Peter's case an individual history that had its dark elements and which needed to be understood and responded to by taking the broader context of his life into account; a set of personal troubles that could have placed him seriously 'at risk' if the significant adults in his life had chosen to ignore that broader context because it was 'his' problem.

There may be instances when, by drawing attention to links between personal troubles and broader institutional and cultural contexts, professionals lend support to some of the scaremongering and demonisation of youth that often occurs in the media and leads to a distorted characterisation of them. Is the only alternative, however, to romanticise young people and to criticise any approach which results in evidence that is in any way unfavourable to young people or problematic – be it disruptive school behaviour, crime, unemployment, suicide, substance abuse or homelessness? The dilemma remains as long as the realities (both positive and negative) of young people's lives get lost in a theoretical debate about the rights and wrongs of different types of academic discourses *about* young people.

Whose solution?

Particularly at a government policy level, the identification of solutions to social problems is a major focus for commissioned research. This targeting of specific groups considered to be 'at risk' has led to a continual narrowing of the terms of reference and the size of the groups affected. This setting of narrow agendas not only underestimates the range of responses that are needed if effective 'solutions' to perceived problems are to be devised, but the types of solutions that appear to 'fit' the narrow target group are likely to fall short of the real needs of all those affected. This is because intervention strategies that are proposed as solutions tend to be dictated to the prospective participants – consistency with policy goals rather than the identified needs of the participants becomes the major determinant of the solutions proposed. This leads to a reliance upon the 'expertise' of outside professionals who have the capacity to develop measurable 'indicators' and to devise technical solutions to the shortcomings and dysfunctional behaviours of the targeted group. As the Grant Foundation's report on youth and America's future pointed out in the late 1980s

> An 80–year emphasis on the 'problems of adolescence' may well have obscured the many abilities of real adolescents and added to the stereotyped view of youth as more often than not 'in trouble'. Often seen as incompetent or requiring adult intervention, young people seldom get the chance to say what they think . . . even programs that focus on prevention rather than remediation can subtly assume the worst about young people, instead of the best. 'Prevention' can imply that, unless 'prevented', the natural path of adolescence is towards pathology rather than toward health. Sometimes the best-intentioned efforts can send the wrong signals.
>
> (Grant Foundation, 1988, pp. 50–1)

A failure to consult with the young people directly affected by strategies of intervention is so commonplace that public authorities and funding bodies even react with some alarm when such a procedure is incorporated into a research design or else see it as imposing an unnecessary delay on the development of a concrete programme. They want solutions and research must provide them with manageable outcomes. Usually there are three elements that are seen as essential constituents of an effective answer: the isolation of specific 'indicators' of the problematic behaviours or conditions that need to be addressed; the use of these indicators to identify the particular 'target group' subject to these conditions; and the development of specific 'strategies of intervention' that will alleviate the problem and, hopefully, reintegrate the targeted individuals back into the mainstream. This has become standard practice in compensatory programmes for 'at-risk' or disadvantaged groups in society, particularly in the field of education. In an extensive review of education programmes for poor students in several industrial societies, Connell's study in the Harvard Education Review sums up how this approach has shaped programmes of public education since the 1960s.

> With this rationale, publicly funded programs were set up in the 1960s and 1970s in a number of wealthy countries, starting with

the United States and including Britain, the Netherlands and Australia. While the details of these programs vary from country to country, they do have major design elements in common. They are 'targeted' to a minority of children. They select children or their schools by formulae involving a poverty-line calculation. They are intended to compensate for disadvantage by enriching the children's educational environment, which they do by grafting something on to the existing school and pre-school system. And, finally, they are generally administered separately from conventional school funding.

(Connell, 1994, pp. 129–30)

While the purpose of such programmes may be both well-intentioned and progressive, Connell suggests that they are 'factually wrong, doubtful, or profoundly misleading'. This is because they bring in solutions imposed on the 'target group' from the outside, without the prior consultation and involvement of those affected, and with the assumption that the 'problem' is isolated to them and has no bearing on existing educational structures and policies which have already failed to meet their needs. He refers to a 'false map of the problem' which assumes

that the problem concerns only a disadvantaged minority; that the poor are distinct from the majority in culture or attitudes; and that correcting disadvantage in education is a technical problem requiring, above all, the application of research-based expertise.

(Connell, 1994, p. 130)

For professionals this pre-set agenda of finding techniques of intervention for what are demonstrably real problems creates genuine concerns. No matter how carefully they take into account the complexities and ambiguities of the issues at stake, the policy demands to provide down-to-earth solutions place constraints on them that lock them into the pre-set agenda.

There is, of course, a political process at work here. Finding a programmatic solution to a complex social problem is a convenient means of making use of limited resources and restricting those resources to 'genuine' cases of need. One social problem affecting the lives of a growing proportion of young people in Western societies that exemplifies this is the issue of homelessness. This is obviously a complex issue, which involves a range of intersecting problems related to family breakdown or conflict, the growth of youth unemployment, the reduced availability of cheap accommodation for young adults and various other forms of social and economic disadvantage. In the United States in the late eighties for example it was estimated that about 1.3 million young people were in emergency shelters or on the streets in the course of a year. If we take account of those drifting in and out of the family home or some form of transient accommodation, it appears that the extent of homelessness among those under 25 in Australia had shown a dramatic increase since the early 1980s and that the actual numbers may be two to three times the official estimates (Dwyer, 1989, p. 7). Official figures in England indicated that between 1978 and 1992 the rate of homelessness had effectively trebled (Hutson and Liddiard, 1994, p. 33). In European countries, an increase of youth homelessness is attributed to the high levels of youth unemployment as well as restrictive state housing policies which make little provision for young single applicants.

Many of the relief or support programmes for homeless youth are provided by charitable agencies and are often directed specifically at those considered most at risk. In the United States in particular these either take the form of education, health or drug rehabilitation programmes or temporary shelters and soup kitchens (Hutson and Liddiard, 1994; Baumohl, 1996). Overall, the complexities involved in the individual cases make it difficult to provide a comprehensive response to the issue.

In addition, it must be noted that the homeless themselves do not necessarily view their situation in negative terms. Some may see themselves as marginalised by the failure of society to provide the necessary employment or housing that young adults are entitled to seek as independent members of society. Others regard squatting and living off the underground economy as a positive response to the need to make their own way in life. There are those who see their choice as a positive solution to an unbearable family situation of rejection and abuse. One British study, for example, found that four out of every ten homeless young women had been victims of sexual abuse at home (Hutson and Liddiard, 1994, p. 61). While Hutson and Liddiard cast doubt on some of the more positive assessments made by the homeless youth they have been involved with, they nevertheless admit that the young people themselves had a different view of their 'problem' from that adopted by the agency workers who were concerned to help them.

It must be remembered that, in talking about their experiences, young people are presenting a picture of themselves and their lives. It is not surprising that this picture is often a positive one. Agency workers, on the other hand, are not talking about themselves when describing homelessness. They are talking about and justifying their work. Herein lies some of the difference.

(Hutson and Liddiard, 1994, p. 137)

Despite all this complexity, responses to the issue by public authorities are demanded, and hence a search for some measurable and clearly defined 'expert' remedy is given major priority. In Australia as elsewhere this has reached the highest levels of national government. In the mid-nineties a parliamentary inquiry into homelessness was established as a follow-up to a 1989 study (Burdekin, 1989), and in its report (Morris, 1995) it drew attention to the role schools could play by being more responsive to the needs of students at risk and thus developing effective programmes of support and 'early intervention'. It paid particular attention to the work of a team of researchers (Chamberlain and Mackenzie, 1996, 1998) who had conducted a major study of over 40,000 secondary students as part of a research programme on youth homelessness.

The researchers were concerned to uncover likely indicators, and sought to identify how experienced welfare professionals would set about determining that particular young people might be at risk of homelessness (1996, p. 12). Guided by the judgements of these professionals, they narrowed down the identification of 'at risk' youth by focusing on the young person's 'situation at home'. There is no doubting that the authors approached the issue of youth homelessness in a markedly professional fashion. They undertook a detailed research agenda to determine the dimensions of the problem, proposed quite specific criteria to identify those potentially at risk, and emphasised the ways in which schools can provide strategies of 'early intervention' to 'care' for their students and thus reduce the potential risks. They even drew attention to what they saw as a policy contradiction (1996, p. 12) between the push for early intervention and the continual cutback in funding for key 'students at risk' programmes in schools. At the same time, there was less awareness of the ways in which inadequacies within schools are actually *part of the problem*. This perpetuates some uncomfortable parallels with the types of compensatory education programmes criticised by Connell that hint at the ways in which the pre-set agenda of research-based 'solutions' has shaped the programmatic outcomes.

First, while the researchers quite rightly based their findings on responses to a large-scale sample of young people, those students were responding to a pre-set agenda which was determined by professional judgements made *about* them by *school* personnel and which assumed that the likely risk factors were entirely attributable to the *home* environment. This effectively put in brackets some of the evidence which emerged in the major 1989 study of homelessness (Burdekin, 1989) which had not only argued against such single-factor explanations but had identified young people's experiences at school as an important contributing factor. Burdekin's Report suggested that bad experiences at school 'can contribute to child and youth homelessness' (Burdekin, 1989, p. 271), and drew attention to the fact that many of the homeless under 15 were not attending school, and some as young as 12 were effectively 'denied access' to education (Burdekin, 1989, pp. 271–2) – thus indicating a very different kind of link between early leaving and homelessness. One of the strongest messages of the report was concerned with the tendency of schools to 'write off' students who do not conform to their mainstream preconceptions. In the light of this, it is informative to note that those schools which have devised specific programmes (Dwyer, 1996a, pp. 33–35) to assist homeless youth have found it necessary to diverge dramatically from standard school procedures – to the extent that

> teachers' attitudes had changed – staff had gradually come to accept that the school has to work in and around the lives of these young teenagers; staff were less likely to just continue to impose school rules and to battle to get students to fit in, and there was less of a 'stockade' feeling amongst staff given that there was less animosity from students. Administrative procedures had become more flexible; for instance, enrolment procedures were more sensitive in eliciting information on the welfare needs of students.
>
> (Batten and Russell, 1995, p. 70)

Our experience during the early 1990s in working with early school leavers confirmed this. We maintained contact with one of the schools working with homeless youth during these years and in fact its first 'homeless' student eventually became one of our own undergraduate students. The story, as reported in one of our working papers, therefore had particular significance for us.

> In 1988, a 17-year-old Year 11 student, a victim of a traumatic family breakdown, appeared before her school counsellor at

Ardoch-Windsor Secondary College in Prahran, Melbourne, with a problem. Her problem was homelessness, which was getting in the way of her desire to complete her education. She was coming to school from a Brotherhood of St. Laurence clothing bin!

The school had not been confronted with the problem of homelessness among students before, but rather than dismissing her, responded as best they could. They extended both physical and emotional support, meeting her basic needs, needs normally met by a supportive family – housing, clothes, food, health needs including dental treatment and glasses, stationery, books and probably most importantly someone to listen to and care about her. In doing this it was soon found that other young homeless people came forward to seek the help they needed to get an education.

The Ardoch-Windsor Programme started with that single student in 1988. In 1989 there were 12 homeless students, in 1990 there were 39, in 1991 there were 78, in 1992 the programme helped over 100 homeless students.

(Holden, 1993, p. 35)

A second problem with the pre-set agenda to develop intervention strategies as a flow-on from the research was the demand for a 'technical' solution. Whatever the intentions of the researchers themselves, the effect of developing a diagnostic instrument for identifying those at risk was that it was used in schools to label and individualise the issue. The schools assumed that if the identified risk factors were overcome or remediated at an individual level, intervention would prove successful. The proposed 'solution' became isolated from a range of other factors which unfortunately are also part of the 'problem'. Again, the findings of the Burdekin Report had already indicated that individualising the issue ignores many of the contextual factors which contribute to homelessness. The report was based on very detailed research which made use of both quantitative and qualitative material, including interviews with homeless youth. There were two major aspects to its evidence. One aspect involved personal inadequacies and the breakdown of interpersonal relationships within family units, while the other covered structural factors that demanded wider solutions – unemployment, housing needs, inadequate income levels, lack of community support and services, cut backs to government funding and rigid school practices. The emphasis on individual 'risk factors' restricts the focus to individual students, and leaves untouched contextual factors that cannot be solved at an individual level.

Obviously these contextual factors cannot be addressed in a pro-grammatic way – they require significant structural interventions which are likely to depend on major political decisions. At the same time at the level of the individual school there is some scope for structural change as the researchers themselves had noted. A failure by teachers to attempt this and instead to rely entirely upon 'inter-vention strategies' consistent with policy goals helps to explain why programmes that prove successful initially – or while the spotlight of trialling and evaluation is on them – rapidly degenerate or meet with resistance. As a major 1994 American review of student-at-risk programmes has observed

> positive effects often 'fade out' when students leave a program, and many programs address only one aspect of a student's diffi-culties with little attention given to the complex web of social forces that influence a student's opportunities and motivation to learn.
>
> (Rossi and Montgomery, 1994, ch. 9)

One-dimensional lives

In reviewing a number of recent studies associated with notions of risk, we have noted the ways in which a focus on particular target groups and particular indicators predetermine the outcomes. It is informative to observe, for example, that despite the obvious oppo-sition that exists between the views of Eckersley and those of his major critics, they are each engaged in attempts to avoid blaming young people for social problems and to find some broader explana-tory context to put the effects of those problems into perspective. Similarly, professionals dealing with homelessness are concerned to find some strategies of intervention that would enable schools to counteract some of the negative experiences influencing young people to leave home. Nevertheless, one of the effects of focusing on the particular issues at stake (such as suicide, crime rates, homelessness, or historical myth-making) is that the issue itself begins to define the young people under consideration, almost as if that is all there is to their lives.

The challenge in this for those involved is that for the purposes of analysis (even if unwittingly) youth with 'problems' become either defined – or defended – as problem youth. One dimension of their lives becomes the deciding factor, and arguments are engaged in about measurable criteria (for the purposes of denial, diagnosis or remediation) determined by professional discourse. The individual is prejudged – or exonerated – and the solution is already constrained by a pre-set adult-driven agenda.

In commenting on youth policy in the United States, Pittman says this in another way.

- We are locked into a mode of linear one-track thinking that suggests that youth problems must be fixed before youth development can occur.
- Precious little is available to help troubled or at-risk youth move from receiving treatment and problem prevention services to exploring opportunities to develop the skills and traits necessary to succeed as adults.
- Too often these youth are denied opportunities to engage in meaningful tasks because we define their needs too narrowly.
- They need the same types of supports and services other youth need.
- A disproportionate share of resources and attention is focussed on the narrow goals of academic training and vocational placement, without understanding the importance of developing 'non-credentialled' competencies such as personal and social skills.

(Pittman, 1992, pp. 13–14)

Similarly, in discussing the initiatives of young people in disadvantaged localities in Britain to find their own answers to the problems confronting them, MacDonald reminds us of

the value in comprehending the parallel transitions young people make in terms of, for example, families and housing (as well as the 'school-to-work' transition) and the connections between them ... how these changes intersect with unwaged domestic work, and the transitions that young people are making in terms of sexuality, marriage and partnerships, family life and parenthood ... If we are to seriously grapple with the diversity and complexity of youth transitions and the way that they lead to social inclusion/exclusion in the longer term, we need to grasp more holistically the relationships between these different aspects and arenas of youth transition.

(MacDonald, 1998, p. 169)

Concern about young people at risk has recently taken on a sense of urgency because of the changed circumstances affecting them. The dramatic changes to the youth labour market, changes in family structures and styles, the increased significance of educational credentials, and public concerns about drugs and crime, mean that those judged to be at risk are likely now to be even more targeted than in the past. Evidence suggests that growing numbers of families are unable to provide now for their teenage children, and that among certain groups of young people there has been an increase of homelessness, substance abuse and life-threatening activity. Circumstances such as these become a focus for a clear policy response, and depending what the particular problem might be the young person who is targeted becomes defined almost exclusively in those terms. It is important to remind ourselves that, however serious the focus of concern, it is not the only dimension to young people's lives. *For them, other dimensions may be even more important*: the negotiation of 'personal' issues such as health and sexuality; relationships, including those in the workplace as well as with other adults and young people in the community and family life; and participation in formal and informal networks, activities, leisure pursuits and risk-taking behaviours. Crucially, these other dimensions cannot be excluded if we are to find effective solutions to the problems that do exist.

8   Life-patterns and careers

- I am slowly heading up that path, a path which is full of learning
  – growing, developing and dynamic with a hint of stability and
  no repetition whatsoever.
- Just because you have left school everyone thinks you are now
  an adult and you're suddenly expected to know all sorts of things:
  how to get your car insured, how to pay tax ...
- I'm too old at 20 to get part-time work – too old and too
  educated, but then I don't have enough experience to get a full-
  time position!
- When I finish studying and have a real life I'll consider myself
  an adult.
- You do your best when you have no idea what will happen next
  ... part of my success has been pure luck, being in the right
  place at the right time. I found it a very up and down period;
  it became really hard to not believe it was a personal thing ...
  for whatever reason you didn't get the job, it hurt.
- I feel that I've made my own way in life – didn't follow everyone
  else into uni or college. Feel good that I did this now, I reckon
  that my own work and life experience is worth more than any
  degree.
- Now I know how it all works, I saw how the others who were
  older and had been there longer with much more experience than
  me were also sacked. I saw how hard it is for them to get work
  as well. I realise now, its not just me it's the system.
- One of the most frightening aspects of this working generation
  would have to be job uncertainty – and all that goes with this.

These statements from participants in our Life-Patterns Project reveal
some of the uncertainties which now affect young people's transitions into adult life. The increasing insistence on prolonging their life

as 'students' well into their twenties complicates their experience of adulthood. New stages of the life-course are being invented (post-adolescence, over-aged young adults) and notions of 'extended transitions' and 'deferred adulthood' are being explored (Jones and Wallace, 1992; Côté and Allahar, 1994; du Bois-Reymond, 1998). And so, instead of rethinking youth (Lesko, 1996a and b; Wyn and White, 1997), and either questioning its continued usefulness as a simple age category or examining the appropriateness of the established markers of both youth and adulthood, a seeming solution is found by elongating the linear sequential model of transition to cover over the inconsistencies that have emerged. This is done despite the accumulated evidence that the sequence has been disrupted.

There are now significant overlaps in the lives of both young and old between characteristics of life that were in former times separated out from each other and assigned to different stages of the life-course. Even the physical attributes of adolescence, middle life and age have been modified in ways that dislocate the established time sequences of 'maturation' and 'ageing' on which the traditional markers relied. At a social level, changes to the significance of studenthood, parenthood, kinship, sibling relationships, leaving home, career, and retirement pose problems for the linear sequence – new forms of family and parenting relationships, delayed entry into and interruptions to career paths, middle-aged adults returning to the classroom for retraining, students as members of the adult labour force, adolescents acting as breadwinners for their unemployed parents, adults in their late twenties remaining in or returning to the parental home. Much of the academic literature and public commentary takes account of these upheavals. There is, however, an obvious reluctance to let go of established assumptions about what 'ought to be' (Côté, 2000, p. 51), and a failure to learn from the ways that those who have grown up in this new kind of social environment are coming to terms with it.

A fundamental reason for this neglect is that by defining youth in terms of 'age' and then prolonging the 'student' years into their twenties, the broader experience and competing life concerns of the actual participants tend to be bracketed out. The narrowly focused imagery of linear pathways is perpetuated despite evidence from researchers in youth studies to the contrary. It is important therefore to attempt to bridge the gap between the psychological, education and economics literature (and the subsequent policy formulations) and contrasting findings from the broader field of youth research. A first step would be to acknowledge the ways in which analyses of young people's lives throughout the 1990s reflect a struggle on the part of researchers to understand increasing complexity. This complexity is apparent in the 'world' in which young people live: including the effects of globalisation on some aspects of youth culture; the restructuring of national and regional economies; the increased significance of educational credentials and the casualisation of the youth labour market. Complexity is also apparent in the way in which young people themselves approach these issues (Furlong and Cartmel, 1997; Wyn and White, 1997; MacDonald, 1998).

The 1990s emphasis on educational 'pathways' in discussions of young people's futures poses a problem here. It tends to provide support for the assumption that to become adults young people's lives must be dominated or structured by a developmental process that steers them towards their goal, in a sequential and linear fashion. Education is seen as an essential ingredient in that process. This assumption is supported by insights drawn from developmental psychology, which assert that young people (adolescents), in order to become normal adults, must complete a particular set of developmental 'tasks', which, if completed in the correct order and under the right conditions, will ensure that normal adulthood is attained. This view is still shared by some youth researchers (e.g. Heaven, 1994), and is still influential in studies of young people's transitions in the United States (Graber *et al.*, 1996). The problem is that the key assumptions underlying this model of youth transitions are difficult to sustain now because of the changes that have taken place in physical maturation and processes of socialisation since that model was initially developed and tested (Holmes, 1995).

Underlying the established approach to adolescent development there has been a combination of structural prerequisites concerning the organisation of society and adult roles that are no longer normative. That approach was a useful one during the industrial era and could be applied with a reasonable degree of accuracy and predictability to determine who was likely to succeed and how, and who might prove to be at risk. The model assumed, for example, that the permanence and stability of the major institutions and functions of society (the family, schools, government services, the industrial base, the labour market and career structures) could be relied on throughout the life-course of any one individual. It also assumed that there were predictable male and female roles for different members of society which the young could be prepared for and grow into. They would thus know what was expected of them, what steps they needed to take, and what skills or even qualifications they needed to develop to enable them to fulfil those roles. It was also assumed that there were standard, accepted and recognisable 'role models' that were an important part of the socialisation process and which provided them with examples of adult life to which they could aspire and which they knew in advance would provide them with an assured life-course throughout their adult years.

What is surprising, even in the current literature on youth transitions, is that the authors acknowledge the extent to which these structural determinants no longer provide a basis of security and predictability for on-coming generations and yet they still measure those transitions in the same ways as if nothing has changed (Holmes, 1995). It is tempting to suggest that those of previous generations whose lives had developed along the 'normal' lines of the established model are reading their own experience of youth into a generation that is facing the transition to adulthood in very different circumstances and on very different terms. Where are the stable and permanent social institutions of today, what are the predictable 'normative' family roles, and where are the appropriate role models, uninfluenced by media or highly commercialised pop culture portrayals, on which the linear sequence can continue to be founded?

A kind of 'border crossing' is the term used by Biklin (1999) to describe the nature of the relationship researchers of youth have with young people. Because they have their own experience of youth behind them, they assume they know its essence. They carry their own past with them into what is now a different territory. Drawing on the post-structuralist articulation of the impossibility of the 'view from nowhere', she explores how researchers' own memories of youth 'infiltrate' their fieldwork and their developing conceptions of the youth they are studying. Her research draws on examples of youth research conducted in Italy, the United States and Australia to reveal the meanings of adult memories for understanding youth, which illustrate the ways in which the memories and positioning of the older adult researcher have influenced the research question, the data collection and the way in which data are interpreted.

For some traditions in youth research this comes as no surprise because they never subscribed to the conventional wisdom anyway. It is important to take account of an alternative tradition within youth research (Coleman and Warren-Adamson, 1992; Looker and Dwyer, 1998b) which contradicts and questions the usefulness of linear and developmental models of how young people 'grow up', and which casts doubt on the certainty of achieving adult status simply after the time designated as 'adolescence' has passed. Indeed, the current uncertainty of outcomes from post-compulsory education opens up a useful link to this alternative tradition.

As we have seen in the first part of this book, detailed research from different countries, which explores the available evidence about young people's actual experience of life, indicates that the complexities involved in growing up are such as to throw doubt on the meanings of 'adult' and 'youth' as entirely separate realities. Some youth researchers draw the conclusion that therefore a rethink is necessary because the circumstances under which people grow up have changed, from a time of relative certainty in which linearity was likely for a majority, to a time when very little is certain (Heinz, 1991; Jones and Wallace, 1992; Chisholm, *et al.*, 1990). Others go further and argue that the linear and developmental model was only ever applicable to a minority of young people, and that the model was clearly based on middle-class, white males in the 1950s (Looker and Dwyer, 1998b; Johnson, 1993; Palmer and Collard, 1993; Mitterauer, 1993). This is not surprising given that, for example, most of the research published in the leading United States academic journals concerned with adolescent development ignored considerable elements of diversity in American society. As Lerner has pointed out, 95 per cent of the articles published in Child Development between 1970 and 1990 had a narrow 'measurement focus', and for at least 50 per cent of the studies the racial or socio-economic status of the children studied was 'not even mentioned'. In the four major journals published by the American Psychological Association

> only about 5.5% of the articles published in the 1970–1974 period pertained to African Americans. And by the end of the 20–year period assessed by Graham (1992), that is, across the final 5 years within this period – between 1985 and 1989 – the percentage of articles about African Americans published across the four journals *decreased* to about 1.5%.
>
> (Lerner, 1995, p. 38, italics in original)

Even allowing for this obvious bias, it is valid to suggest that within the research data there is sound evidence for a rethink of the concept of youth in the 1990s. There is consequently a need to redress the tendency in much of the educational literature to accept youth simply as an age category with entirely predictable outcomes (Wyn and White, 1997), without reflecting sufficiently on the fact that the very concept of 'youth' has a history and meaning of its own, shaped through specific social and political processes.

Findings on emerging educational patterns in Germany are informative in this regard. In Germany in the past, a strongly institutionalised apprenticeship system had provided comparatively smooth and predictable access for young people into the adult workforce. However, while as recently as 1998 at least two-thirds of the school-leaving cohort 'showed a strong interest in apprenticeship training' (Heinz, 2000, p. 167), job outcomes had become much less certain, with a rise in the 18–25-year-old jobless rate from 8.5 per cent in 1993 to over 12 per cent by 1998, and a decline in post-apprenticeship job continuity from 60 per cent in 1995 to 45 per cent in West Germany in 1997. Heinz points out that, compared to their parents or grandparents, young Germans today face greater variability in the 'timing of job entry, marriage and parenthood' so that 'it is more difficult to predict the most likely career of young adults on the basis of social origin, level of education and credentials, because the timing and duration of transitions to employment are becoming more individualised in European societies' (Heinz, 2000, p. 164).

This complexity and increasing unpredictability of educational outcomes is evident in other studies of young people which take a broad sweep, exploring the patterns which occur over large populations. Jones and Wallace's study of young people in the UK during the 1980s is a good example (Jones and Wallace, 1992). In a study of 'youth, family and citizenship', they find that the events which mark young people's transition into adulthood are no longer predictably ranged along a continuum. For example, leaving home, an important signifier of adult status in the UK, traditionally associated with getting a job, has become an unpredictable, drawn-out process. There is increasing dependence of young people on their families, well into their twenties. This extension of the period of youth means that there are problems with definitions of adulthood, and that

> some writers, particularly in France and Germany, have started talking of 'post-adolescence' as a newly-emerged stage of the life course characterized by the extension of education and extended dependency on parents beyond the age of 18 – and sometimes into the 30s.
>
> (Jones and Wallace, 1992, p. 103)

Jones and Wallace conclude that there has been a decreasing 'connectedness' of transitions to adulthood, resulting in an increasing diversity of form and variability of patterns across social groups. For researchers, this means that it is increasingly difficult to make accurate assessments about young people's outcomes simply from looking at the patterns that occur. The meaning of these patterns to young people is fundamental to understanding outcomes, so that the perpetuation of the hard-set normative model of transition can even colour their own understanding of themselves. Jess is now in her late-twenties, but as she points out:

> It's taken me a long time to think of myself as an adult. I am sometimes inspired at just how old I am, or how old others perceive me to be. This could be because it's only been lately that I've also abandoned some of the trappings of 'childhood' (full-time study till late 1999) or adopted some of the trappings of 'adulthood' (I recently obtained my first full-time job) . . . I have always felt 'left behind' . . . as my peer-group settled down, got married, or found a long-term defacto or same sex partner. It made me feel like a failure as an adult that there were kinds of success that held secrets to which I was not privy.

Complex lives

A major problem associated with recent upheavals in the life-courses of young people in Western societies is that it unsettles and calls into question many of the basic assumptions and procedures adopted in established research concerning the young. There is now an uneasy relationship emerging between the pre-set agendas of quantitative analysis and the anomalies that can arise when qualitative approaches such as interview procedures are also adopted for the same study. In referring to the way in which this tension has affected youth research in Nordic countries, Gudmundsson refers to the misleading opposition that is set up between what he calls 'soft culture' and 'hard social facts'.

> Although interdisciplinarity and the combination of various methods have characterised the youth research field, there is a recurrent tendency to reproduce the iron curtain of habitual science between 'soft humanistic' approaches and 'hard sociological' approaches. The latter consist of quantitative research based on large surveys . . . often using advanced statistical analysis . . . By this distinction, the bulk of Nordic youth research is labelled as 'soft' approaches, anything from ethnographic research to interpretation of rock texts, from studies of life stories

to analyses of media genres ... the focus has been on a crude distinction between 'soft' and 'hard' approaches, which among other things means ignoring the extensive research crossing this border.

(Gudmundsson, 2000, p. 137)

In our experience in the Life-Patterns Project we have found that these two different research approaches can prove to be complementary, particularly when the interviews are used to elucidate or explain the anomalies that occur. Increasing complexity and also the possible inconsistencies in the data have forced us to question our own assumptions. Once we began to review our survey data in the light of the interview material we became aware of a number of different patterns of response that pointed to a range of attitudes and perspectives on the part of the participants that could not be explained by recourse to the linear model of transition.

The evidence has forced us to accept that, if complexity is now an important element for a proper understanding of the real-life context of the post-1970 generation, we need to reconceptualise their life-patterns and give greater weight to this process of complex negotiation of a life-path. Even though the young people we are examining in our research may for example have study pathways in common with each other this does not make them a homogeneous group. Study is but one element in their lives and the ways they combine or balance that with their other commitments take on a wide range of different meanings in different cases. In both our survey data and interview evidence, there were, for example, some respondents who were clearly career-orientated and had a definite goal in mind, while some regarded study and the gaining of qualifications as unimportant, and were concentrated on getting a job – however routine it might be – and having a regular income from it. Others made it clear that their decisions about both study and work were contingent upon remaining in – or returning to – their local rural community. There were some also whose main priority in life was marriage, family and children, and for them study and work were temporary or subordinate considerations.

In an attempt to allow for this complexity and diversity, we therefore re-examined the data to differentiate between the various 'life-patterns' manifested in the responses of the participants. We developed this analysis in collaboration with a Canadian researcher (Looker and Dwyer, 1998b) and came to the conclusion that there are five major patterns which capture the range of perspectives being adopted. There is certainly evidence of:

Vocational focus:	respondents who display a focus on gaining qualifications to enable a career choice to be made;
Occupational focus:	respondents who still give priority to finding a job even independently of completing post-school studies (they give priority to work, with other life-choices subordinate to that);
Contextual focus:	respondents who emphasise the 'life' context chosen (such as family, community, religious or political involvement, lifestyle, or 'field' of work);
Altered patterns:	those who have made definite changes in their study, career or life-options (they reconsider their original route and change to another destination), and
Mixed patterns:	respondents with a preference for maintaining a balance of commitments in their lives (they place equal value or emphasis on a range of activities or goals).

We have used these five variations in the responses to various items in our survey data to test the relative merits of the images of 'linear pathways' by comparison with the more complex 'life-patterns' that young people are constructing for themselves. However, as we have noted elsewhere

> It would be wrong to imply that this range of patterns in transitions is unique to the post-1970 generation of students in Western societies. Examples of each of the five have always been part of the total picture of any age-group in transition, although it seems likely that in the past the first two had normative significance. Our reason for explicitly extending the categories of analysis is because of the increasing artificiality of assuming the type of linear sequence restricted to vocational and occupational pathways and outcomes.
>
> (Looker and Dwyer, 1998b, p. 16)

If the linear images of the policy documents are presumed to represent the mainstream we would have expected, for example, that the majority of the respondents would be included under either the 'vocational focus' or the 'occupational focus'. Our provisional analysis of the survey evidence did not support this. The initial analysis indicated

Table 8.1 Priorities 1996–9 (VOCAM)

Priority concern	1999 n = 1296	1997 n = 1334	1996 n = 1908
Pursuing a career in area of interest (V)	19	15	27
Holding a job with economic security (O)	10	27	13
The broad context (e.g. family, lifestyle, 'field' of work) (C)	24	13	10
To rethink priorities and make new choices (A)	9	1	6
A balance of commitments rather than just one aspect (M)	37	44	43

a more diverse understanding of the ways in which the participants were defining their own transitions into adult life. We have tested that typology again in 1997 and 1999. It is clear that, as our participants have moved beyond full-time study, they have re-examined their priorities in life and shifted their perspective. The variations since 1996 are shown in table 8.1.

It seems likely that the increased emphasis in 1997 on the occupational focus of 'holding a job' was related to the fact that this was a period of job-hunting after completion of post-school studies. It is also probable that the decline in the emphasis on 'pursuing a career' is related to experience of the new realities of the labour market. What is most significant is that a majority of both males and females now include themselves in the final three categories, even though more males (37 per cent) than females (25 per cent) still favour the first two priorities.

What is particularly challenging from this provisional analysis is that a minority of young people could be said to have experienced a linear progression through post-compulsory education, with a strong vocational focus. By contrast, the options of the vast majority in the study are characterised by clearly divergent patterns. Their own perspectives on their experiences suggest that, even if only at the pragmatic level of coping with the constraints confronting them because of changed economic and social circumstances, the ways in which they are negotiating and constructing the central elements of their lives and their identity do not conform neatly to the underlying assumptions influencing current policy formation.

Steve puts it this way:

> I'm an automotive engineer, working on the designs of the interior trims in cars, boats and trains. I did Year 12 and went to University where I studied full time for one and a half years. After the one and a half years I decided to also start working in the textile industry ... did it for about 12 months. Started in the crappiest of the crap jobs and just worked my way up. It was hard to do both work and study; for example my employer was happy for me to take time off from work so I could study, but I always had to make up for it.
>
> Once I finished study I got work in maintenance in a textiles plant; it was good in that I managed to use some of the design work I did in university. I started doing more textile courses as well as a business course by correspondence – this was hard too, you have gotta be really motivated to do it. After four years I left that work; I got a better-paid job as a shift supervisor but the work was crappier – I guess I took it because I just wanted to get out of what I was doing. I lasted in that for nine months.
>
> Right now I'm working in development, which is good because it uses all of my previous studies and experience; you need to have a design background, and a production background. On top of that, though, I've started up a small business with some mates where we make products out of stuff – you know, like company logos and toys and boardgames. We make a good profit out of it. Oh yeah, and I'm also an officer in the army reserve which keeps me occupied on the weekends.
>
> You have to have diversity these days if you want to build a successful career. Going back, looking at the changes in the last 20 to 30 years you can't just focus on the one career anymore, you really have to be able to do a million and one things these days.

Career choices

For the post-1970 generation the meaning of career has changed. The patterns of work, the clear separation of public and private roles for men and women, the prospect of permanent full-time employment and uninterrupted career paths until retirement age that were taken as gospel truth in the industrial era have been significantly transformed during their lifetime. What their parents saw as a guaranteed and largely predictable future as they entered into their early adult years is a recollection from the past and not a 'living memory' as far as their own offspring are concerned. As Sennett (1998, p. 22) has noted, today 'a young American with at least two years of college can expect to change jobs at least eleven times in the course of working, and change his or her skill base at least three times during those forty years of labor'. If this is the prospect, what does career now mean?

For the participants in our Life-Patterns Project this has become an issue that they face as a day-to-day reality. Most of the participants have now completed their post-school studies. Like their counterparts in other nations, they are unquestionably the most highly qualified generation, both in terms of numbers of graduates and levels of qualification, in Western history. Again like their counterparts elsewhere, they have fulfilled their end of the bargain and responded to the challenge that 'the teenage years should be a period in which to invest in education and training' (Commonwealth of Australia, 1994, p. 90). Many of them are beginning to ask what kind of return they have received on their investment.

At a research level, a number of different Canadian authors argue that the expectation of career fulfilment is still a legitimate concern but that either a longer time-frame or a redirection of career options is needed to allow for successful outcomes (Trottier *et al.*, 1996; Anisef *et al.*, 1996; Livingstone, 1998; Côté and Allahar, 1994; Krahn and Lowe, 1991). Underlying the patterns of change in the pathways of young people in English-speaking nations, there is an increasing mismatch between levels and types of qualifications and the employment or career outcomes of education within three years after entry into the labour market. The Canadian data suggest that only one graduate in three sees a direct link between their university education and the labour market, and that they face 'vocational integration problems: job instability, underemployment, "inappropriateness" of their training in relation to the job, disparity of integration conditions according to the field of studies' (Trottier *et al.*, 1996, p. 92).

That study by Trottier *et al.* (1996) involved a detailed statistical analysis of the 'vocational integration of university graduates', and examined the career outcomes of bachelor students three years after they graduated. The authors developed a threefold typology: the integrated; those in the process of integration; and the inactive. They concluded that 'for close to half, job instability 2 years after graduation is a predominant phenomenon' (p. 104). The threefold typology consisted of the following categories:

1   the integrated were those who within three years of graduating had achieved a permanent full-time job envisaged as a career

choice – 'even if the job is not the one he or she initially hoped for' (p. 94);

2   those in the process of integration were either not working full time, or were in a temporary position, or else had a full-time job which was not envisaged as their career job; and

3   the final group were said to be inactive because of their non-involvement in the labour market (often because they were continuing with post-graduate studies).

Figure 8.1 displays the variations of 'the integrated' for gender and areas of specialisation.

The conditions prevailing within the new labour market in Western nations raises a problem regarding this Canadian analysis. It adopts an assessment of career outcomes which requires graduate jobs to be both permanent and also full time. The increasing emphasis on flexibility and contingency as a result of new employment practices, however, calls these elements into question. The assumed one-to-one relationship between notions of 'career' and 'permanent full-time' employment is difficult to sustain in the contemporary labour market. It also makes it difficult to strike a balance between objective and subjective definitions of what constitutes career 'success'.

This can be illustrated by reference to the findings from our annual survey in 1998 at which stage the participants were seven years beyond completion of high school and well into their mid-twenties. Also by that stage the vast majority were at least three years beyond

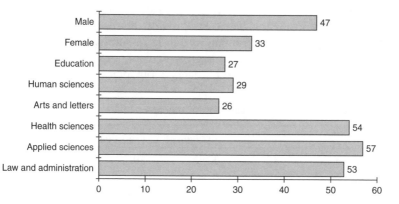

Figure 8.1 Vocational integration of 3-year Canadian graduates (%)
Source: Trottier *et al.*, 1996, p. 98.

the completion of their initial tertiary qualification. The survey included a number of questions concerning the employment history of the participants. We found, for example, that the majority (57 per cent) had had more than one job since the beginning of 1996, and about 5 per cent had had more than five. The majority of respondents were currently in full-time jobs (67 per cent), with 15 per cent in casual or irregular jobs and as many as 8 per cent with a number of jobs. There were 5 per cent unemployed looking for work and 5 per cent who saw their main work as family or home commitments. Most (59 per cent) reported that their jobs were 'permanent' by this stage, with a further 11 per cent in renewable-contract positions. Even though a significant number had found positions that were both full time and permanent, it is important to note that this did not necessarily mean that the jobs were in their preferred career area. Only 48 per cent considered that this was the case, although a further 20 per cent saw their job as a 'stepping-stone' one related to that career. Having a job in their 'preferred career area' did not mean that it was as yet seen by them to be a real 'career job'.

Related to this uncertainty is the fact that different fields of study have quite different employment prospects. For example, in 1997, 75 per cent of those with a business qualification described their jobs as 'permanent' but only 51 per cent saw these as jobs in their 'preferred career area', whereas for health professionals 70 per cent were working in their preferred area but only 54 per cent had permanency. Our 1998 survey confirmed this and indicated that areas such as trades or business/economics which had the highest 'permanency' outcomes had the lowest 'field-related' and 'career-position' outcomes, while the reverse was true of those qualified in the fields of education or nursing. Table 8.2 provide the contrasts between the top six of the areas of training in our 1998 sample.

Perhaps partly related to this growing complexity is the fact that, while gender is still a factor affecting outcomes, the influence of

Table 8.2 1998 qualifications and job outcomes (%)

	Frequency	Permanent	Field-related	Career job
Maths/science	139	53	60	55
Education	75	45	80	79
Nursing etc.	129	57	85	75
Computing etc.	74	77	70	70
Business	209	78	61	68
Trades	61	85	61	67

parental background or socio-economic status is much less evident. If we look back over the history of the various groups in our sample there is clear evidence that young people from more advantaged family backgrounds were *initially* more likely to gain access to university pathways and the more prestigious courses within them. On the down side, those from less advantaged backgrounds were more likely to be over-represented among those who failed to gain post-school qualifications and among those who failed to find careers for themselves.

However, our data also indicate that once particular individuals have crossed the 'threshold' of post-school study, other factors come into play. Data related to 'vocational integration' (those with permanent full-time career jobs) for our 1999 sample are given in table 8.3.

Surprisingly, those from government schools do just as well on integration levels as those from the more prestigious private schools (47 per cent from each) and those from vocational colleges by 1999 had done somewhat better than their university peers (53 per cent versus 47 per cent). While males were more likely than females to achieve 'vocational integration', socio-economic status (SES) or family background (professional/managerial fathers or university-educated mothers) had become a less likely indicator of successful career outcomes. This is in line with the Canadian research on vocational integration which led its authors to observe that their hypothesis concerning the advantaged position of those from higher SES backgrounds 'was not verified', and that this was probably because the determining factor governing outcomes was not status but 'that the

Table 8.3 Per cent vocational integration (1999)

	%
Males	51
Females	46
Government schools	47
Catholic schools	48
Private schools	47
Non-English-speaking parents	43
From metropolitan city	50
Professional/managerial father	49
University-educated mother	42
University qualified	47
College qualification	53
Total sample	47

positions to which they aspire require a specific level of training and special skills' (Trottier *et al.*, 1996, p. 104).

Rethinking careers

This growing uncertainty about 'career' raises questions about the relationship between having a 'full-time' job, having a 'permanent' job, and deciding when a job moves beyond being one with 'career prospects' to one that is a career. As a result our current generation of graduates is showing signs of rethinking what 'career' means for them. They are beginning to discover that, given the move to more flexible and deregulated labour markets, outcomes from post-compulsory education are now less straightforward and take longer to achieve.

In 1998, at most 69 per cent were able to report that they either had a career job or one that had genuine career prospects. By 1999, that combined total had risen to 75 per cent. What is significant with regard to their subjective assessments of vocational integration is that by this stage 64 per cent were ready to state that they had now achieved an 'ongoing career' for themselves. As can be seen from the table there was little variation on this score between the responses of the males and females (table 8.4).

What these figures show, therefore, is a 17 per cent divergence between subjective assessments (64 per cent) and the objective classifications shown in table 8.3. The gap is at least partly related to the job situations of the women in the sample who have a higher representation (22 per cent) than men (4 per cent) in the combined fields of health and education, which suffer from a lack of permanency and therefore do not fulfil the objective criteria for vocational integration. Although these graduates are likely to be employed in

Table 8.4 Career outcomes (1999)

	Male	Female	Total
I would consider it as an ongoing career	65	63	64
Not currently a career position but has genuine 'prospects'	11	12	11
It doesn't yet offer 'career prospects' but may in the future	8	8	8
It is unlikely to develop career prospects	7	7	7
None of the above	8	10	10

their respective industries, the lower permanency levels reflect the changes that have taken place in those sectors. The shift towards short-term contracts for both nurses in the health system and teachers in the education system is thus shown in the fact that, while many of them are professionals, fewer of them have permanency in their long-term future. Nevertheless, it is important to note that even for the males in the sample there remains an 14 per cent discrepancy between their subjective and objective assessments.

In other words, this shift to short-term contracts in particular professional fields is not sufficient to explain the full extent of the divergence between the subjective and objective findings. A further reason can be found in the fact that as many as 15 per cent of those who nominate a current job as one they see as a genuine career were in fact only working in it part time. It is worth asking why at this stage would some participants regard part-time employment as sufficient justification for claiming to have an ongoing career? Part of the explanation lies in the fact that amongst them there is a group of people making up 8 per cent of our sample who currently have more than one job – one of which is in their area of specialisation with a renewable contract. There are, for example, graduate nurses who have regular but part-time work in childcare or as nannies and who supplement their income doing restaurant or bar work in another part-time job in the evenings. Or there are a few accountancy graduates who keep the books on a part-time basis for small business firms and work as croupiers at night in the local casino. Others are relief teachers, part-time research workers in an 'out-sourced' consultancy, or apprentices who only get occasional jobs in their trade.

Our interview material suggests a further explanation. It reveals that the shift towards a more contingent and flexible workforce is not simply a factor affecting the objective conditions under which people are now expected to work, but that it has also led to a more contingent or flexible attitude on the part of employees towards *their own definitions* of work and career. Thus, 'career' means something different now and measuring it in terms of 'permanency' or 'full-time commitment' fails to capture the way many of our participants are organising their lives. As we saw in the typology of five life-patterns we examined earlier, by 1999 the majority were indicating that their ideas about future careers were much broader now, and there is an adoption of 'mixed patterns' of job and life commitments – having 'many irons in the fire' has for an increasing number of young people become a 'fact of life'. The broader three 'choice' priorities are now preferred options for as many as seven out of every ten in our sample.

This broadening of outlook and the mixing of commitments are more common than is realised. There are, for example, increasing numbers of young adults who are using unpaid volunteer work as a means of access to a career path so that when the opportunity arises even a renewable and regular part-time job is read as proof of success. For others, having a number of different career options serves a similar purpose – so that 'permanence' for them is not the defining element – 'it will not be a job that I will have to do for ever'.

At this stage in their lives, having completed their initial post-school studies and entered their late twenties, for the majority of our respondents, however, 'having a steady job' is still the number-one priority, but it is important to note that even in their case this does not necessarily equate with pursuing a career. If the meaning of jobs and career has changed, then a different understanding of the 'work ethic' is also at stake.

In our year 2000 annual survey we followed up some of these issues. One question, for example, asked them what they considered important in deciding on a career job. The responses indicate that what matters the most to over 90 per cent of the sample is that the job 'is a secure one' and that features such as 'responsibility over others' (42 per cent males, 36 per cent females) or 'high status' (39 per cent males, 32 per cent females) are the least favoured items of all. It is also interesting to note the contrast between the 90 per cent support for a job that 'makes me think a lot' as against the 60 per cent options for one that 'has flexible hours' on the one hand or one that is 'busy and demanding' on the other. The various options are given in table 8.5.

Table 8.5 Favoured aspects of a career job – 2000

n = 1109	*High support*
The job is a secure one	1025
It makes me think a lot	1001
It pays well	989
Is full time	861
Requires organisational skills	836
Is busy and demanding	664
Lets me work on my own	646
Has flexible hours	636
Involves responsibility over others	422
It is a 'high-status' job	385

Choice or constraint?

- I love my job but the hours I work make it hard to balance other parts of my life. Overtime has been an expected part of all my jobs – and quite frankly I'm tired of this. In five years of full-time work I've worked an extra year of overtime (unpaid). My work is very rewarding, but the workload is immense.
- You need a clear focus on personal goals, together with continuing with your own personal development. It is important though to keep a balance of life aspects so that you don't lose things of high value in your life, i.e. relationships, personal well-being.
- I am looking for a new job; although the money is good, the hours are too long; now I am a father, my family is my first priority and I want to spend more time with them.
- My work priorities and career goals are different – my job is only to earn enough money to live.
- My mother thinks success is about having my car paid off; she thought leaving to go to a job with less pay was madness.
- These days your employer can't promise you a job for life, but through education and training they can give you the skills to get ahead. Spending two to five years with the same firm and then moving on is good and brings outside knowledge to your new organisation.
- Unfortunately, despite all the promises there was no new contract when the last one ran out, so I have had to take on work I have no experience or qualifications in, working for a bunch of cowboys who would sack me in a minute if I spoke up about anything.

In raising the idea of choice biographies, the German theorist Ulrich Beck also commented that the pressures to conform to the established expectations of industrial society continued to exert a strong influence on people's lives. As we have seen, authors such as Côté and Allahar (1994) from Canada or Furlong and Cartmel (1997) from the UK present convincing evidence that there is a deceptive element in the supposed increase in individual opportunity and 'choice' for the post-1970 generation once we examine their actual job outcomes. If they appear to be broadening their options and placing equal emphasis on a range of factors that do not fit neatly into the linear model of transition from study to work, from dependence to independence, from 'growing up' to 'settling down', is this really a matter of personal choice or a matter of necessity because of the constraints and uncertainties they face?

It is difficult to answer this question as long as we continue to insist on the established categories used to examine young people's career transitions. In the past, the theories of social stratification and class analysis that have been used to explain predetermined or background influences on people's life-chances have made use of the concept of 'social mobility' to allow for variations and unexpected outcomes which suggest that life is not as predetermined as the structural categories seem to imply. Particularly in studies of intergenerational change, the concept has been used to explain how people from working-class or underprivileged backgrounds have succeeded in an 'upward' move on the social scale, or for those from more privileged backgrounds there has been some recognition of 'downward' mobility from their class position. At times in locality studies reference might also be made to 'lateral' moves of people from one region to another, but usually within structural analysis social mobility is essentially a uni-dimensional and hierarchical concept and the possibility of horizontal mobility is not part of the equation. If, however, mixed patterns involving a range of educational, occupational, lifestyle, personal relationship and locality choices are now assuming greater significance (or are more openly acknowledged) in the lives of young people, the concept of social mobility needs to be broadened to allow for these other kinds of priorities which in effect cut across the pre-set hierarchical categories on which structural analysis relies. If the assumption is made that educational and occupational aspirations and choices are the only elements that matter (Andres *et al.*, 1999), it is not surprising that other elements are excluded from both the data-gathering and the analysis, and that self-fulfilling prophecies inevitably result.

The evidence from our Life-Patterns Project suggests to us that, in the light of the international evidence, what our respondents are telling us about their lives is not simply a matter of necessity, but is derived from a more critical assessment of the gap between what they were led to believe and expect about adulthood and what they have experienced as they entered upon it. One of the effects of their prolonged entry into career paths has been that they have had more time than previous generations did to assess and balance their priorities concerning adult life. Ironically, their experience in the deregulated labour market has, if anything, served to reinforce the belief that the other areas of their lives are of at least equal importance. Terms like 'generation on hold', 'post-adolescence' and 'over-aged young adults', that have been used in the international literature to explain the delaying of traditional outcomes, tend (perhaps unintentionally) to perpetuate the assumption of the linear two-dimensional sequence –

by conveying an impression that these groups of young people will somehow or other eventually arrive at 'normal' adulthood defined in terms of the industrial era and their parents' expectations of them. The type of taken-for-granted structural determinism which still dominates in some fields of youth research and which Rudd and Evans (1998) have expressed concern about regarding British research traditions also appears to assume that this is 'inevitable'. It is worth noting here some of the evidence which emerged in the American study of teenagers at work in North Carolina.

> The pursuit of autonomy in horizontal mobility also represents a reaction against traditional working-class attitudes that preach the American Dream as a lifelong march up the social ladder, which translates into upward social mobility from one generation to the next. From this point of view, worker loyalty (whether to company or union) is traded for increments in status or wages. Born into the downward turn of industry and labor, none of the teens I spoke with had any interest in factory work. Nor did they see themselves entering a company and working their way up to a supervisory position. 'It's all the same', said one. 'You get laid off before you get anywhere'.
>
> (Willis, 1998, p. 352)

Those teenagers were refusing to accept the experience of a past generation as 'normative', and like many in our own study were in the process of exploring a different balance of life-patterns. If the evidence suggests that they are of their own accord already reassessing their work ambitions and their own processes of transition, the possibility must at least be investigated that they are also already in the process of redefining the meaning of adulthood for themselves. It is obvious that for many in this generation personal fulfilment is not being defined solely in 'career' terms. In the past 'who people are' may have been defined by what they do (or don't do) in their jobs, but certainly for our participants it is clear that occupational destiny is not all there is to life. They define themselves in terms of a blending of 'being' and 'doing', as can be seen from the personal goals they emphasised in our year 2000 survey (table 8.6).

Even though our participants are reassessing for themselves the place that career concerns have in their lives, this still leaves us with a question about the implications of the disjuncture between educational achievement and labour-market uncertainties which has at least partly contributed to that reassessment.

Table 8.6 Important goals in adult life

n = 1113	Males (%)	Females (%)
Financial security	93	96
Special relationship with someone	90	94
Care and provide for a family	75	82
Working for a better society	60	68
Pursue a life of pleasure	62	65
Make a lot of money	57	48
Help people who are in need	42	56
Enjoy an affluent lifestyle	49	46

The question is an important one because the disjuncture is not simply one that affects educational policy and economic outcomes but one which has serious implications regarding social policy as well. First, it points to the demise of the utilitarian compromise. For much of the twentieth century, English-speaking nations relied on that compromise to avoid social upheaval and promote the welfare of citizens (Hobsbawm, 1994; Rowse, 1978). Liberal democratic traditions were developed which held out the promise of fulfilment of the utilitarian goal of 'the greatest happiness for the greatest number'. One of the main assumptions underpinning utilitarian policies was that education modified the extremes of either classic capitalism or state socialism and served as a vehicle for upward social mobility. There was an expectation that a one-to-one relationship existed between levels of educational attainment and long-term career prospects, with supplementary opportunities at the lower skilled and unskilled levels of the labour market for those without suitable credentials.

Education was defined as both a public good and a means of personal fulfilment. It had economic utility as well, but the compromise allowed for its purpose of social mobility. This perhaps explains why American researchers continue to use social mobility as a point of reference regarding educational outcomes, even though they acknowledge that the increasing flexibility and impermanence of employment outcomes make such mobility much more uncertain. Instead of therefore questioning its continuing usefulness as a basis for analysis, Schneider and Stevenson, for example, persist with it and then, criticising young Americans for being 'directionless', they assert that most high school students 'have high ambitions but no clear life plans for reaching them' and thus are 'drifting dreamers' with 'misaligned ambitions' (1999, p. 7). Is it really appropriate to criticise the current generation on the basis of expectations of this kind from the past? It may well have been true that expectations about educational participation – particularly during the unique period of economic growth of the 1950s and 1960s – had offered the promise at a national level that it guaranteed the fulfilment of the utilitarian goal. Many of the younger generation of that period saw and enjoyed the resulting benefits. One reason for the demise of utilitarianism, however, is that education also offered and promoted a belief in achievement, or the rewarding of individual 'merit', and appeared to justify the subsequent cult of managerial and leadership expertise (Dwyer, 1994a) – the emergence or selection of the 'best and the brightest'. Those who benefited then are now the first to pontificate about 'user pay' principles, conveniently forgetting the scholarship schemes and open-door university policies that helped get them where they are today. From their leadership positions in industry and higher education they advocate a much narrowed definition of education in instrumentalist terms for the purposes of economic advantage.

The utilitarian hope may still be alive amongst present-day students and their very supportive families, but it would be a mistake to under-estimate how instrumentalist and subordinated to corporatist economic goals current educational policies are. It is clear that in English-speaking nations such as Australia, Canada, the US and the UK the major emphasis at a policy level on increased participation in education and training derives, not from a belief in it as a human endeavour of personal growth, but from the prevailing economic belief that it will serve as the key to future economic growth. Pro-longed education or training may continue to be held out to young people as important for their identity formation and as a guarantee of their future employment and livelihood, but it is also part of the 'sorting' process advocated by the Organization for Economic Cooperation and Development (OECD) for 'flexible' labour markets – and thus 'unrelated to the quality of the skills actually created' (OECD, 1987, p. 71).

There is a cruel irony in this vision of the future. While we can acknowledge the intrinsic merits of education for the coming gener-ation and for national well-being, the fact remains that currently significant structural changes are occurring within the labour markets of these nations in ways that are at odds with the policy provisions advocated within the educational market. The real meaning of the 'highly skilled and flexible' workforce of the future is that the 'flex-ible' demands of economic markets are irreconcilable with what the 'highly skilled' have been led to expect for themselves on utilitarian grounds as the predictable outcome of their successful participation in the market of education. There is a continuing divergence between current adult employment trends and trends affecting youth pathways into adulthood.

Secondly, however, there are implications in the truth that throughout the life of this post-1970 generation developments in the global economy have had far-reaching cross-national effects on the lifestyles and consumer interests of all generations – but particularly on the young. They have been cultivated – and in this sense enculturated into an individualised sense of 'choice'. They were not only candidates for the labour market but were a market in their own right; and so their tastes, their interests, their leisure pursuits and their assumed 'drives' were courted and pursued. They had identities that were to be shaped, labelled and expressed, even though as students they were told to 'keep their eye on the main chance'.

In other words, even in terms of the linear model of 'transition', outcomes for the post-1970 generation depend therefore not on their educational achievements alone, however admirable or desirable they might appear, but on how these balance and blend with other aspects of their personal lives. Alongside what has been an unprecedented and significant intergenerational investment in education as a public good and a means of career fulfilment, there has been a shaping of other dimensions of their lives that were marketed as intrinsic to their identity formation. They have learnt their lessons well, even if we seem to have missed much of the irony of this *American Beauty*.

There is something ironic, too, in the fact that the widening of 'choice' in young people's lives has in some sense served to compensate for the increase of personal insecurity within the labour market. 'Self-reliance' would seem to have become a major survival strategy, and one that is sometimes read as an indication that the current younger generation is a much more conservative one than its predecessors. But, as one of the post-1970 generation puts it,

> There is no question that many young people have compensated for the fact that they don't trust politicians or corporations by adopting the social-Darwinist values of the system that engendered their insecurity: they will be greedier, tougher, more focused. They will Just Do It. But what of those who didn't go the MBA route, who don't want to be the next Bill Gates or Richard Branson? Why should they stay invested in the economic goals of corporations that have so actively divested them? What

is the incentive to be loyal to a sector that has bombarded them, for their entire adult life, with a single message: Don't count on us?

This issue is not only about unemployment per se. It would be a grave mistake to assume that any old paycheck will buy the level of loyalty and protection to which many corporations – sometimes rightly – were once accustomed. Casual, part-time and low-wage work does not bring about the same identification with one's employer as the lifelong contracts of yesterday.

(Klein, 2000, pp. 268–9)

Despite, therefore, the growing emphasis that seems to be placed on choice, self-reliance and mixed patterns of life, it is still important to ask questions about the future career outcomes for this generation. What exactly is envisaged by a 'highly skilled and flexible workforce'? Skilled it will be – the education participation rates will deliver on that. But what kind of flexibility is to be utilised – the capacity of a skilled generation to undertake a variety of tasks and apply a range of skills within their chosen careers, or their capacity to reconcile themselves to limited opportunities and thus 'to turn their hands to what is on offer'? And what kind of workforce is in prospect – ongoing full employment for full-time workers based on their proven skill levels and educational attainment, or a 'flexible' workforce in terms of transitions between or combinations of limited-term full-time contracts, periods of part-time positions and an adjustment to the realities of occasional underemployment or unemployment? On what current model are we to vision the archetypal worker of the twenty-first century – the self-employed professional, the tenured academic or permanent public servant, the person 'on call' or the casual service provider, the itinerant worker, or perhaps the creative artist on an employment/unemployment rollercoaster?

Questions such as these are central to the 'deferred agenda' of post-compulsory education and training policy to which this generation has been subjected. As the time comes to demand a return on the significant investment that has been made in their education, the questions will inevitably be raised despite the very different reality that might be uncovered in response. What will emerge to replace the utilitarian compromise of the past and the corporatist ideology of the present is difficult to predict, but it will necessarily be based on an unpredictable labour market, despite a much more highly-educated generation of adults. A dangerous combination, which confronts the post-1970 generation with the challenge of forging a future based on different assumptions, options and hopes from those currently on offer to them from the leaders and policy-makers from a self-rewarding but passing generation.

Epilogue

Looking back over a ten-year period of accumulated research about young people in a variety of Western nations has proved to be a challenging but rewarding task. Partial recollections of significant patterns in the various studies needed to be tested and re-examined, and possible links between the findings from separate projects demanded further analysis. In addition, as we went back over the material we became increasingly conscious of the ways in which changes in youth policy, increased educational participation and shifts in economic indicators were often at odds with the experience, expectations and priorities of the participants themselves. We believe that these concerns come through in our reworking of the evidence, but suggest that there are three themes that stand out once the findings of the different studies are put together. First, an awareness and experience of foreclosed options appears as a consistent thread over the whole decade; second there was a discernible shift by the end of the decade towards more complex life-patterns and a blending or balancing of a range of personal priorities and interests; and third the need to give 'active voice' to young people about the dramatic social and economic changes they have been subjected to is unmistakable in the light of the increasing disparity between the propaganda of policy and their own experience of its outcomes.

Foreclosed options

Despite the complexity and diversity of experience that have characterised the various research studies we have examined over the past decade, they have all revealed a consistent concern about foreclosed options among the participants. Our 1991 study of secondary school students from largely stable family backgrounds identified significantly high levels of pessimism about the uncertain job futures that

they shared with those of their generation who were seen as 'casualties of change'. Our 1990–3 longitudinal study of early school
leavers, which kept in contact with them at three-monthly intervals
over a three-year period, confirmed the uncertainty about job
outcomes, even though their lack of success in achieving a secure
livelihood for themselves did not appear to have discouraged them
to the extent that we might have expected. The one thing they seemed
to agree upon was that they had entered 'uncharted territory'. In our
larger longitudinal study which is still in progress, the participants
had initially displayed a degree of optimism about their future chances
– largely because most of them had been fortunate enough to enter
upon a course of study which held the promise of successful career
pathways into the future. However, by the time they had completed
their courses many of them had begun to echo the notes of pessimism
that had been voiced by the school students who had participated in
our 1991 study.

At another level, however, there was a contradictory undercurrent
of response from all our studies which was confirmed by comparable
international findings and which was becoming increasingly insistent:
that this particular generation was persisting with a positive view of
its own choices despite the foreclosed options they faced in the labour
market. For many writers there was a strange paradox in this. Thus,
because of the clear gap between the high career hopes of young
Americans and the realities of the labour market, some American
authors (Schneider and Stevenson, 1999) saw the gap as evidence of
an 'ambition paradox' and proof that this current generation is 'directionless'. Faced with similar ambition-gaps in their country, British
authors find them either 'perplexing' (Rudd and Evans, 1998) or
evidence that young people today underestimate the extent to which
structural factors such as social class and gender continue to predetermine their life-chances (Furlong and Cartmel, 1997). Yet, when
we examine what young people themselves say about their experience, these explanations appear to be missing something. If it is true
that the need to make your own choices in life is now a central aspect
of young people's experience, learning to live with inconsistency is
an inevitable consequence, and many of their comments suggest that
they are aware of this. They may have accepted a definition of their
futures in terms of economic security and career success, but at the
same time they are giving notice of other priorities in their lives that
enabled them to adjust to foreclosed options. This is evident from
the obvious similarities between the comments of teenagers of North
Carolina (Willis, 1998), students in schools in Manchester, England

(Raffo and Reeves, 2000), 'post-adolescents' in Holland (du Bois-Reymond, 1998) and unemployed graduates in their late twenties in Australia (Dwyer *et al.*, 1998a). Willis even suggests that there is an element of 'horizontal mobility' in the way they adjust to foreclosed options – 'the particulars of a job matter less than their ability as employees to move across a field of jobs' (1998, p. 351).

Nevertheless, there are also some signs of cynicism, anger and disillusionment regarding the unfulfilled promises made to them about their career options. Throughout the whole of their lives, educational goal-setting has been put at the service of prevailing economic fashions, with little consideration given to the impact this would have on those at the receiving end. In their early years education policy was being strongly influenced by the adoption of human capital theory as a justification for increased public expenditure. By the late seventies and with the onset of economic recession, human capital theory lost favour and the emphasis shifted to the importance of market forces and principles of individual effort and self-reliance (Dwyer *et al.*, 1984).

At the same time, major OECD reports on youth policy (Henry, 1996) placed considerable emphasis on promoting post-compulsory education as a key to future economic prospects. Thus, since the mideighties in Western countries, there has been a substantial redefinition of the agenda for youth and education policy with particular emphasis on the post-compulsory years. What is advocated now is a carefully planned and managed national policy to produce a skilled workforce that has the necessary flexibility and adaptability to cope with, and advance, the knowledge society of the future. This tightening of national planning for education since the mid-eighties has turned once again to human capital theory but has redefined it in terms of the deregulated economy (Marginson, 1993). A new economic consensus that espouses deregulation at a national level and economic exposure to global markets has combined the two key ideas of 'globalisation' and 'privatisation' – the duty of government is to ensure the proper setting of policy goals but their fulfilment ultimately depends on 'user pay' principles and the play of the market at the local and individual level. A whole generation now has been on the receiving end of this shifting play of policy forces. It is hardly surprising, then, that they have emerged into adulthood with a strong emphasis on individual 'choice' but also a heightened awareness of the 'unpredictability' of outcomes.

And so, despite the high hopes about the 'knowledge society' that continue to be voiced within the forum of education, young people themselves are much more aware that the realities of the workplace in the 'service society' are being transformed regardless of educational outcomes. Even the highly qualified are entering into a radically restructured labour market in which greater flexibility and contingency are at play, and for whom a dilemma arises because the meaning of career has changed. Although the images (and advice) they are offered with regard to transitions between study and work still promise a world of predictability of outcomes, permanence of career and security in future prospects, we know for a fact that 'contingent' work now encompasses 30 per cent of the US workforce and 'casual' positions have accounted for 62 per cent of job growth in Australia since the mid-eighties. A detailed analysis of labour-market trends for young adults in Australia (Wooden and VandenHeuvel, 1999, p. 47) reveals that, 'perhaps surprisingly and certainly of concern, given the emphasis placed on educational attainment and qualifications, data on changes in the occupational distribution between 1993 and 1998 suggest a general trend toward lower-skilled jobs for both young men and young women'. Despite their criticisms of the 'drifting dreamers' in their study, the American authors of *The Ambitious Generation* note that today's teenagers:

> see their future work lives as filled with promise and uncertainty. They believe in the value of technology, in the importance of being flexible, and in the need for specialisation; they also believe that they will change jobs frequently and change careers occasionally. Teenagers accept the volatility of the labor market and believe that the way to create a personal safety net is to obtain additional education.
>
> (Schneider and Stevenson, 1999, p. 11)

The problem for the post-1970 generation in Western societies is that they are becoming increasingly aware of the fact that, unlike their predecessors, they are entering adult life as a venture into uncharted territory, whereas the ideology of education and economic planning continues to profess a one-to-one link between qualifications and ongoing career attainment. In the face of this they are making their own pragmatic assessments, but whether they will persist with an accommodation to foreclosed options by pursuing alternative avenues of personal or 'private' interest, or whether resentment about false promises of fulfilment will shape their 'public' or political responses in the future remains a matter of concern.

Multi-dimensional lives

Our research does indicate that those alternative avenues of personal interest are of increasing importance to our participants. There is a definite shift towards more complex life-patterns and multi-dimensional lives, which suggests that they are beginning to rethink the priorities and expectations their parents had encouraged in them. The message we derive from the responses in our Life-Patterns Project to both the large surveys and the interviews is that, whether by choice or constraint, they are already moving beyond the narrow career investments to which they had been led to aspire while still at school.

The changed experience of young women is an important ingredient in this shift of perspective. As we saw in chapter 6, they are the ones for whom increasing participation in post-compulsory education and also in the labour market has been the most dramatic. Despite these added dimensions to the lives of young women of this post-1970 generation, they continue to insist on the importance of what might be considered as either 'traditional' roles – their personal relationships, the prospect of family life, the opportunities for 'private' time with family and friends, notions of 'care' for those who are close to them – or a sense of a balance of personal commitments which blend together the 'private' and 'public' dimensions that were so separated along gender lines in the industrial era. The males in our Life-Patterns Project are also aware of these new dimensions, but for them foreclosed options within the labour market propose a greater threat to what many of them still see as their traditional roles. It is interesting to note, however, that despite this in our sample only about one-third of them are narrowly focused on the model of industrial manhood.

It is important not to exaggerate the significance of this shift or to set up new stereotypes – male and/or female – to replace the old. One of our main reasons for developing a diverse fivefold typology of life-patterns in attempting to make sense of what the participants in our study were telling us, was that they had displayed a broad range of responses about individual priorities in life. Some were more focused on career or on work than others, and some were in the process of changing their priorities for the future, even though it was evident from our findings that the largest grouping – for both males and females – was made up of those adopting 'mixed patterns'.

One of the difficulties we have been confronted with in this research arises from the fact that, apart from education and employment, data on the other important dimensions of young people's lives have proved difficult to document. The old linear categories continue to dominate within most of the large-scale statistical data-bases, and evidence about young people's personal lifestyles, leisure interests and even family priorities tend to be piecemeal, sporadic or market-driven. Apart from a longitudinal study of the leisure patterns of young people in Scotland (Hendry *et al.*, 1993) and a series of studies in other European countries (Gudmundsson, 2000; Mommaas *et al.*, 1996) and also the work of Roberts in Britain (Roberts, 1997) much of the available evidence tends to approach leisure as one side of the work/non-work binary – as a kind of left-over or peripheral category of analysis, which has often ignored the leisure aspects of women's lives because they did not fit the neat work/non-work distinction (Deem 1986). Lifestyle of course is much more than leisure, but the questions asked in many surveys continue to be preoccupied with the old agenda, and conceptually dubious labels such as Generation X and Generation Y are used as cover-all labels which homogenise the real diversity of young people's experience. The labels tend to be applied to rather than derived from young people themselves and, until much more participatory research is done which builds on their own priorities and interests, the gaps in our knowledge about broader dimensions of their lives and how they balance a range of commitments are likely to persist.

There is, therefore, an urgent need to devise new research approaches that can build on the changes that have affected the processes of transition. In the course of this book we have criticised the established linear model of youth transitions derived from the industrial era and have argued that a shift of perspective on youth research is long overdue. We have acknowledged that the structural conditions of that era still persist and factors such as gender, family background and educational attainment still influence the life-course of particular individuals and their ability to gain access to whatever career paths the post-industrial labour market might have to offer. At a theoretical level we have made use of Beck's concept of the risk society as the best means of differentiating between the normal biographies that are still written into many analyses of young people's lives and the choice biographies which represent more clearly the ways in which they are balancing a new life-context for themselves. At the same time, the gaps and inconsistencies in the research data have made it clear to us that contemporary analysis is still too strongly influenced by the discrete transitional categories which are part of the research tradition.

Instead of examining the interconnections and interplay between the different aspects of life, it has become accepted practice to separate them out and concentrate on 'transitions': from school to work, from youth to adulthood, from dependence to independence, from being single to being married, from initial training to ongoing career, and as a result these sequentially separate categories still dictate much of the evidence. Issues related to gender, class and ethnicity are still too often dealt with by means of a binary or two-dimensional analysis – males or females, middle or working class, whites or minorities, public or private (domestic) responsibilities and roles; not which males, females or minorities, nor what kinds of blending or balance of the public and private dimensions of life now shape the priorities, choices and measures of individual and socially approved 'success'. While the evidence definitely shows that an increasing number of the post-1970 generation are developing mixed patterns of life for themselves, how the interconnections between different aspects of their lives are likely to affect their futures and whether some patterns or combinations are likely to prove more lasting in the long term still remain at issue until models of analysis are developed to provide an effective means of evaluating these interconnections and patterns. A first step would be to involve young people much more directly as active partners in the research process, to help us to move beyond the pre-set adult-driven agendas.

Active voice

A major question we have puzzled over many times during the writing of this book is why studies of adolescent development and youth transitions, which recognise the widespread upheavals affecting all aspects of the lives of the young people they are studying, nevertheless continue to analyse and interpret their lives with reference to norms of development and transition based on the very different life experience of the past. One possible answer lies in the obvious success of the established frameworks and the informed understanding they provided of youthful transitions in the industrial era. In each nation and in each school of thought valuable insights were developed which have been used to extend our knowledge on specific aspects of young people's lives. Unfortunately, along with the established success of particular frameworks of research there has also been a considerable degree of academic closure which has prevented inroads being made into the prevailing modes of thinking. Measuring new research against the established literature and the authoritative traditions of a partic-ular nation or a particular discipline has the effect of reducing divergent evidence to what is at best a subtext or else a contextual issue that leaves the accepted wisdom intact. This certainly helps to explain why many of the studies we have examined on the same youth issues but published in different journals or different countries refer almost exclusively to a closed corpus of source material. Often little recognition is given to comparable studies which emanate from a different national setting or a competing academic tradition. The European writings are different from their British counterparts; both are very different from what is written about young people in the United States. Still more surprising, even within the different nations there are competing schools of thought which again rely on quite separate sources and 'authorities' and which present almost contradictory impressions of the lives of the very same younger generation. The bibliographies display the closure.

Nevertheless, this heavy reliance on the exclusive authority of particular academic and national traditions points to what in our view is a more fundamental explanation specific to the area of youth studies. Naive as it might sound, the big problem with young people is that they are not adults, but instead the objects of intensive adult scrutiny and concern. For this reason it would appear naive to suggest that they might know more about what is happening in their own lives than adults who after all were once young themselves. Not only that: for experienced researchers in the field of youth it appears self-evident and certainly far more reliable to measure the experience of youth against the time-tested norms and models because, as they themselves know, the 'experience' of youth is essentially transitory and episodic. On this basis, divergent evidence – such as findings which suggest that that experience has changed fundamentally because of what has occurred over the last quarter century – can legitimately be treated as equally 'transitory and episodic'.

The difficulty is that once the cross-cultural evidence is examined and critically assessed, and once the inherent contradictions in the established literature between the strands of 'crisis' and the 'normative' modelling are taken seriously, the need to pay more attention to evidence from young people and not merely evidence about them on pre-set adult-driven agendas becomes decisive. It is not a question of naively accepting what they have to say, or of ignoring their failings and the inadequacies in their accounts, but it is a question of researching *with* them to uncover the real significance of the changes that they – unlike ourselves – have spent their *whole* lives within.

At a recent major conference on 20–24-year-olds in Australia (Dusseldorp Skills Forum [DSF], 1999), a range of significant and substantial research papers was presented which drew on the (almost exclusively Australian) available contemporary evidence. At an objective level, much of the data presented confirmed the kinds of conclusions we have arrived at in this book, although most of it was based on almost exclusively statistical data-sets rather than on the alternative strands of participatory research. At the subjective level of young people's agency, however, the statistical data and analysis presented a one-sided picture. The undercurrent of choice and complexity evident in a variety of international studies and also communicated by the participants in our longitudinal study was lacking, and an impression was created of passive recipients – expressed in a mechanical metaphor of up and down escalators conveying them to their separate fates in 'the deepening divide'. It brought to mind the comment of Rudd and Evans (1998) about similar analyses of youth transition in the UK, which

> underestimate the degree of choice or agency evident in such processes and there have been few attempts to explain the apparent incompatibility between young people's perceived feelings of autonomy and control and the alleged over-arching often unmediated, influence of 'deterministic' social structures on their lives.
>
> (1998, p. 60–1)

The large-scale statistical data are clearly important for documenting outcomes from the generation as a whole, but this evidence *about* them needs to be balanced by evidence *from* them. Otherwise we run the risk of categorising the risk generation as the 'at-risk' generation, because our data-bases assume an 'almost deterministic macro-sociological perspective of "propulsion" into career trajectories and their associated occupational outcomes, with very little control over the processes on the part of the young people themselves' (Rudd and Evans, 1998, p. 60). The overview of the conference findings hinted at this (DSF, 1999, p. 24).

> Policy development in Australia tends to be rooted in institutional and bureaucratic bases that encourage one dimensional views of young people ... Public policy needs to focus on intermediary structures and agencies that bridge the different worlds inhabited by young people, which deal with the whole of their life experience not just one part of it.

More explicitly, at the conclusion of the conference one of the key speakers drew attention to the largely one-sided preoccupation of the research agenda and expressed concern that two days had been spent talking about young people rather than hearing from young people.

> I think a criticism I have about the last two days is that we have been talking about young adults, and I believe we should be talking with young adults. My experience is that they are highly articulate, they know what their problems are and they have a fair idea about what the solutions could be. They should be involved in any policy development that involves what is going to happen to the future of work and learning for them. They are very clear from the very disadvantaged to the most advantaged about what is wrong with the current system and what changes need to be made to make it work. It would be my ardent hope that one of the next steps of the Dusseldorp Skills Forum would be to actually consult with young adults, and that no policy either from government or any other institution be developed without consultation with young adults. People say that young adults are our future, but *young adults are also our present* and that needs to be acknowledged.
>
> (DSF, 1999, p. 219, our italics)

In our major projects we have maintained a commitment to consulting with the participants in a variety of ways to help shape our research agenda and ensure that their own priorities and interests become the focus of our questions and the substance of our reports. At times this is a difficult approach to adopt, particularly in the quantitative aspects of longitudinal studies, because the need for consistency and comparability of evidence from one year to the next tends to pre-set the agenda in a prescriptive rather than responsive way. Still, we are convinced that if we had not provided at least some degree of active voice to the participants our findings would have been very different – and our questions would have neglected or failed to open up lines of inquiry which have proved most revealing and incisive.

In a joint article we have discussed this issue in some detail elsewhere (Looker and Dwyer, 1998b, pp. 16–18), but would insist here that precisely because the predictability of the old-style linear model of transition is questionable it is now more important than ever to devise ways of uncovering the complexity and ambiguity of transition in post-industrial society. Many of the uncertainties, shifts, tensions and overlapping of interests that young people are experiencing in their daily lives can only be revealed and understood by letting them identify for the researcher what is really important for them and what sense they are making for themselves of the risks and dilemmas in their lives. As we have noted in commenting on the theoretical analysis provided by Furlong and Cartmel, there are definite signs of ambiguity in the efforts young people are making at an individual level to shape adult futures for themselves. If we make the assumption that what they are aiming for is the pre-set agenda of 'normal' adulthood based on the industrial society of the past, it is fair to conclude that they do not have the degrees of individual choice that would enable them effectively to escape the constraints of predetermined conditions of social origin, privilege or disadvantage. But how true is that assumption? We cannot simply take the pre-set agenda for granted; we need to test it against young people's own agendas.

There is a genuine issue of generational change at stake here. If the wide-ranging social and economic changes that have occurred during the post-1970 period in Western societies have changed the conditions of life and future prospects for *both* young and old in those societies, we need to develop new research frameworks of inquiry and analysis that enable us to question assumptions which measure outcomes with reference to the norms of the past. Otherwise we portray members of this generation as uncritical recipients of education and training, or docile and accepting employees for the future, and passive victims of discourses that proponents from a prior generation proclaim to them as inevitable truth and reality. There is a danger here that the experience of a past generation is accepted as 'normative', and in effect belittles the ongoing significance in the new life-patterns that young people today are shaping for themselves.

Bibliography

Adkins, L. (1995) *Gendered Work: Sexuality, Family and the Labour Market*, Buckingham, Open University Press.

Ainley, J. (1998) School Participation, Retention and Outcomes, in Dusseldorp Skills Forum (ed.), *Australia's Youth: Reality and Risk*, Sydney, Dusseldorp Skills Forum.

Ainley, J. and Sheret, M. (1992) *Progress through High School: A Study of Senior Secondary Schooling in New South Wales*, Research Monograph no. 43, Hawthorn, Australian Council for Educational Research.

Ainley, P. (1998) Towards a Learning or a Certified Society? Contradictions in the New Labour Modernization of Lifelong Learning, *Journal of Education Policy*, 13(4), pp. 559–73.

Allahar, A. and Côté, J. (1998) *Richer and Poorer: The Structure of Inequality in Canada*, Toronto, Lorimer.

Amato, P. (1987) *Children in Australian Families*, Sydney, Prentice Hall.

Andres, L., Anisef, P., Krahn, H., Looker, D. and Theissen, V. (1999) The Persistence of Social Structure: Cohort, Class and Gender Effects on the Occupational Aspirations and Expectations of Canadian Youth, *Journal of Youth Studies*, 2(3), pp. 261–82.

Andres Bellamy, L. (1993) Life Trajectories, Action, and Negotiating the Transition from High School, in P. Anisef and P. Axelrod (eds) *Transitions: School to Work in Canada*, Toronto, Thompson.

Anisef, P. and Axelrod, P. (1993) Universities, Graduates and the Marketplace, in P. Anisef and P. Axelrod (eds) *Transitions: School to Work in Canada*, Toronto, Thompson.

Anisef, P., Ashbury, F., Bischoping, K. and Lin, Z. (1996) Post-secondary Education and Underemployment in a Longitudinal Study of Ontario Baby Boomers, *Higher Education Policy*, 9(2), pp. 159–74.

Anisef, P., Axelrod, P., Baichman-Anisef, E., James, C. and Tunittin, A. (2000) *Opportunity and Uncertainty: Life Course Experiences of the Class of '73*, Toronto, University of Toronto Press.

Australian Curriculum Studies Association (ACSA) (1996) *From Alienation to Engagement, Vols 1, 2 and 3*, Belconnen, Australian Curriculum Studies Association.

Australian Education Council (AEC) Review Committee (B. Finn, chair) (1991) Young People's Participation in Post-compulsory Education and Training, report, Canberra, Australian Government Publishing Service.

Ayman-Nolley, S. and Taira, L. (2000) Obsession with the Dark Side of Adolescence: A Decade of Psychological Studies, *Journal of Youth Studies*, 3(1), pp. 35–48.

Ball, S., Maquire, M. and Macrae, S. (2000) *Choices, Pathways and Transitions Post-16*, London, Routledge and Falmer.

Baker, M., Carne, S. and Ha, V. (1995) *Life after Graduation*, Parkville, Institute of Applied Economic and Social Research, University of Melbourne.

Bank, B. J. (1999) Some Dangers of Binary Thinking: Comment on 'Why Smart People Believe that Schools Shortchange Girls', *Gender Issues*, Spring, pp. 83–6.

Batten, M. and Russell, J. (1995) *Students at Risk: A Review of Australian Literature, 1980–1994*, Hawthorn, Australian Council for Educational Research.

Baumohl, J. (1996) *Homelessness in America*, Phoenix, Oryx Press.

Beck, U. (1992) *Risk Society: Towards a New Modernity*, London, Sage.

Beresford, Q. (1993) The Really Hard Cases, *Youth Studies Australia*, 12(4).

Bessant, J. and Hil, R. (eds) (1997) *Youth, Crime and Media*, Hobart, National Clearing House for Youth Studies.

Bessant, J. and Watts, R. (1998) History, Myth Making and Young People in a Time of Change, *Family Matters*, 49, pp. 5–10.

Bessant, J., Sercombe, H. and Watts, R. (1998) *Youth Studies – An Australian Perspective*, Sydney, Longmans.

Biklin, S. K. (1999) 'Narrative Constructions of Memory in Ethnographies of Youth', paper presented at Annual Meeting of the American Educational Research Association, Montreal.

Blackman, S. (1998) The School: 'Poxy Cupid!' An Ethnographic and Feminist Account of a Resistant Female Youth Culture: The New Wave Girls, in Skelton, T. and Valentine, G., 1998 (eds), *Cool Places, Geographies of Youth Cultures*, London, Routledge, pp. 207–28.

Bowles, S. and Gintis, H. (1976) *Schooling in Capitalist America*, New York, Basic Books.

British Youth Council (1992) *The Time of Your Life? The Truth about Being Young in 90s Britain*, London, British Youth Council.

Burdekin, B. (chairman) (1989) *Our Homeless Children – Report of the National Inquiry into Homeless Children*, Human Rights and Equal Opportunity Commission, Canberra, Australian Government Publishing Service.

Bureau of Labor Statistics (1999) *Report on the American Workforce*, Washington, US Department of Labor.

Bynner, J., Chisholm, L. and Furlong, A. (eds) (1997) *Youth, Citizenship and Social Change in a European Context*, Aldershot, Ashgate.

Byrne, S., Constant, A., and Moore, G. (1992) Making Transitions from School to Work, *Educational Leadership*, 49(6), pp. 23–6.

Canadian Labour Force Development Board (CLFDB) (1994) *Putting the Pieces Together: Toward a Coherent Transition System for Canada's Labour Force*, Ottawa, Canadian Labour Force Development Board.

Catan, L. (1998) Review: Youth, Citizenship and Social Change in a European Context, *Journal of Youth Studies*, 1(3), pp. 349–51.

Chamberlain, C. and Mackenzie, D. (1996) School Students at Risk, *Youth Studies Australia*, 15(4), pp. 11–18.

Chamberlain, C. and Mackenzie, D. (1998) *Youth Homelessness: Early Intervention and Prevention*, Sydney, Australian Centre for Equity through Education.

Chaney, D. (1996) *Lifestyles*, London, Routledge.

Chisholm, L. (1997) Initial Transitions between Education, Training and Employment in Learning Society, *International Bulletin of Youth Research* (International Sociological Association), 15, pp. 6–16.

Chisholm, L. Buchnen, P., Kruger, H. and Brown, P. (eds) (1990) *Childhood, Youth and Social Change: A Comparative Perspective*, London, Falmer.

Church, A. and Ainley, P. (1987) Inner City Decline and Regeneration: Young People and the Labour Market, in P. Brown and D. Ashton (eds) *Education, Unemployment and Labour Markets*, Lewes, Falmer.

Cohen, P. (1997) *Rethinking the Youth Question: Education, Labour and Cultural Studies*, London, Macmillan.

Cohen, S. (1972) *Folk Devils and Moral Panics: The Creation of Mods and Rockers*, London, MacGibbon and Kee.

Coleman, J. (1974) *Youth: Transition to Adulthood. Report of the Panel on Youth of the Resident's Science Advisory Committee*, Chicago, Chicago University Press.

Coleman, J. and Warren-Adamson, C. (eds) (1992) *Youth Policy in the 1990s*, London, Routledge.

Commission on the Skills of the American Workforce (1990) *America's Choice: High Skills or Low Wages!* Commission on the Skills of the American Workforce, Rochester.

Commonwealth of Australia (1994) *Working Nation: Policies and Programs*, Canberra, Australian Government Publishing Service.

Commonwealth Schools Commission (1980) *Schooling for 15 and 16 Year Olds*, Canberra, Australian Government Publishing Service.

Commonwealth Schools Commission (1984) *Girls and Tomorrow: The Challenge for Schools*, Canberra, Australian Government Publishing Service.

Connell, R. (1994) Poverty and Education, *Harvard Education Review*, 64(2), pp. 125–49.

Connell, R., Ashenden, D., Kessler, S. and Dowsett, G. (1982) *Making the Difference*, Sydney, Allen and Unwin.

Côté, J. (2000) *Arrested Adulthood*, New York, New York University Press.

Côté, J. and Allahar, A. (1994) *Generation on Hold: Coming of Age in the Late Twentieth Century*, Toronto, Stoddart.

Crowhurst, M. (1999) Are You Gay Sir? Part 1, *Melbourne Studies in Education*, ed. J. Wyn, 40(2), pp. 89–104.

Davies, Bronwyn (1993) *Shards of Glass*, Sydney, Allen and Unwin.

Deem, R. (1986) *All Work and No Play?* Milton Keynes, Open University Press.

Department of Employment, Education and Training (DEET) (1987) *Completing Secondary School in Australia: A Socio-economic and Regional Analysis*, Canberra, Australian Government Publishing Service.

Department of Employment, Education and Training (DEET) (1990) *Higher Education Series: Urban and Rural Participation*. Canberra, Australian Government Publishing Service.

Department of Employment, Education and Training (DEET) (1993) *The Australian Youth Survey*, Profile 2, Canberra, Australian Government Publishing Service.

Department of Employment/Department of Education and Science (1991) *Education and Training for the 21st Century*, London, HMSO.

du Bois-Reymond, M. (1998) 'I Don't Want to Commit Myself Yet': Young People's Life Concepts, *Journal of Youth Studies*, 1(1), pp. 63–79.

Dusseldorp Skills Forum (1999) *Australia's Young Adults: The Deepening Divide*, Sydney, Dusseldorp Skills Forum.

Dwyer, P. (1989) A Summary and Analysis of the Burdekin Report, in National Clearing House for Youth Studies (ed.) *Responses to Burdekin*, Hobart, National Clearing House for Youth Studies.

Dwyer, P. (1994a) The New Managerialism and the Rhetoric of Outcomes in Post-compulsory Education Policy, *Discourse* 15(2), pp. 13–21.

Dwyer, P (1994b) Participation or Forced Retention? Some Implications of Improved School Participation Rates, *Unicorn*, (20)2, pp. 58–66.

Dwyer, P. (1995a) Pathways in Post-compulsory Education – From Metaphor to Practice, *Australian Journal of Education*, 39(2), pp. 126–45.

Dwyer, P. (1995b) Postcompulsory Education in Australia and the Domination of Truth, *Journal of Education Policy*, 10(1), pp. 95–105.

Dwyer, P (1995c) Disjuncture between Pathways Policy and Student Outcomes: Experience of Early School Leavers, *Australian Journal of Education*, 39(3), pp. 265–78.

Dwyer, P. (1996a) *Opting Out: Early School Leavers and the Degeneration of Youth Policy*, Hobart, National Clearing House for Youth Studies.

Dwyer, P. (1996b) Finn Pathways, Employment and Disaffiliated Youth: The Deferred Agenda, in J. Spierings *et al.* (eds) *Jobs for Young Australians*, Adelaide, Social Justice Research Foundation, pp. 110–18.

Dwyer, P. (1997) Outside the Educational Mainstream: Foreclosed Options in Youth Policy, *Discourse*, 18(1), pp. 71–85.

Dwyer, P. and Wyn, J. (1998) Post-compulsory Education Policy in Australia and its Impact on Participant Pathways and Outcomes in the 1990s, *Journal of Education Policy*, 13(3), pp. 285–300.

Dwyer, P., Wilson, B. and Woock, R. (1984) *Confronting School and Work*, Sydney, Allen and Unwin.

Dwyer, P., Harwood, A., Poynter, G. and Tyler, D. (1997) *Participant Pathways and Outcomes in Vocational Education and Training: 1992–1995*, Research Report 14, Melbourne, Youth Research Centre, pp. 1–56.

Dwyer, P., Harwood, A. and Tyler, D. (1998a) *Life-Patterns, Choices, Careers: 1991–1998*, Research Report 17, Youth Research Centre, University of Melbourne, pp. 1–59.

Dwyer, P., Stokes, H., Tyler, D. and Holdsworth, R. (1998b) *Negotiating Staying and Returning*, East Melbourne, Victoria Department of Education, pp. 1–74.

Dwyer, P., Harwood, A., Costin, G., Landy, M., Towsty, D. and Wyn, J. (1999) *Combined Study and Work Paths in VET: Policy Implications and Analysis*. Leabrook, National Centre for Vocational Education Research.

Eckersley, R. (1988) *Casualties of Change: The Predicament of Youth in Australia*, Commission for the Future, Canberra, Australian Government Publishing Service.

Eckersley, R. (1998) Rising Psychosocial Problems among Young People, *Family Matters*, 50, pp. 50–2.

Elder, G. Jr, (ed.) (1985) *Life Course Dynamics: Trajectories and Transitions*, Ithaca, Cornell University Press.

Epstein, D. (1997) Boyz' Own Stories: Masculinities and Sexualities in Schools, *Gender and Education*, 9(1) pp. 105–11.

Erikson, E. (ed.) (1965) *The Challenge of Youth*, New York, Doubleday.

Evans, K. and Heinz, W. (1994) *Becoming Adults in England and Germany*, London and Bonn, Anglo-German Foundation.

Evans, G. and Poole, M. (1991) *Young Adult's Self-Perceptions and Life Contexts*, London, Falmer.

Featherstone, M. (1991) *Consumer Culture and Postmodernism*, London, Sage.

Fensham P. (ed.) (1986) *Alienation from Schooling*, London: Routledge and Kegan Paul.

Finnegan, W. (1998) *Cold New World*, New York, Random House.

Freeman, R. and Katz, L (1994) *Working under Different Rules*, New York, Rusell Sage.

Furlong, A. and Biggart, A. (1999) Framing 'Choices': A Longitudinal Study of Occupational Aspirations among 13- to 16-Year-Olds, *Journal of Education and Work*, 12(1), pp. 21–36.

Furlong, A. and Cartmel, F. (1997) *Young People and Social Change: Individualisation and Risk in Late Modernity*, Buckingham, Open University Press.

Galbraith, J. K. (1992) *The Culture of Contentment*, Harmondsworth, Penguin.

Gilbert, R. and Gilbert, P. (1998) *Masculinity Goes to School*, Sydney, Allen and Unwin.

Giroux, H. A. (1996) *Fugitive Cultures: Race, Violence, and Youth*, New York, Routledge.

Goldscheider, F. and Goldscheider, C. (1999) *The Changing Transition to Adulthood*, Thousand Oaks, Sage.

Graber, J., Brooks-Gunn, J. and Petersen, A. (eds) (1996) *Transitions through Adolescence*, Mahwah, Lawrence Erlbaum Associates.

Graham, S. (1992) Most of the Subjects were White and Middle Class, *American Psychologist*, 5, pp. 629–39.

Grant Foundation (1988) *The Forgotten Half*, Washington, Grant Foundation.

Green, A. (1991) The Reform of Post-16 Education and Training and the Lessons from Europe, *Journal of Education Policy*, 6(3), pp. 327–39.

Greenberger, E. and Steinberg, L. (1986) *When Teenagers Work: The Psychological and Social Costs of Adolescent Employment*, New York, Basic Books.

Gregory, R. (1995) Higher Education Expansion and Economic Change in Australia, *Australian Bulletin of Labour*, 21(4), pp. 295–322.

Gregson, J. (1995) The School-to-Work Movement and Youth Apprenticeship in the U.S.: Educational Reform and Democratic Renewal? *Journal of Industrial Teacher Education*, 32(3), 7–29.

Griffin, C. (1993) *Representations of Youth*, Cambridge, Polity.

Gudmundsson, G. (2000) Youth Research at Crossroads: Sociological and Interdisciplinary Youth Research in the Nordic Countries, *Journal of Youth Studies*, 3(2), pp. 127–45.

Hall, G. Stanley (1904) *Adolescence: Its Psychology and its Relation to Physiology, Anthropology, Sociology, Sex, Crime, Religion and Education*, 2 vols, New York, Appleton and Co.

Hamilton, S. and Hamilton, M. (1992) A Progress Report on Apprenticeships, *Educational Leadership*, 49(6), pp. 44–7.

Haveman, R. and Wolfe, B. (1994) *Succeeding Generations*, New York, Russell Sage Foundation.

Haworth, J. T. (1997) *Work, Leisure and Well-being*, London, Routledge.

Heaven, P. (1994) *Contemporary Adolescence, a Social Psychological Approach*, Melbourne, Macmillan.

Heggen, K. and Dwyer, P. (1998) New Policies, New Options: Learning from Changing Student Transitions at two Ends of the World, *Journal of Research in Post-Compulsory Education*, 3(3), pp. 261–77.

Heinz, W. R. (2000) Youth Transitions and Employment in Germany, *International Social Science Journal*, 164, pp. 161–70.

Heinz, W. R. (ed) (1991) *Theoretical Advances in Life Course Research*. Weinheim, Deutscher Studien Verlag.

Henderson, I. (1999) Secret Million Can't Find Work and Most of Them are Women, *The Australian*, 10 March.

Hendry, L., Shucksmith, J., Love, J. G. and Glendinning, A. (1993) *Young People's Leisure and Lifestyles*, London, Routledge.

Henry, M. (1996) OECD and Educational Policy Development in Australia, *Discourse*, (17)1, pp. 101–6.

Hobsbawm, E. (1994) *The Age of Extremes*, New York, Pantheon Books.

Holden E. (1992) *Getting a Life: Pathways and Early School Leavers*, Working Paper no. 9, Melbourne, Youth Research Centre.

Holden, E. (1993) *Services and Early School Leavers*, Working Paper no. 10, Melbourne, Youth Research Centre.

Holden, E. and Dwyer P. (1992) *Making the Break – Leaving School Early*, Working Paper no. 8, Melbourne, Youth Research Centre.

Holmes, G. (1995) *Helping Teenagers into Adulthood*, Westport, Praeger.

Hutson, S. and Liddiard, M. (1994) *Youth Homeless, The Construction of a Social Issue*, London, Macmillan.

Ianni, F. and Orr, M. (1996) Dropping Out, in Graber *et al.* (eds) *Transitions through Adolscence*.

Istance, D., Rees, G. and Williamson, H. (1994) *Young People Not in Education, Training or Employment in South Glamorgan*, Cardiff, South Glamorgan Training and Enterprise Council/University of Wales.

Jencks, C. (1973) *Inequality: A Reassessment of the Effect of Family and Schooling in America*, London, Allen Lane.

Johnson, L. (1993) *The Modern Girl, Girlhood and Growing Up*, Sydney, Allen and Unwin.

Jones, G. (2000) Experimenting with Households and Inventing 'Home', *International Social Science Journal*, 164, pp. 185–94.

Jones, G. and Wallace, C. (1992) *Youth, Family and Citizenship*, Buckingham, Open University Press.

Jordan, A. (1995) Review, *Social Security Journal*, June, pp. 167–70.

Kenway, J. and Willis, S. (1995) *Critical Visions. Rewriting the Future of Work, Schooling and Gender*, Canberra, Commonwealth of Australia.

Kenway, J., Willis, S., Blackmore, J. and Rennie, L. (1994) Making 'Hope Practical' Rather than 'Despair Convincing': Feminist Post-structuralism, Gender Reform and Educational Change, *British Journal of Sociology of Education*, 15(2), pp. 187–210.

Klein, N. (2000) *No Logo*, London, Flamingo.

Krahn, H. and Lowe, G. (1991) Transitions to Work: Findings from a Longitudinal Study of High School and University Graduates in Three Canadian Cities, in D. Ashton and G. Lowe (eds) *Making Their Way: Education, Training and the Labour Market in Canada and Britain*, Toronto, University of Toronto Press.

Lamb, S. (1994) Dropping Out of School in Australia: Recent Trends in Participation and Outcomes, *Youth and Society*, 26(2), pp. 194–222.

Lamb, S., Dwyer, P. and Wyn, J. (2000) *Non-Completion of School in Australia: The Changing Patterns of Participation and Outcomes*, Camberwell, Australian Council for Educational Research.

Land, H. (1996) The Crumbling Bridges between Childhood and Adulthood, in J. Brannen and M. O'Brien (eds) *Children in Families, Research and Policy*, London, Falmer.

Lasch, C. (1995) *The Revolt of the Elites*, New York, Norton.

Lerner, R. M. (1995) *America's Youth in Crisis*, Thousand Oaks, Sage.

Lesko, N. (1996a) Denaturalising Adolescence: The Politics of Contemporary Representations, *Youth and Society*, 28(2), pp. 139–61.

Lesko, N. (1996b) Past, Present, and Future Conceptions of Adolescence, *Educational Theory*, 46(4), pp. 453–72.

Levin, M. A. and Ferman, B. (1985) *The Political Hand – Policy Implementation and Youth Employment Programs*, New York, Pergamon.

Levine, D. (1994) The School-to-Work Opportunities Act: A Flawed Prescription for Education Reform, *Educational Foundations*, 8(3), pp. 33–51.

Lingard, R. and Rizvi, F. (1992) A Reply to Barcan: Theorising the Ambiguities of Devolution, *Discourse*, 13(1), pp. 111–23.

Livingstone, D. (1998) *The Education-Jobs Gap: Underemployment or Economic Democracy*, Boulder, Westview Press.

Looker, E. D. and Dwyer, P. (1998a) Education and Negotiated Reality: Complexities Facing Rural Youth in the 1990s, *Journal of Youth Studies*, 1(1), pp. 5–22.

Looker, E. D. and Dwyer, P. (1998b) Rethinking Research on the Education Transitions of Youth in the 1990s, *Journal of Research in Post-Compulsory Education*, 3(1), pp. 5–23.

Lunt, P. and Livingstone, S (1992) *Mass Consumption and Personal Identity*, Buckingham, Open University Press.

McDonald, K. (1999) *Struggles for Subjectivity*, Cambridge, Cambridge University Press.

McDonald, P. (1997) *Young People in Australia Today: A Socio-demographic Perspective*, Canberra, Research School of Social Sciences, Australian National University.

MacDonald, R. (1991) Risky Business? Youth in the Enterprise Culture, *Journal of Education Policy*, 6(3), pp. 255–69.

MacDonald, R. (ed.) (1997)*Youth, the 'Underclass' and Social Exclusion*, London, Routledge.

MacDonald, R. (1998) Youth, Transitions and Social Exclusion: Some Issues for Youth Research in the UK, *Journal of Youth Studies*, 1(2), pp. 163–75.

McLaren, A. T. (1996) Coercive Invitations: How Young Women in School Make Sense of Mothering and Waged Labour, *British Journal of Education*, 17(3), pp. 279–98.

MacLaughlin, M. (1999) Comparing Learning and Work for Young Adults in Australia and Canada, in Dusseldorp Skills Forum (ed.) *Australia's Young Adults: The Deepening Divide*, Sydney, Dusseldorp Skills Forum.

McLoyd, V. and Steinberg, L. (1998) *Studying Minority Adolescents*, Mahwah, Lawrence Erlbaum Associates.

McRobbie, A. (1997) Bodies, Space, Capitalism: Girls and Youth Cultures in Contemporary Britain, in D. Morley, C. Sparks and T. Hanada (eds) *Cultural Studies, East and West*, London, Routledge.

Males, M. (1998) *The Scapegoat Generation: America's War on Adolescents*, Monroe, Common Courage Press.

Males, M. (1999) *Framing Youth: 10 Myths about the Next Generation*, Monroe, Common Courage Press.

Mann, D. (1986) 'Can We Help Dropouts? Thinking about the Undoable', in G. Natriello (ed.) *School Dropouts-Patterns and Politics*, New York, Teachers' College Press.

Marginson, S. (1993) *Education and Public Policy in Australia*, Cambridge, Cambridge University Press.

Marginson, S. (1999) Young Adults in Higher Education, in Dusseldorp Skills Forum (ed.) *Australia's Young Adults: The Deepening Divide*, Sydney, Dusseldorp Skills Forum.

Martino, W. (1999) Disruptive Moments in the Education of Boys: Debating Populist Discourses on Boys, Schooling and Masculinities, *Discourse*, 20(2) pp. 298–294.

Miles, S. (1995) Towards an Understanding of the Relationship between Youth Identities and Consumer Culture, *Youth and Policy*, 51, pp. 35–45.

Miles, S. Cliff, D. and Burr, V. (1998) 'Fitting In and Sticking Out': Consumption, Consumer Meanings and the Construction of Young People's Identities, *Journal of Youth Studies*, 1(1) pp. 81–96.

Miller, P. (1990) Training in the Youth Labour Market, *Labour, Economics and Productivity*, 2, pp. 1–26.

Mills, C. Wright. (1959) *The Sociological Imagination*, Oxford, Oxford University Press.

Mishel, L., Bernstein, J. and Schmitt, J. (1999) *The State of Working America 1998–99*, Ithaca, Cornell University Press.

Mitterauer, M. (1993) *A History of Youth*, G. Dunphy, (trans.), Oxford, Blackwell.

Mizen, P., Bolton, A. and Pole, C. (1999) School Age Workers, *Work, Employment and Society*, 13(3). pp. 423–38.

Mommaas, H., van der Poel, H., Bramham, P. and Henry, I. P. (1996) *Leisure Research in Europe: Methods and Traditions*, Wallingford, CAB International.

Morris, A. (chair) (1995) *Report on Aspects of Youth Homelessness*, Canberra, Australian Government Publishing Service.

Mortimer, J. T. and Finch, M. D. (eds) (1996) *Adolescents, Work and Family: An Intergenerational Developmental Analysis*, Thousand Oaks, Sage.

Murray, C. (1984) *Losing Ground: American Social Policy 1950–80*, New York, Basic Books.

Murray, C. (1990) *The Emerging British Underclass*, London, Institute of Economic Affairs.

Murray, C. (1994) *Underclass: The Crisis Deepens*, London, Institute of Economic Affairs.

Nava, M. (1984) Youth Service Provision, Social Order and the Question of Girls, in A. McRobbie and M. Nava (eds) *Gender and Generation*, London, Macmillan.

Nagel, U. and Wallace, C. (1997) Participation and Identification in Risk Societies: European Perspectives, in J. Bynner., L. Chisholm. and A. Furlong (eds) *Youth, Citizenship and Social Change in a European Context*, Aldershot, Ashgate.

Nickell, S. and Bell, B. (1995) The Collapse in Demand for the Unskilled and Unemployment Across the OECD, *Oxford Review of Economic Policy*, 11(1), pp. 40–62.

Organisation for Economic Cooperation and Development (OECD)/Centre for Educational Research and Innovation (CERI) (1983)*Education and Work: The Views of the Young*, Paris, OECD/CERI.

Organisation for Economic Cooperation and Development (OECD) (1987) *Structural Adjustment and Economic Performance*, Paris, OECD.

Palmer, D. and Collard, L. (1993) Aboriginal Young People and Youth Subcultures, in R. White (ed.) *Youth Subcultures, Theory, History and the Australian Experience*, Hobart, National Clearinghouse for Youth Studies.

Parliament of the Commonwealth of Australia (1996) *Truancy and Exclusion from School*, Canberra, Australian Government Publishing Service.

Pittman, K. (1992) From Deterrence to Development, in Council of Chief State School Officers, *Investing in Youth: A Compilation of Recommended Policies and Practices*, Washington.

Power, C. (1984) Factors Influencing Retentivity and Satisfaction with Secondary Schooling, *Australian Journal of Education*, 28(2).

Preston, A. (1997) Where Are We Now with Human Capital Theory in Australia? *The Economic Record*, 73(220), pp. 51–78.

Probert, B. and MacDonald, F. (1999) Young Women: Poles of Experience in Work and Parenting, in Dusseldorp Skills Forum (ed.), *Australia's Young Adults: The Deepening Divide*, Sydney, Dusseldorp Skills Forum.

Probert, B. and Wilson, B. (eds) (1993) *Pink Collar Blues, Work, Gender and Technology*, Melbourne, Melbourne University Press.

Raffo, C. and Reeves, M. (2000) Youth Transitions and Social Exclusion: Developments in Social Capital, *Journal of Youth Studies*, 3(2), pp. 147–66.

Rattansi, A. and Phoenix, A. (1997) Rethinking Youth Identities: Modernist and Postmodernist Frameworks, in J. Bynner, L. Chisholm and A. Furlong (eds) *Youth, Citizenship and Social Change in a European Context*, Aldershot, Ashgate.

Redhead, S., Wynne, D. and O'Connor, J. (1997) (eds) *The Club Cultures Reader*, Oxford, Blackwell.

Redpath, L. (1994) Education – Job Mismatch among Canadian University Graduates: Implications for Employers and Educators, *Canadian Journal of Higher Education*, (24)2, pp. 89–114.

Reed, L. (1999) Troubling Boys and Disturbing Discourses on Masculinity and Schooling: A Feminist Exploration of Current Debates and Interventions Concerning Boys in School, *Gender and Education*, 11(1), pp. 93–110.

Rifkin, J. (1995) *The End of Work*, Putnam, New York.

Roberts, H. and Sachdev, D. (eds) (1996) *Young People's Social Attitudes*, Ilford, Bernados.

Roberts, K. (1997) Work and Leisure in Young People's Lives, in J. T. Haworth (ed.) *Work, Leisure and Well-being*, London, Routledge, pp. 145–64.

Rosenthal, D., Moore, S. and Buzwell, S. (1994) Homeless Youths: Sexual and Drug-related Behaviour, Sexual Beliefs and HIV/AIDS Risk, *AIDS Care*, 6, pp. 83–94.

Rossi, R. and Montgomery, A. (1994) *Education Reforms and Students at Risk: A Review of the Current State of the Art*, McREL: Mid-Continent Regional Educational Laboratory, US Department of Education, Washington, located at http://www.mcrel.org.

Rowe, K. (1992) *Victorian Profiles Program 1991: Technical Report*, Melbourne, University of Melbourne, Centre of Applied Educational Research.

Rowse, T. (1978) *Australian Liberalism and National Character*, Melbourne, Kibble.

Rudd, P. and Evans, K. (1998) Structure and Agency in Youth Transitions: Student Experiences of Vocational Further Education, *Journal of Youth Studies*, 1(1) pp. 39–62.

Schneider, B. and Stevenson, D. (1999) *The Ambitious Generation*, New Haven, Yale University Press.

Senate Standing Committee on Employment Education and Training (SSCEET) (1992) *Wanted: Our Future*, Canberra, Parliament of the Commonwealth of Australia.

Senior Secondary Assessment Board of South Australia (1994) *SSABSA Statistics 1992, Participation and Performance*, Wayville, SSABSA.

Sennett, R. (1998) *The Corrosion of Character*, New York, Norton.

Shears, L. and Matthews, J. (1983) *Youth Policies*, Melbourne, Office of Co-ordinator General of Education.

Smith, C. and Rojewski, J. (1993) School-to-Work Transition, Alternatives for Educational Reform, *Youth and Society*, 25(2), pp. 222–50.

Spierings, J., Voorendt, I. and Spoehr, J. (1996) *Jobs for Young Australians*, Adelaide, Social Justice Research Foundation.

Stern, D., Bailey, T. and Merritt, D. (1997) *School-to-Work Policy Insights from Recent International Developments*, Berkeley, National Center for Research in Vocational Education.

Stern, D., Mcmillion, M., Hopkins, C. and Stone, J. (1990) Work Experience for Students in High School and College, *Youth and Society*, 21(3), pp. 255–389.

Strauss, A. (1987) *Qualitative Analysis for Social Scientists*, Cambridge, Cambridge University Press.

Sum, A., Harrington, P. and Goedicke, W. (1987) One-fifth of the Nation's Teenagers, *Youth and Society*, 18(3).

Swadener, B. B. and Lubeck, S. (1995) (eds) *Children and Families 'at Promise'*, Albany, State University of New York Press.

Sweet, R. (1992) Can Finn Deliver Vocational Competence? *Unicorn*, 18(1), 31–43.

Sweet, R. (1993) Changing Patterns of Work and Education, in D. Anderson and C. Blakers (eds) *Youth, Transition and Social Research*, Canberra, Australian National University Press.

Sweet, R. (1997) *School-Industry Programs*, Sydney, Dusseldorp Skills Forum.

Teese, R. (2000) *Academic Success and Social Power*, Melbourne, Melbourne University Press.

Teese, R., Polesel, J., and McLean, G. (1993) *Locational Disadvantage in Educational Outcomes: A Geographical Analysis of Curriculum Access and School Success in Victoria*, Melbourne, Youth Research Centre.

Teese, R., Davies, M., Charlton, M. and Polesel, J. (1995) *Who Wins at School?*, Canberra, Commonwealth of Australia.

Teichler, U. (1989) Research on Higher Education and Work in Europe, *European Journal of Education*, 24(3), pp. 223–48.

Trottier, C., Cloutier, R. and Laforce, L. (1996) Vocational Integration of University Graduates: Typology and Multivariate Analysis, *International Sociology*, (11)1, pp. 91–108.

United States Department of Labor (1999) *Futurework: Trends and Challenges of Work in the 21st Century*, Washington DC, US Department of Labor.

Van Roosmalen, E. and Krahn, H. (1996) *Boundaries of Youth, Youth and Society*, 28(1), pp. 3–39.

Walker, J. (1986) *Louts and Legends: Male Youth Culture in an Inner City School*, Sydney, Allen and Unwin.

Wallace, C. (1989) Social Reproduction and School Leavers: A Longitudinal Perspective, in K. Hurrelmann and U. Engels (eds) *The Social World of Adolescents: International Perspectives*, New York, de Gruyter.

Wexler, P. (1992) *Becoming Somebody: Toward a Social Psychology of School*, London, Falmer.

White, R. (1994) The Making of a Youth Underclass, Policy Issues Forum, *Journal of Social Policy Issues*, Autumn, pp. 22–8.

White, R. (1995) *Young People, Social Resources and the Underground Economy*, Melbourne, Youth Research Centre.

Whyte, S. and Probert, B. (1991) *Young Workers in Technologically Advanced Industries*, Hobart, National Youth Affairs Advisory Scheme/National Clearinghouse for Youth Studies.

Williams, T., Long, M., Carpenter, P. and Hayden, M. (1993) *Entering Higher Education in the 1980s*, Canberra, Australian Government Publishing Service.

Williamson, H. (1996) Policy Responses to Youth Unemployment: Cultures, Careers and Consequences for Young People, in J. Spierings *et al.* (eds) *Jobs for Young Australians*, Conference Proceedings, Adelaide, Young Australians Conference Organising Committee.

Williamson, H. (1997) 'Status ZerO Youth and the 'Underclass': Some Considerations', in R. Macdonald (ed.) (1997) *Youth, the 'Underclass' and Social Exclusion*, London, Routledge, pp. 83–95.

Willis, P. (1977) *Learning to Labour: How Working Class Kids Get Working Class Jobs*, Farnborough, Saxon House.

Willis, S. (1998) Teens at Work, Negotiating the Jobless Future, in J. Austin and N. M. Willard, (eds) *Generations of Youth. Youth Subcultures and History in 20th Century America*, New York, New York University Press.

Withers, G. and Batten, M. (1995) *Programs for At-Risk Youth: A Review of American, Canadian and British Literature since 1984*, Hawthorn, Australian Council for Educational Research.

Women's Bureau (1993) *Women's Employment and Education Experience in the Recession and Recovery*, Canberra, Australian Government Publishing Service.

Wooden, M. and VandenHeuvel, A. (1999) The Labour Market for Young Adults, in Dusseldorp Skills Forum (ed.) *Australia's Young Adults: the Deepening Divide*, Sydney, Dusseldorp Skills Forum.

Wright, A., Headlam, F. and Ozolins, U. (1978) *Outcomes of Schooling: Aspects of Success and Failure*, Canberra, Australian Government Publishing Service.

Wyn, J. (1994) Young Women and Sexually Transmitted Diseases: the Issues for Public Health, *Australian Journal of Public Health*, 18(1), pp. 32–9.

Wyn, J. and Lamb, S. (1996) Early School Leaving in Australia: Issues for Education and Training Policy, *Journal of Education Policy*, 11(2), pp. 259–68.

Wyn J. and White, R. (1997) *Rethinking Youth*, London, Sage.

Wyn, J. and White, R. (2000) Negotiating Social Change – The Paradox of Youth, *Youth and Society*, 32(2), 165–83.

Wyn J., Stokes H. and Stafford J. (1998) *Young People Living in Rural Australia in the 1990s*, Research Report 16, Melbourne, Youth Research Centre.

Wynne, D. (1998) *Leisure, Lifestyle and the New Middle Class*, London, Routledge.

Yates, L. (1997) Gender, Ethnicity and the Inclusive Curriculum: An Episode in the Policy Framing of Australian Education, in C. Marshall (ed.) *Feminist Critical Policy Analysis*, London, Falmer.

Yates, L. and Leder, G. (1996) *Student Pathways. A Review and Overview of National Databases on Gender Equity*, Canberra, Commonwealth of Australia.

Index

adulthood and youth 1–2, 25–34, 49–50, 55–6, 65, 76–80, 95–6, 119–21, 127, 131, 170–4, 188–90, 199–201, 205
age and youth 33, 55–6, 76–9, 125, 127, 170, 171, 173
Ainley, P. 59–60, 85, 121
Andres, L. 31, 101–2, 117, 128, 188
Anisef, P. 61, 77, 180
at risk categories 42–4, 55–6, 57–8, 85–6, 113, 145, 148–9, 150–1, 154, 163–4, 165
Australia: early school leavers 37–41, 46–56, 73, 74, 112, 156, 164; education policy 18, 37–8, 41, 51–9, 63–5, 78,120, 191, 193, 197; priorities of youth 1–2, 26–32, 104–11, 168, 177–8, 190, 199–201; retention rates 60, 63–5, 72, 99, 100, 112; youth labour market 2, 38, 60, 84, 106–13; see also choices of youth

Beck, U. 83, 86–9, 187, 200
Bessant, J. 154–6
Britain 2, 20, 25, 38–41, 43, 53, 59–60, 66–7, 77, 79–85, 91–2, 112, 123, 125, 146–7, 162, 174, 187, 189, 196, 203

Canada 2, 20, 61–3, 69–73, 79–83, 101–2, 110–11, 117–18, 128, 132, 180–1, 187
careers 12–18, 49–56, 61, 101–2, 108–12, 118, 120–2, 179–82, 184–5, 190–1, 193

Chaney, D. 88, 94
Chisholm, L. 79, 81, 85, 95, 173
choices of youth 4, 11–13, 15, 20–5, 28–32, 41, 47, 77–8, 83, 86–9, 91–6, 123, 128–9, 162, 174–5, 176–9, 184–5, 187–9, 190, 192, 199–201
Connell, R. 58, 135, 160–1, 163
Côté, J. 34, 62, 69–73, 79, 90, 96, 170, 180, 187

du Bois-Reymond, M. 12, 27–8, 79–84, 88, 94, 123, 128, 170, 197

Eckersley, R. 154–5, 166
education: inequalities 29, 93, 117–18; outcomes 3, 12–18, 49–56, 61–6, 72–4, 99–102, 114–22, 133–5, 179–82, 183–5, 190–1, 193; policy 3, 25, 31, 33–4, 37–41, 51–6, 100, 159, 161, 163, 191, 197; post-compulsory participation 1, 37–41, 63–5, 70–4, 82, 99, 100, 111, 113, 120, 134, 180–3, 190–1, 197; re-entry 36–7, 54–6; retention rates 60, 63–5, 72, 99, 112, 149; and transitions 3, 9–13, 35–39, 82, 99
employment: and careers 12–13, 16–18, 65–6, 75, 179–82, 190–1, 193; and early school leavers 35–8, 43, 49–50, 68; and financial security 26–7, 30, 186;

employment (*continued*)
  and flexible labour markets 3, 15,
  17–18, 32, 60–3, 78, 120–22,
  171, 179, 181, 185, 191, 193,
  198; knowledge society 17, 59,
  69, 74, 121, 191, 193, 197
Europe 2, 20, 28, 71, 79–83, 90,
  119–120, 128, 162, 172, 174,
  175–6, 197
Evans, K. 12–13, 79–84, 89, 90,
  92, 123, 189, 196, 203

family: changes 77–8, 86–7, 93, 96,
  146–7, 168, 170; influences
  101–2, 103–4, 142, 152, 157–9,
  164, 168; living with parents
  19–20, 116, 174; parental
  support 19, 35, 47, 50, 75, 93;
  pressures 28–9, 48; priorities
  26–7, 105, 187 190
females: and careers 21–3, 31, 51,
  61–2, 104–6, 128, 132, 184–5,
  199–201; and education 72–4,
  117–18, 128, 133–6, 199; and
  identity 77, 104–5, 124–6,
  128–9, 136–7, 140–1, 199–201;
  and sexual relations 137–9, 144;
  see also gender
Finnegan, W. 41–3, 46, 85, 93, 123
Furlong, A. 70–1, 79, 87, 89, 91,
  92, 93, 95, 123, 171, 187, 196,
  205

gender: and identity 77, 124–6,
  128–9, 136–7, 140–1, 171;
  diversity 21–3, 31, 51, 61–2,
  104–6, 117, 133–6; inequalities
  61–2, 72–4, 118, 124, 129–30,
  182–3, 184–5
Giroux, H. A. 85, 92, 150, 152–3
Gudmundsson, G. 90, 175–6, 200

Heggen, K. 71, 119–20
Heinz, W. 79, 173, 174
Holden, E. 4, 47–50, 53–4, 165
homelessness 43, 161–5

identity formation 1, 25–34, 46,
  52–6, 77–9, 91, 124–6, 128–9,
  136–7, 144, 170–5, 177–8,

188–90, 191, 192, 199–201,
  205
inequality: class 29, 45, 71–2, 73,
  88–9, 133–4; educational 29, 73,
  93, 117–18, 133–4; gender 51,
  61–2, 72–4, 124, 129–30,
  182–5

Jones, G. 20, 170, 173, 174

Kenway, J. 128, 129
Klein, N. 32, 192–3

Lamb, S. 73–4, 133
Lerner, R. M. 85–6, 150–2, 173
Lesko, N. 78–9, 170
Life-Patterns Project 4, 9–13,
  18–21, 26–32, 80, 84, 113–22,
  169, 175, 176–9, 181–2, 183–7,
  188–90, 196
lifestyles and leisure 2–3, 14, 26–8,
  34, 77, 88, 90, 94–5, 126, 137,
  192, 199–201
Looker, E. D. 4, 71, 79–83, 89,
  123, 172, 173, 176, 177, 204

MacDonald, R. 43, 67, 91, 123,
  146–7, 156, 167, 171
mainstream 37, 39, 45, 57–63, 66,
  85–6, 93, 112–13, 141, 145, 154,
  164, 177–8
Males, M. 57, 154, 155
males: and careers 21–3, 31, 61–2,
  104–6, 182–5; and education
  72–4, 117, 132–6; and identity
  77, 104–6, 129, 131; and sexual
  relations 137–9; *see also* gender
marginalisation of youth 41–3,
  46–56, 65–9, 93
Marginson, S. 73, 124, 130, 197
media and youth 14, 57, 132–3,
  152–3, 155–6, 159

pathways of youth 4, 11–13,
  16–21, 31–4, 43, 49–56, 65–8,
  78–83, 170–1, 176–9, 179–82,
  190–1, 193, 199–201
Pittman, K. 167
priorities in life 1, 26–32, 104–6,
  168, 177–8, 190, 199–201

research: and the 'at risk' 42–4,
85–6, 92; blindspots 30–1,
89–90, 93–5, 128, 139, 142–3,
147–8, 152, 159, 160, 167, 172,
175–6, 188, 199–200, 202, 204;
cross-cultural 3–4, 46, 101, 103,
202; linear assumptions 30–1, 76,
78, 160, 167, 172, 177–8, 188,
200; national traditions 2–3,
85–6, 91, 92, 95, 175–6, 201–2;
participant 4, 31, 89–95, 128,
139, 152, 160, 165, 200, 202,
204–5
rural disadvantage 71, 118, 120

Schneider, B. and Stevenson, D.
12–18, 26, 32, 58, 80–1, 84–5,
93, 99, 190, 196, 198
schools: and age 25, 55–6, 78–9,
127; and dropouts 35–7, 45–6,
47–56, 73–4, 99, 112; and
homelessness 161, 163–6; and
hopes 104, 106–13; and identity
140–1; and performance 25,
35–7, 39, 47–9, 52, 78–9, 133–5,
149, 150, 157–9, 164; and re-
entry, 36–7, 48–51, 54–6; and
retention rates 63–5, 149
Sennett, R. 179–80
service society 17, 59, 61, 74–5, 198
social mobility 15–18, 63, 123,
142, 188, 190–1, 203; and
horizontal mobility 27, 126, 130,
188–9, 197
structural influences 29, 73, 80,
88–90, 91, 117–18, 123, 129–30,
133–4, 143, 171–2, 182–3, 188,
196, 200–1, 203–5
study/work combinations 15–24,
81–2, 88, 124–5, 126, 127, 179
Sweet, R. 132

Teese, R. 70–1, 133–5

underclass debates 67, 145, 146–7,
150, 156

unemployment 12, 19, 43, 48, 60,
67, 68, 71, 74, 77, 92, 106–13,
146–8
United States 2, 13–18, 20, 25, 27,
32, 38, 41–6, 56, 60–3, 65–6, 73,
79–81, 84–6, 93, 112, 123, 125,
142, 146–7, 150–4, 162, 171,
173, 189, 196

vocational integration 180–1, 183–5

Wallace, C. 85, 173, 174
White, R. 13, 43, 136, 139, 154,
170–73
Williamson, H. 39–40, 43, 53, 67
Willis, S. 25, 27, 90, 123, 126–8,
189, 196–7

Yates, L. 133, 134–5
youth: and adulthood 1, 25–34,
49–50, 55–6, 77–83, 127, 131,
170–4; alienation 41–3, 148–9,
157–9; and globalisation 2, 33,
63, 101, 103, 119–22, 145, 171,
192, 197; and knowledge society
17. 59–63, 69, 74, 121, 191,
193; optimism 41, 83–5, 92–3,
106–7, 123–4, 162–3, 196; peer
groups 14, 29, 44, 52–3; policy
4, 18, 37–41, 51–9, 63–5, 78,
120, 191, 193, 197; priorities 1,
11, 26–32, 91, 104–6, 168,
177–8, 190, 199–201; and social
change 1–3, 32–4, 41–3, 76–83,
87, 95–6, 100, 119, 169, 177–8,
190–3, 199–201, 204–5; training
programmes 53, 60, 66–70;
transitions 1, 32–4, 37–41, 55–6,
65–7, 79–83, 87, 91, 96, 113–15,
125–6, 167, 169, 170–3, 176–9,
190–4, 199–201; uncertain
futures 1, 9–13, 15–18, 30–2, 41,
49–56, 60–3, 74–8, 106–13,
120–2, 182, 189, 191, 193,
198
Youth Research Centre 4